Facing the Nuclear Heresy:
A Call to Reformation

W9-AGK-912

First Church of the Brethren
1340 Forge Road
Carlisle, Pennsylvania 17013

Facing the Nuclear Heresy:
A Call to Reformation

G. Clarke Chapman

Foreword by
Jürgen Moltmann

BRETHREN PRESS
Elgin, Illinois

Facing the Nuclear Heresy: A Call to Reformation

Copyright © 1986 by G. Clarke Chapman

BRETHREN PRESS, 1451 Dundee Avenue,
Elgin, IL 60120.

All rights reserved. No portion of this book may be reproduced in any form or by any process or technique without the written consent of the publisher, except for brief quotations embodied in critical articles or reviews.

Cover design by Kathy Kline

Foreword translated from the German by Hedda Durnbaugh

Library of Congress Cataloging-in-Publication Data

Chapman, G. Clarke, 1934–
    Facing the nuclear heresy.
    Bibliography: p.
    Includes index.
    1. Nuclear warfare—Religious aspects—Christianity.
2. Arms race—Religious aspects—Christianity.
I. Title.
BR115.A85C48   1986   261.8′73   85-31417
ISBN 0-87178-225-1

Manufactured in the United States of America

CONTENTS

PART II, Preparing for Reformation: A Paradigm Shift

PART III, Preparing for Reformation: A New Lifestyle

Foreword

Clarke Chapman has written a necessary book. It is written against the resignation with which all of us are gradually accommodating ourselves to the thought of the bombs and missiles of the nuclear arms race, a resignation that allows us to live in the knowledge that the crime of destroying humanity and all life on earth could be visited on us at any moment. No one would have thought it possible in 1945 after Hiroshima and Nagasaki, and yet it happened. Every year the shadows of the threatening nuclear holocaust are growing, but we call it only "nuclear deterrence" and stake our "security" on it. The worst is that one gradually becomes accustomed to it. One grows blind and blunted, no longer aware of the enormity of the nuclear mass murder which could break in upon us at any time and the responsibility for which we must share, because we do not (or at least not emphatically enough) protest against it. Everyone who raises a voice against this universal delusion and the profound dulling of hearts is like a prophet among a hardened people. Such a person has little prospect of visible success but is nevertheless compelled to cry out for conscience's sake.

Clarke Chapman belongs to this catagory. His book is indeed like "the voice of a preacher in the desert." His book cannot be recommended for its beautiful content, nor can it be recommended because it is entertaining to read. On the contrary, his subject, "nuclearism," is singularly horrible and his presentation of it awakens consciences. However, his subject, "nuclearism," determines the reality of our life in all areas, and his presentation is true to fact. Thus his book is neither beautiful nor entertaining, but it is true because it reveals our reality for what it is, and it calls us to a decision for life before death overcomes us all. It is a necessary book.

In this foreword I should like to deal with several points that appear significant to me in my situation in West Germany. In the debate between the groups of the Christian peace movement and the established churches, as well as the political parties, about *Nachrüstung* (i.e., stepping up armaments for the alleged purpose of catching up with the opponent) with Pershing II rockets and cruise missiles, the question is still whether Christian groups and churches can or ought to take a stand on such military and purely political issues at all. Those who are in favor of *Nachrüstung* deny the churches and the faithful the right to interfere in such "worldly" matters. They deplore therefore the "politicization of the church" through the peace movement. And it is true that during the 1950s and 1960s we ordinarily considered nuclear armaments as an ethical-political problem. We spoke then about "political obedience" by the faithful when calling for resistance against such armament with "weapons of mass-destruction," as we called atomic bombs.

Clarke Chapman in this book, however, makes it quite clear that "nuclear armament" is only part of a "hidden religion," namely the religion of nuclearism. It is the religion of a profound fear which calls for ever more security. It is the religion of power, of superpower, and of divine omnipotence on earth. However, the self-deification of the superpowers, who proclaim themselves messianic nations for the rest of humanity, is possible only if these superpowers allow for the nuclear inferno of the entire earth in their calculations. At the core of their system of "nuclear deterrence" is terror. Clarke Chapman dares to call this new "nuclear religion" a "heresy." If it is indeed a heresy, then it will challenge the true Christian faith to confession. If this nuclear heresy is the "religion" prevailing in a given nation, then all true Christian churches are called upon to put any kind of tolerance and pluralism aside and become "confessing churches" who unequivocally confess Christ in word and deed and who unequivocally reject the "nuclear heresy" in word and deed.

Several Christian peace groups and the Reformed Church in Germany, to which I belong, have already arrived at this point. As early as 1958 the fellowship groups of the old "Confessing Church" in Germany rejected nuclear armament and proclaimed the *status confessionis*. In their "Ten Theses" they stated: Those who believe in Christ and confess him must reject nuclear armament because they cannot raise the threat of mass murder. When journalists at that time asked the aged Karl Barth whether he agreed with these theses, he answered with an unequivocal Yes. He was well able to do so because he had written those theses himself. In 1981 the Reformed Alliance in Germany proclaimed again the *status confessionis* in a public declaration against *Nachrüstung*. Nuclear mass destruction represents the direct denial of all three articles of the Christian faith: faith in the Creator, in the Reconciler, and in the Savior of the world. One year later the Protestant Church in East Germany declared: The system of nuclear deterrence violates the Christian faith in spirit, logic, and practice. The consequence of all three declarations is that Christians can participate neither in the construction, nor in the threat, nor finally in the deployment of this inhuman and ungodly system, but must resist it wherever they can.

One might, of course, argue that "heresy" is merely an internal problem of Christianity and of the church and that, therefore, this concept does not really apply to this new, apocalyptic "political religion" of the superpowers. If I understand Clarke Chapman correctly, he uses this concept of "heresy" in order to call the Christian faith to a public confession in this existential question which confronts humanity. Probably he means to say more than that. The elevation — with the aid of nuclear terror — of the superpowers to the status of divine omnipotence is not only a "heresy," it is *blasphemy*. And because it has the potential of being the ultimate blasphemy of humanity on earth, it is the apocalyptic blasphemy, that is to say, the blasphemy of the Antichrist. If this is correct, then every Christian who takes his or her faith seriously, knows what must be done, for God will not be mocked.

Clarke Chapman's book does not end with this apocalyptic vision. His book is rather a book of hope. He is looking for the portents of a new reformation of the Christian churches. He finds it in the fact that many Christian peace groups and entire denominations today are heeding the witness of the so-called old "peace churches," namely the Mennonites, the Quakers, the Brethren, and others, and that they no longer shove them aside as sects. He finds the portents for a new reformation of the churches also in the rediscovery of the peace witness of the Old Church of the first three centuries before the turn to Constantinianism. He finds the new signs also in the formation of "confessing churches" in the race struggle in South Africa and in the struggle for human rights in the countries of the Third World. Perhaps we are indeed witnessing today the decline of an obsolete form of the Christian church and of Christian life, and the beginning of a new form of the presence of Christ in our world. Christ becomes present wherever faith is professed and lived in answer to being concretely called to profession and obedience. This occurs in the "First World" through the blasphemous system of nuclear deterrence. It occurs in the Third World through the inhuman economic system which spreads hunger and famine. It occurs in the "Second World" through the godless dictatorship of ideology and the political party system which murders the soul. On all these fronts we find today the portents of a new, credible presence of the church of Christ.

Clarke Chapman sees these portents of a new hope not only in the Christian churches. He also surveys human society and finds signs of a renewal of humanity that would lead from the traditional violent societies with which we are familiar, and under which we suffer, to peaceful and just societies that are capable of survival. Harboring these hopes, is he chasing hollow illusions? Is he a utopian? I do not think so. His commitment to nonviolence and peace and his rejection of the heresy of nuclearism are part of the only realism of life left to us in this situation which is so severely threatened by death. The system of nuclear deterrence, the system of worldwide economic exploitation, the system of oppression by dictatorship—all of these are the bad dreams, the negative utopias, the images of death which oppress life today. There is still time to free ourselves from them. There is still time to wake up, to live in the light of God's approaching day, and to love life.

Jürgen Moltmann
University of Tübingen

Preface

Testimonials from Some Worshipers of the Bomb

"The atomic bomb is a marvelous gift that was given to our country by a wise God."
— Phyllis Schlafly, of The Eagle Forum[1]

"Developing nuclear weapons was part of God's plan. Nuclear war may be fulfillment of prophecy. Before we go, they go. I can do that in all good Christian conscience."
— Ed McAteer, of The Religious Roundtable[2]

"I want to come out No. 1, not No. 2" [in a nuclear war].
— James Edwards, Secretary of U.S. Department of Energy, upon witnessing a nuclear test, Nevada, 5 August 1982.[3]

"I am here to report to the Senate and the American people that the atomic bottlenecks are being broken. There is virtually no limit and no limiting factor upon the number of A-bombs which the United States can manufacture, given time and given a decision to proceed all out. . . . We must have atomic weapons to use in the heights of the sky and the depths of the sea; we must have them to use above the ground, on the ground, and below the ground. An aggressor must know that if he dares attack he will have no place to hide. . . . Mark me well: massive atomic deterring power can win us years of grace, years in which to wrench history from its present course and direct it toward the enshrinement of human brotherhood."
— Senator Brien M. McMahon, speech to the U.S. Senate, 18 September 1951.[4]

"I wonder if we have ever thought about the greatest tool that we have. That power of prayer and God's help. If you could add together the power of prayer of the people just in

this room, what would be its megatonnage?"
— President Ronald Reagan, National Prayer Breakfast, 2 February 1984. [5]

"If they had enough atomic bombs, they could use them to clean out a nation. The man that made that bomb was a man after my own heart. I love him. I don't care if he was a nigger. I'd love his neck."
— Virginia farmer, interviewed in 1946. [6]

"it would be so exciting
it would be so powerful
it would punish us for our sins
things wouldn't be so boring anymore
we could get back to basics
we would remember who we love
it would be so loud
it would be so hot
the mushroom clouds would rise up
we could start over
we wouldn't have to be afraid of it anymore
we wouldn't have to be afraid anymore
we would finally have done it better than Raskolnikov
it would release our anger in the ultimate tantrum
then we could rest."
— Alia Johnson, "Why We Should Drop the Bombs" [7]

PART I
Nuclearism Confronts the Church

1

Nuclearism as a Religion

For Richard Barnet, it was the scene with the general that was the eye-opener. He remembers it vividly, for it drew to a focus a disillusionment that had grown during his two years in Washington D.C. — first in the State Department and then in the Arms Control and Disarmament Agency. The time was during the Kennedy administration. Barnet was fresh out of Harvard, having finished a graduate research project eventually published as *Who Wants Disarmament?*. Now he was getting an unsettling answer to his question. The more he worked in corridors of governmental power, the more it appeared that, in effect, very few want it — even among those who nominally are in charge of such matters. It was for him a shock to see the casual, even arrogant manner in which colleagues discussed plans which assumed many millions might die in the course of advancing our own national interest. Barnet felt surrounded by symptoms of a profoundly spiritual sickness.

It came to a head when this Air Force general arrived to demonstrate a new early warning system. He was proud of a technology which allegedly would give the President several extra minutes to decide about launching a massive nuclear reprisal. For Barnet, who is now a senior fellow at the Institute for Policy Studies in Washington, this incident crystallized a new insight that would last him a lifetime: "There was no way to argue with the man or his system, to make him see that he was offering illusion instead of security. The biblical language of idolatry made far more sense as a description of what was happening than the language of nuclear strategy. There was no way out of the race to destruction except somehow to transcend it."[1]

The young policy analyst had just found himself in the intractable presence of what is, in effect, an alternate religion — a self-contained complex of faith assumptions, complete with reinforcing rituals, codified lifestyle, and a missionary zeal. "Within the hermetic system of nuclear rationality, there were no solutions"; indeed only an altogether new vision could provide a "way out," a means to "transcend" the dilemma. Barnet concludes, "The idea that profound conversion was necessary before a sane national security policy was possible made me very uncomfortable and still does."[2] And well it might! The clash of incompatible belief systems is always disquieting, and conversion is painfully exacting in its drive to reintegrate the self in all its aspects around a new vision. But herein also lies hope for the nuclear age.

The Bomb as a Religious Issue

It is curious that the growing threat of major nuclear war is not widely perceived as more than a moral problem, but indeed a directly religious one. Religion, of course, deals with our relationship to the Holy and with the redemptive consequences that follow, while morality deals with more derivative matters of valuing and behaving. Since 1945 the Bomb has often been debated as an ethical issue, but rarely as a religious one. Why is that? Why this reluctance to push a discussion of values and their adjudication to its source: a tenacious underlying view of ultimate reality?

By two functional criteria of religion, namely wholeness and ultimacy, our preparations for planetary suicide would appear to a neutral observer as quite devout. The claim to deal with the whole of reality, first of all, is a trait that distinguishes religion from other facets of culture. The sacred does command an all-encompassing vision and it plumbs the totality of our being. What is merely partial or fragmentary cannot qualify. And whatever lays counterclaims to the wholeness of life, such as totalitarian ideologies aspire to do, should logically be renounced — not as simply a cultural phenomenon but as an outright religious rival.

The Bomb comes close to such an encompassing claim. Alan Geyer, for instance, recalls that Karl Barth criticized the churches' failure to condemn nuclear armament as the greatest infidelity since the failure of most Christians to take a firm stand against Nazism. "That comparison is appropriate," Geyer continues, "because it points to the totalitarianism of both Nazism and nuclear weapons."[3] The "totalitarianism" of the Bomb derives from our recognition of not only the unprecedented magnitude of its explosive power, but also a widening range of thermal, electromagnetic, and ionizing radiation effects. These consequences are so vast and so complex in their interactions that the very life support systems of the planet may be undermined. It is the potential "totalism" of these fearful weapons, the boundlessness of their likely impact on global life, that distinguishes them from other modern devices of mass destruction. This is what also confers upon them a virtually religious status.

A second functional characteristic of religion is ultimacy: whatever is acknowledged finally as affecting our deepest weal or woe and on which we accordingly lavish our utmost loyalties. In expounding on the First Commandment, Martin Luther put it bluntly: "a god is that to which we look for all good and where we resort for help in every time of need: to have a god is simply to trust and believe in one with our whole heart. . . . Now, I say, whatever your heart clings to and confides in, that is really your God. . . ."[4] Luther, together with many sixteenth-century Reformers, would insist that if the heart clings to a misplaced absolute, the resulting idolatry not only is expressed in false beliefs but also a false heart. Calvin would add that the true knowledge of God and the true knowledge of humanity are closely related. The converse would be that idolatry and an existence in estrangement are corollaries, that worship of false gods both expresses and reinforces the distortion of human life. The Old Testament, for instance, is keenly aware of this mutuality in fallenness. Not only are idols merely human artifacts of lifeless metal or stone, but "their makers grow to be like them, and so do all who trust in them" (Ps. 115:8, NEB; see Isa. 44:9-20). False ultimates exact a heavy cost indeed on the lives of their proponents!

Paul Tillich took up this functional characteristic in his well known definition of religion as "ultimate concern." "Ultimate," moreover, is analyzed as having both objective and subjective dimensions: that which is in itself unconditional and holy, and also the centering passion and awe which a person directs towards it.[5] Various loyalties may approximate either of these two dimensions, but only the (genuine) Ultimate can unite them into an ecstatic, centered act of the whole person. Again the critique of idolatry is implicit: when any finite object or lesser cause is elevated to the status of absolute, it will have a fragmenting effect on the believing self.

The Bomb verges on claiming such ultimacy, in both the dimensions described by Tillich. First, objectively, it certainly affects that which is ultimate — at least of this finite and habitable world. That is, the cumulative effects of thousands of nuclear explosions would not only injure the *totality* of the biosphere, but also put at *ultimate* risk its very continuation. Such hypothetical fears have reached the level of virtual certainty since 1983. It was then that scientists announced the results of a wide range of studies using computer analyses of various physical models. They predict that any large scale nuclear war could damage irreversibly the earth's climate and ecology by triggering a "nuclear winter."[6] The widespread fires from the ruins of targeted cities and industries would send pillars of smoke and soot into the atmosphere; these would spread until at least the northern hemisphere was plunged into darkness and freezing cold for a period of many months or years. Water supplies would freeze, vegetation and crops die, and then the animals and humans who depend on them. Even when the atmosphere became clear enough to allow some sunshine to return, it would also permit the earth's surface to be bathed with dangerous ultraviolet-B radiation. Little life could withstand this combined onslaught on the environment.

Objectively, therefore, our world could end because of nuclear war. Within history, at any rate, there could be nothing more ultimate. To be sure, most of us have contemplated our personal deaths, or pondered the mass death of many people. This mental exercise, unpleasant though it is, is possible because such death occurs within the ongoing context of survivors and societies. But it is almost incomprehensible to try to imagine human extinction. There is neither a framework nor precedent for it.

It is one of Jonathan Schell's more original contributions in *The Fate of the Earth* that he is able to bring some clarity to this mental limit. "Death is only death; extinction is the death of death," however, or the "second death — the death of mankind."[7] That would be categorically different from a mass slaughter, no matter how numerous the victims. It would extinguish our irreplaceable "common world," that fragile web of culture, meaning, and human response which alone gives some sense to any aggregate of individual deaths. That is why Schell argues so eloquently against the arms race. There can be no grounds whatsoever, either in national self-interest or in morality, to risk human extinction, since both national interest and morality presuppose ongoing human existence.[8] True, nuclear war *might* not kill us all; but it very well *could*. To behave in ways which even remotely increase the possibility of human extinction is to gamble with the final crime against the future, against the waiting generations yet unborn. Nothing, says Schell, is worth the heightened risk of such finality, although he writes as a social scientist and not as a theist. But through his discussion we can see that the nuclear threat does indeed raise the issue of ultimacy in its full objective sense, at least within the limits of history. Extinction cannot fail to be a religious question.

The other dimension of ultimacy is the subjective — as Tillich puts it, whatever ultimately concerns a person. Here it is even more clear that religious allegiance is at work. Each of us can testify that our sense of awe is aroused by these genuinely "awe-ful" weapons. We find a numinous fascination in watching the film footage of test explosions, or the special effects contrived by film makers in fictionalized stories of holocaust. In our hearts most of us experience a vicarious thrill of forbidden boundaries transgressed when we hear of new instances of scientists or national leaders dabbling with human destiny, or skirting another crisis which might well have unleashed global catastrophe. While custom and etiquette frown on open discussion or emotion about such topics, the images of annihilation nevertheless are stored up in the public memory. Often it is in unconscious ways that they break through and surface—in dreams, for instance, or art, or in the simple yet candid drawings of young children, unskilled in dissimulation.

It is quite understandable why the Bomb elicits such reverence. Ultimate concern, in its subjective dimension, is always directed toward that which is perceived to affect us ultimately, for good or for ill. The words of Bernard Brodie, one of the earliest and most influential nuclear strategists, contain an unexpected tone of wonder and awe: "Everything about the bomb is overshadowed by the twin facts that it exists and that its destructive power is fantastically great."[9] On several levels such profound feelings of ultimacy toward nuclear weapons are shared by the public. They resemble, for instance, many of the classic descriptions of religious experience. There is a sense of mystery before the incalculable, a fear and yet fascination with unknown and invisible forces of enormous potency, apprehensions of creaturely helplessness mingled with a vicarious sense of sharing in exhilarating power, and the thrill of veiled anticipations of cosmic nemesis.[10]

These feelings also resemble themes common to the mind's dream life. Psychoanalyst Edward Glover points out that images of world-destruction are familiar to those who study the unconscious mind and especially the fantasies of the insane. He worries that modern weapons of extermination are so "well adapted" to these secret lusts. "The capacity so painfully acquired by normal men to distinguish between sleep, delusion, hallucination and the objective reality of waking life has for the first time in human history been seriously weakened."[11] Moreover, John Sanford comments from his Jungian perspective on the life of the psyche that a cleavage has been developing for some time in the Western mind. "Rejected and separated from consciousness, the unconscious turned hostile and in our century has erupted in barbaric wars, crime, and the sickness of soul so characteristic of our times."[12] The struggles of the unconscious are perceived by the ego as something invaded by death. So our society is pervaded by fantasies and dreams of menacing invasions—by criminals, aliens from outer space, or an enemy nation . . . and finally by Doomsday itself.

Further evidence is found in those TV productions, popular films, comic strips, and other forms of mass entertainment which attest and play upon such intimations in the public mind. Indeed the more successful ones are those which are best attuned to preconscious hopes and anxieties, images and ritualized acts, and which go on to articulate them in satisfying detail. Direct portrayals of nuclear holocaust are considered too horrific by film producers. But they well know the public fascination for dramatizations of smaller, more manageable catastrophes, perhaps mere components of a holocaust, suitably scaled down or sublimated. So our mass entertainments often feature plots about natural disasters, invasions of earth by extraterrestials, violence originating from the supernatural, or purgation and rebirth through some sort of bloodbath. Fans of pop culture will recognize, of course, that such themes also existed before Hiroshima. But certainly the years since 1945 have seen these scenarios and images increase substantially—both in frequency and in explicit portrayals.

Clearly then, if these criteria of religion (wholeness and ultimacy in both objective and subjective forms) are placed alongside descriptions of the clusters of mythic images and attitudes commonly held concerning nuclear weapons, there is a striking congruence. It appears that, in effect, a new religion has been born in our time.

Indeed the Bomb confronts us with far more than a *moral* dilemma ("What should we do?"), perplexing and urgent though that is. We are confronted also with a *religious* challenge ("Who are we?" "To whom/what do we owe final allegiance?"). It is this dimension which has all too seldom been recognized since the day the first mushroom cloud rose over the New Mexico desert—the climax of the project to which Robert Oppenheimer had enigmatically given the code name "Trinity."

Accordingly, on the grounds both of totalism and of ultimacy, we are thrust by nuclear technology into the arena of outright theological controversy, whether we like it or not. We dare not ignore this challenge any longer. Least of all should we be lulled by the frequent claim that religion is no

longer a factor in our secular age. As Gibson Winter says, in
reviewing his lifework as a social ethicist,

> The pretension to "secularity" merely conceals the
> "faith" of the Western world, its belief in progress
> through domination and accumulation. As long as
> this faith is concealed, the technological elites can
> purport to operate with a purely neutral, instrumen-
> tal reason as they reckon the tens of millions that
> they will have to destroy in order to save their way
> of life. Every people lives its symbols, some symbols
> that further life and some that destroy life. Talk
> about secularity merely conceals the symbols and
> leaves them unreflected.[13]

Uncertain Quests for a New Vision

The covert idolatry of our situation is recognized clearly
by Dale Aukerman, in his moving and provocative book,
Darkening Valley: A Biblical Perspective on Nuclear War.
"War, now nuclear war, is the key issue not only for survival
but also for coming to grips before God with who we are."[14]
So who are we? On the one hand, war has always been the
most extreme unveiling of the sinister depths of the human
heart. As Karl Barth also pointed out, "It only needed the
atom and the hydrogen bomb to complete the self-disclosure
of war in this regard."[15] Just as the boundaries to human existence were symbolically burst in Eden by the primal sin
committed by our ancestral parents, so now the boundaries
of human disobedience have been physically burst at
Almagordo by the limitless destruction achieved by our
human intelligence.

But on the other hand, continues Aukerman, the figure
of Jesus Christ has always been the most profound unveiling
of God. Here is the divine self-disclosure of judgment and yet
of boundless compassion. To this merciful unmasking of
God's very presence, we humans in our defiance responded in
turn by unmasking ourselves — in direct violence against God.
The last word, however, comes not from the anguish of the
cross but the victory of the resurrection. So now in the
nuclear age, to talk about war means that we must also talk

about God. That means reflection on just who God is, who we are and who we shall become, and what is after all the final reality in a world within which Christ both died and rose to new life.

It was of course this religious dimension of the nuclear threat which Richard Barnet had finally recognized in his frustrating years in Washington: "There was no way out of the race to destruction except somehow to transcend it." The nuclear peril stems from our conventional models for understanding the way the world works, and so these models themselves must be transformed or replaced. To "transcend" an insoluble dilemma, we need a new vision of what is "really real." But a transcending vision is already a virtual definition of religion. That is, it is a mode of understanding which is in some sense "ecstatic," or "standing outside of" the customary ways of perceiving what is around us.

In the nuclear age the classic formulation of this need is an early statement of Albert Einstein: "The unleashed power of the atom has changed everything except our ways of thinking. Thus we are drifting toward a catastrophe beyond comparison. We shall require a substantially new manner of thinking, if mankind is to survive."[16] Similar calls for a new approach to thinking have recently been issued, for instance, by leading psychologists, scientists, teachers, and statesmen.[17] On a more immediate level, this quest is reflected in the "Avoiding Nuclear War" program of the Carnegie Corporation, which since 1984 has made large grants to several academic centers of international studies. "What is being attempted, in effect, is a remapping of the entire field of study . . . with the intention of disclosing new ways of defining and maintaining security in a world brimming with nuclear weapons."[18] Such "remapping," however, can only transform the concept of security if it is grounded in a more encompassing vision, a vision which in the last analysis must be religious — that is, wholistic and ultimate. The Second Vatican Council, for instance, recognized this twenty years ago, stating that the technology and likely effects of total warfare now "compel us to undertake an evaluation of war with an entirely new attitude."[19]

But just how has Christian theology responded to the

urgent need to rethink things in the nuclear age? The answer must be that, its response has been immediate, but sporadic and primarily at the ethical level.

From the first announcements of Hiroshima and Nagasaki, clergy and theologians of all faiths raised a mighty chorus of warnings of the awesome power and unprecedented responsibility now resting in human hands. As early as March of 1946 the "Calhoun Commission," appointed by the then Federal Council of Churches of Christ in America, reconvened and issued a document, *Atomic Warfare and the Christian Faith*. Participants included some of the great names of North American religion of the time, such as the Niebuhr brothers, John C. Bennett, Nels Ferré, and Douglas Steere. After observing that human freedom "is more decisive and dangerous than we had suspected," the report gave one of the first articulations of the terrible question: "If a premature end of history should come . . . the problem then is whether beyond the end of history God's justice and mercy are still a ground for hope, or whether the stultification of human life by a premature end is to be feared."[20]

After the early years of the atomic age, however, theology for the most part found little new to add, and its interest in the nuclear threat did little more than coincide with the periodic rise and fall of public attention to such matters. Moreover, throughout the subsequent decades it is clear that most religious discussion has remained at the level of ethics, rather than theology as such. That is, the churches have contributed to the moral debates on possible uses, misuses, or even renunciations of nuclear weapons, and they have repeatedly exhorted decisionmakers to accountability and caution. The forces unlocked from the atom have been viewed as one more problem in the application of morality, comparable for example to arguments about population control or genetic engineering. But rarely has such discussion considered the Bomb as a challenge to fundamental concepts of God or humanity.

This has been typically the case, even in the latest spate of religious publications about the arms race, which began in the late 1970s. It has been the *moral* issues that have dominated the churches' ventures in peace education or in scholarly exchange—issues such as MIRV'd missiles, a nuclear freeze, counterforce targeting, arms control, first strike technology, economic and psychological effects of the Cold War, and now proposals for outer space ("Star Wars") weaponry.

A case in point is the well known 1983 pastoral letter on war and peace from the U.S. Catholic bishops. [21] There are of course a number of respects in which it has made a landmark contribution: in weighing the limits of the strategy of deterrence, in coming close to discrediting any conceivable use of nuclear weapons, in struggling to balance traditional Catholic moral theology with renewed attention to biblical principles, in its recognition of pacifism as a genuine Christian option (for individuals, anyway), in its publicly open style of writing and revising the several drafts, including the solicitation of testimony from all sides, and in its irenic presentation as a teaching tool for Catholics and non-Catholics alike. [22] The creative substance of the pastoral is contained in its middle two sections, under the headings of "problems," "principles," "proposals," and "policies." Here, as these topics suggest, the subject matter is ethical: the morality of deterrence or possible uses of atomic weapons. [23] The distinctively religious challenge of the Bomb, however, is not examined. References to God, Christ, fallenness, and redemption are brief, conventional, and confined almost to the extent of quarantine to the early pages of the opening section of the pastoral. We can be thankful that the Catholic bishops recognized the urgent need to address public policy and to educate the laity, and that they have risen so well to the occasion. By default, however, the Bomb is viewed as a moral problem, not really as a religious one.

Two Apocalyptic Visions

Although this trend has continued through four decades, recently the exceptions have been growing. To these we now turn our attention.

A pioneering work is *Darkening Valley* by Dale Aukerman, pastor and peacemaker in the Church of the Brethren. While pondering various biblical images in a post-Hiroshima world, he raises basic theological topics such as idolatry, eschatology, an analysis of the dynamics of sin, and the relentless question of theodicy: "Why the possibility for the Bomb?"[24] The book is a collection of essays, largely in the style of meditations, and using the primary language of devotion and straightforward biblical imagery rather than the analytical language of systematic theology. Here it is the age-old foes of sin, death, and idolatry which are named, but with their familiar menace heightened by the newly unleashed power of the atom. Here too are the biblical themes of shalom, judgment, the gift of faithful obedience, and final consummation as God's response.

With understated elegance Aukerman reflects again and again on the momentum and self-deceit of sin, and on our solidarity with Cain as murderer and with Jesus as the ever-present victim. There is a fine discussion of Romans 13, and of the fallacies behind the common argument, "What if an intruder molested your family?" The depth of Aukerman's convictions is reflected in the apocalyptic intensity with which he writes. This style, together with the clear and principled pacifism of his Anabaptist heritage, may have the effect of limiting his readership to the already convinced. But those who delve into his pages will find they can no longer postpone grappling with the nuclear issue on a theological level. As such this marks something of a breakthrough in our generation.

Another exception, at least in part, comes from an unlikely source. Jonathan Schell, as we have noted, is certainly no theologian. Indeed his few references to religious concepts suggest that he has little interest in biblical matters, or theism of any sort. Concerning the latter, he manages to recommend to his readers the ungainly principle of "respect for God or nature, or whatever one chooses to call the universal dust that made, or became, us."[25] Schell's undergirding philosophy is aptly characterized by Stanley Hauerwas as "apocalyptic humanism," a branch of the wider segment of anti-nuclear thinkers he labels as "Survivalists."[26] This broader group is so named because they make a sharp distinction between conventional and nuclear warfare, and they do so to underline their supreme appeal for humanity's survival as a recently endangered species. Without that survival, it is said, there can be no ground or norm for any values in an otherwise amoral, uncaring universe.

Schell's tone is apocalyptic, and his style eloquent. Within his admittedly humanist framework, however, and indeed because of it, he does illuminate a topic that is properly theological: the singular status of the possibility of human extinction. This theme lends a stark clarity, as we have noted already, to the dimension of ultimacy — one of the functional fundamentals of religion. Surely, therefore, believers in the Incarnation can join with believers in humanism to this extent: we must recognize the absolute finality and possible nihilism with which nuclear extinction threatens the precious gift of life on earth.

It may seem that Aukerman and Schell, therefore, offer a study in opposites: the religious pacifist and the urbane humanist. But it is all the more remarkable that each in his own way represents some sort of breakthrough of the irrepressible theological question into discussions of the nuclear threat. Whereas, formerly, this was recognized mainly by premillennialist preachers and by the holocaust fantasies of pop culture, now we are witnessing the emergence of the latent religious claims of the Bomb to a wider audience.

Autonomy and Critical Reason

It was a dramatic moment at the 1982 annual meeting of the American Academy of Religion, the major gathering of college and university religion professors from around the nation. At the podium was Gordon Kaufman of the Harvard Divinity School, who used the opportunity of the AAR presidential address to reflect publicly on Jonathan Schell's description of humanity's "utterly new historical situation." A challenge was issued to scholars in religious studies to lend their talents to the search for fresh solutions. Since then, in the 1984 Ferguson lectures at Manchester University, Kaufman has developed his own ideas more fully.[28]

Immediately one sees how profoundly he is moved by the uniqueness of the nuclear age and the serious possibility that humanity may disappear from the earth. But, he argues, Western religion offers only two ways of interpreting our crisis, both of them equally irresponsible. Either it is said that nuclear holocaust must be God's will (and to hinder it would be to trifle with the divine plan — so the Hal Lindseys, for instance), or that God somehow will forever prevent holocaust from happening. Both alternatives unfortunately obscure the "stark fact of total human responsibility for the earthly future of humanity"[29] by means of traditional but now alienating notions of God's sovereignty and personhood.

In fact, says Kaufman, theism as such has become dubious. It arose from ancient myths ("dualistic and asymmetrical" in their archaic worldview) of a creator/father/king deity, which are no longer binding today.[30] Moreover, such notions blind us to the organic nature and long evolutionary past of humanity and to our corresponding duty to cultivate ecological harmony with the biosphere. Kaufman's solution is, in effect, a form of demythologizing (to use a term he would not claim). That is, "God" must be reconceived as that symbol which both relativizes and humanizes our lives as responsible beings. Likewise Christology must be stripped of its monarchial imagery and exclusivist claims to mediate salvation. Jesus instead is the prototype of service and self-sacrifice for the sake of "wider loyalty to on-going life."[31]

These recent proposals by Kaufman should be understood against the backdrop of his earlier theological work. From the outset he has been keenly aware of the problems posed to faith by relativity, the absolute relatedness and mutuality of all finite things, whether in nature or in history.[32] So his career has been characterized by a quest for a theological method adequate to find meaning in a pluralistic world — a world that seems bound only by the achievements of science and critical analysis. Procedurally his Archimedean point remains the responsible human self.

But long before this self was agitated into nuclear urgency by reading *The Fate of the Earth*, Kaufman was committed to a form of Kantian epistemology. That is, the mind can never know external reality as such, but is ceaselessly active in constructing its own pictures of reality in responding to perceived experience. Knowledge is an unending creativity of the mind struggling to impose meaning on its data, and truth must be judged pragmatically, in effect, as whatever renders contemporary experience as intelligible and of value. The theologian's task, accordingly, is neither to "hand on" Christian tradition nor merely "apply" it to recent problems, because that would be to devalue and subsume actual experience to some abstraction. Instead, we are reminded, "theology is human work, . . . primarily a work of the imagination."[33] As such, it is charged with interpreting the particularities of life here and now in light of symbolic reference points—in our case the mental constructs "God" and "Christ."

In his later writings Kaufman has progressively heightened the role of the subjective self and its conceptual activity, and correspondingly diminished the scope of the objective (divine) Self to be known. Back in 1968 he had stressed "the ultimate authority of God's revelatory act over every phase of theological work"[34] and balanced the experiential grounds of theology with sufficient confidence in God's accessibility to permit some 170 pages to be written (in language reminiscent of Karl Barth) about the triune Lord. Thereafter the title of his 1972 book, *God the Problem*,[35] suggested his growing misgivings about God-language and its warrants. But there he does argue that it is still linguistically defensible to retain the personal category of God as "agent." Properly interpreted, this symbol is not mythological after all, but "analogical," as a comprehensive imaginative construct which can point us to that which is most real: the sense of final limits yet source of value in life.

By his next book[36] Kaufman rejected more sharply any talk of divine self-disclosure, since "revelation" as a term is said to beg the question of what is meant by "God" and is itself a mental construct to be evaluated critically and pragmatically. Not revelation but imagination becomes the operative term in his thought—hence the title of his 1981 book, *The Theological Imagination: Constructing the Concept of God*, in which he also asserts that theology has outgrown the need for "mythopoeic" imagery. And now in his *Theology for a Nuclear Age*, even references to God as "agent" are absent, as is other personalistic language of the more restrained or "analogical" variety.[37] In his passion to avoid both authoritarian dualisms or human complacency, Kaufman would have us demythologize virtually all personal categories for God. What presently remains is "an ultimate point of reference for human existence" which is to unite two indispensable functions: a relativizing of all finite being and a humanizing of mortal life.[38]

In sum Kaufman is increasingly an heir of Enlightenment rationalism. His methodological pilgrimage was already far advanced, but now it apparently has been accelerated by reflecting on Jonathan Schell and the nuclear peril. For our purposes here, his work is of interest for two reasons: both because of what he does and because of what he fails to do. Let us look at each, in turn.

What he does is significant. Kaufman is one of the few non-fundamentalist theologians to face the possibility of nuclear holocaust as not simply a moral issue but as a theological one. From now on, this will be harder for the theological scholars, religious professionalism, and the church at large to ignore. For that we should be grateful to him.

To be sure, the *manner* in which he chooses to cast the challenge should be questioned — and is worth a short digression to do so. For Kaufman portrays the essential problem as a primal, even authoritarian power struggle. That is, humans have for a long time — but especially since 1945 — been snatching more and more ability for domination, so God acordingly must have less of it. In effect, because global Doomsday is at last in human hands, God's sovereignty is discredited. The world conflagration of ancient myths has become a serious possibility at any moment, but now it is so because of human technology and thus exclusively as a human responsibility. It is unthinkable that God would either cause or condone such final horror, so the role of God is shifted to that of fellow victim rather than divine perpetrator. From now on, we are told, for us to retain notions of God's omnipotence, providence, or majesty is not only outmoded, but an act of bad faith. What Kaufman means is that traditional theism offers to superpatriots and right-wing religious crusaders a tempting cover for their all too human spite and folly. This warning is well taken, and it discloses the integrity and moral energy of his argument.

But to applaud Kaufman for raising the theological issue is not to say we should approve of his way of doing it. For in fact his propensity to cast the issue as a contest over autonomy rests on a prior assumption. It takes for granted that "agency" — the power to act and to take responsibility for doing so — is a fixed commodity, an indivisible good which humans seize only at the expense of God. We recognize here a favorite theme of critics of religion in the eighteenth century, when technological mastery over the forces of nature was accelerating. It assumes a dichotomy between divine and human agency, a kind of seesaw effect or tug of war, which is featured in the Prometheus legend — and admittedly in some biblical references to divine jealousy (for instance, Gen. 11:1-9). That apparently is the context for Kaufman's thinking, as well as for the whole tradition of Enlightenment criticism on which he relies.

However, I would reply by pointing out that the Promethean struggle to vindicate a contested human autonomy is certainly not the only way to portray agency. In fact to read the New Testament is to find oneself not in a tug of war between divine and mortal freedom to act, but instead to glimpse the mysterious possibilities of their concurrence — extending from the Incarnation through the Spirit-filled community. If God is seen primarily not as the great Monopolist of power, but rather as the liberating source of loving freedom, then the antitheses of Enlightenment rationalism are surmounted. The whole discussion accordingly shifts to a different level. For instance, both Dietrich Bonhoeffer and Jürgen Moltmann, each of whom suffered under Nazism and war and have certainly no less cause than Kaufman to be alarmed over human irresponsibility, offer us valuable clues precisely in this direction.[39] In that case, the way to equip the responsible self to avert a technological Doomsday would be less a "demythologizing" of God-language, and more an "ideology critique" of human loyalties and covert self-interest.

Nevertheless, as has been said, what Kaufman does accomplish is significant: he recognizes the nuclear threat to be an outright religious issue, and he warns against human complacency and bad faith through any misuse of theistic symbols. This then brings us to the other side of our evaluation: what he fails to do. There is, in fact, no explanation in Kaufman's work for why the Bomb itself is the focus for a new religiosity. He points to extinction as the fate to be avoided at all costs (including the sacrifice of traditional theism), but he seems unable to account for why the very means to such extinction holds such a fearful fascination and exhilaration for its "worshipers." We may be reminded thereby that the rationalist critique of theism, from the Age of Enlightenment through Protestant liberalism, has often been embarrassed after attempting a clean sweep, only to find that alternate religious loyalties have crept in the back door. So today we should ask why it is that humanity seems to seek and serve so avidly the very weapons that may destroy us. Surely such self-contradictory behavior is a problem for more than the social sciences or ethics, but also for theology—especially when we consider the dimensions of totality and ultimacy which are associated with the Bomb. To push onward toward such analysis, then, we must leave Kaufman and look elsewhere.

Death Anxiety and Symbol Formation

We begin with Robert Jay Lifton, a research psychiatrist at Yale University who is best known for his 1962 studies of survivors of the Hiroshima bomb.[40] This experience has impelled him over the years to expand his findings into a range of articles and books which probe our attitudes towards death, as well as the effects on the psyche of living in a post-Hiroshima world. He goes beyond the older Freudian views that one's own death is so unimaginable that the mind tries to repress all thought of it. Instead Lifton stresses the positive role of symbols in helping both the conscious and the unconscious to transcend that personal finality. He sees "the symbolizing process around death and immortality as the individual's experience of participation in some form of collective life-continuity," of which there have been historically five modes.[41]

The biological mode of symbolic immortality is expressed in the confidence of living through one's children and their descendants. The religious mode consists of rituals and formal beliefs about an afterlife. Creative works that live on through artifacts, the arts and sciences, or other service to humanity, forms a third mode. Fourth is nature itself, which is seemingly eternal; Hiroshima survivors often comforted themselves with the ancient saying, "The state may collapse but the mountains and rivers remain." Finally and most fundamentally, there is the altered state of consciousness which Lifton calls "experiential transcendence," such as induced states of momentary ecstasy through drugs, meditation, or various disciplines.

We depend on these symbolic affirmations of life-continuity for our sense of inner well-being. But especially the first four of the five have been steadily eroded and impoverished in modern times, which in turn unleashes an ominous sequence of reactions in the unconscious.[42] This dislocation of vital symbols opens the way for what Lifton calls "ideological totalisms," which rush in to fill the dreaded vacuum. Such totalisms vainly promise symbolic immortalities by "an all-or-none subjugation of the self to an idea-system,"[43] such as a fascist or totalitarian state. This fatal remedy is supported both by victimization, since absolute claims to virtue require a contrasting image of incarnate evil as a scapegoat, and by the distinctively modern blend of passion and numbing that permits mass violence to be organized. Readers of Lifton cannot mistake the religious implications of this analysis for an understanding of totalitarianism: it is an idolatrous answer to the death anxieties of vulnerable modern humans, once desymbolization has reached a certain stage. Lifton goes beyond a critique of police state ideologies, however. By 1945 technology had cleared the way for the ultimate extension of this totalism (even in constitutional societies), namely "nuclearism."

Lifton's work has helped us arrive at a name for what has thus far been described as the religious challenge posed by atomic weapons. We have sketched the functional characteristics of wholeness and ultimacy, and that tenacious hold which the Bomb has on its adherents' loyalties — all of which the Catholic bishops' pastoral letter, Jonathan Schell, and Gordon Kaufman seem unable to explain. But now the complex of ambivalent attitudes towards nuclear weapons may be accounted for under the hypothesis that we are actually dealing with a covert religion. Or at least the phenomena described by Lifton suggest something close to an alternate religion, once we look beyond the conventional indicators of the major historic faiths in the West: formal scriptures, creeds, houses of worship, and clergy. Explicit forms of such identifying features represent one way, but not the only way, in which human spirituality comes to expression — for good or ill.

To resume a description of Lifton's analysis, here is his definition of this final modern totalism:

> *nuclearism*: the passionate embrace of nuclear weapons as a solution to death anxiety and a way of restoring a lost sense of immortality. Nuclearism is a secular religion, a total ideology in which "grace" and even "salvation" — the mastery of death and evil — are achieved through the power of a new technological deity. The deity is seen as capable not only of apocalyptic destruction but also of unlimited creation. And the nuclear believer or "nuclearist" allies himself with that power and feels compelled to expound on the virtues of his deity. He may come to depend on the weapons to keep the world going.[44]

To enter this or any other religion usually entails a conversion experience. In the case of nuclearism this means "an immersion in death anxiety followed by rebirth into the new world view. At the heart of the conversion experience is an overwhelming sense of awe — a version of Freud's 'oceanic feeling' in which one's own insignificance in relationship to the larger universe is so extreme as to feel oneself, in effect, annihilated."[45]

That awe shines through the strikingly religious language used by early witnesses to atomic explosions. For example Lifton notes that a "language reminiscent of a 'conversion in the desert'" and "images of rebirth" are found in the words of a science writer, William Laurence, in describing the Almagordo test: "On that moment hung eternity. Time stood still. Space contracted to a pinpoint. It was as though the earth had opened and the skies had split. One felt as though he had been privileged to witness the Birth of the World. . . . The big boom came about a hundred seconds after the great flash — the first cry of a newborn world. . . ."[46] The same writer compared it also to witnessing the Second Coming of Christ.

Elsewhere Lifton has extended a description of the numinous awe inspired by the Bomb to include the rest of us who have never been eyewitnesses. For us, our fear is amorphous, corresponding to the invisibility of the dreaded radiation; we have a sense of mystery because the precise effects cannot be known; we feel a presence of nemesis and of being related to the infinite by tapping an ultimate force of the universe; and we sense our creatureliness and absolute vulnerability.[47]

It is ironic that such religiosity is devoted to the Bomb. For that weapon is the culminating achievement of those very historical processes that have eroded the traditional modes for symbolizing the sense of immortality and larger connectedness. Under the nuclear threat it is impossible to be confident of posterity, for instance, or of cultural and social achievements that will endure, or even of the capacity of nature to survive.[48] Nor can we rely on conventional religious beliefs in an afterlife, if we accept the report of survivors of Hiroshima, for whom traditional religious symbols and doctrine suddenly were emptied of meaning at the very time they were most needed.

The only mode remaining, experiential transcendence or ecstatic "high states" of consciousness, therefore, must bear the additional weight in meeting our needs for psychic nurture. This helps explain, by the way, the restless demands of our generation for new thrills, heightened sensory awareness, or exotic personal experiences; these are in a complex sense religious quests for transcending the anxiety of extinction. "So 'flexible' is the human mind that it can, in this way, contemplate annihilation as a joyous event, more joyous than living with the sense of being meaninglessly doomed."[49] The danger grows that the weapons themselves may be subconsciously perceived as "the most Dionysian stimulants of all."[50] That would tempt humans to indulge themselves in the ultimate orgy—as is reflected in the apocalyptic ending of the classic film, *Dr. Strangelove or How I Learned to Stop Worrying and Love the Bomb*, where the bomber pilot straddles the nuclear weapon and rides it down to its target with a wild Texas yodel.

And so, as Lifton remarks, "The weapon itself comes to usurp all of the pathways to symbolic immortality."[51] The

heritage of images for death and immortality that formerly
sustained us has become contaminated with forebodings of
holocaust. Lately many people have turned in frustration to
conservative religions that promise security from nihilism.
But this resurgence of traditionalism will be ineffectual, Lifton believes, for "as death imagery comes to take the shape of
total annihilation or extinction, religious sybmolism becomes
both more sought after and more inadequate."[52]

When basic symbols lose their nurturing power and
plausibility in a culture, one desperate response is — so to
speak — to turn up the volume. It is no wonder that all over
the world in the 1970s and 1980s there has been an upsurge of
fundamentalist religion and politics. "Fundamentalism is a
form of totalism with a very specific response to the loss of
larger human connections. It is a doctrinal restatement of
those connections in which literal, immutable words (rather
than the original flow of vital images) are rendered sacred
and made the center of a quest for collective revitalization."[53]
However Lifton does not dwell long upon the dangers of,
say, Protestant literalists who understand little of the profound nature of symbolization, and who thereby only make
the problem worse. His real concern lies elsewhere, and so
with disconcerting nonchalance he takes up this religious
term primarily to bend it to his earlier point of reference:
"Nuclearism, then, is the ultimate fundamentalism of our
time. The 'fundamentals' sacrilized [sic] are perverse products
of technicism and scientism — the worship of technique and
science in ways that preclude their human use."[54]

Finally, this summary of Lifton should take note of
some of the psychic traits associated with nuclearism, the new
totalism. Lifton sees two major categories of these consequences: "Dislocation creates a special kind of uneasy duality
around symbolization: a general sense of numbing, devitalization, and absence of larger meaning on the one hand; and
on the other, a form of image-release, an explosion of
symbolizing forays in the struggle to overcome collective
deadness and reassert larger connection."[55]

To take the latter one first, the "image-release" and flood
of "symbolizing forays" characterize what Lifton labels as the
Protean self of the modern age. Like the figure in ancient

mythology who changed shape at will, so the self nowadays seems embarked on an endless series of experiments in seeking identity. Belief systems, careers, marriage partners, or lifestyles often are switched with bewildering ease. Fads come and go, discordant ideas may be held simultaneously, or ever new personal experiences sought in unending quests for rebirth. Because one's outer, public world is no longer coordinated with one's inner, symbolic world, a sense of absurdity prevails — and the best defense mechanism becomes a tone of mockery affected towards every experience.[56] It seems that ony old, stable societies are able to breed durable personal identities in their members. But we moderns find ourselves overwhelmed by the nuclear threat, the cultural dislocation of our symbols, and the flood of unrelated fragments of imagery from our mass communications. No wonder a person's role or identity may change as abruptly as turning the channel switch on one's TV set!

The other main category of effects of the Bomb on us all, "psychic numbing," moves in the reverse direction. Alongside the excitation of multiple images and successive self-identities — what Lifton calls "an explosion of symbolizing forays" — there is also an implosion. That is, we find a widespread muting and repression of affect, a sense of inner emptiness and devitalization.

Lifton first noted this general "psychic shut-down" in his early research: "We thus encounter in both Hiroshima and concentration camp survivors, what can be called a pervasive tendency toward sluggish despair — a more or less permanent form of psychic numbing which includes diminished vitality, chronic depression and constricted life space, and which covers over the rage and mistrust that are just beneath the surface."[57] But psychic numbing is not limited to victims of catastrophe. In one degree or another similar reactions to death anxiety have been reported also in empirical studies of people who earlier had taken part in 1950s nuclear air-raid drills, or in recent questionnaires given to school children.[58] Assailed by images of grotesque annihilation, the mind's protective mechanisms act quickly to block painful feelings or impressions. For those present at, for instance, Hiroshima, it means the mind is telling itself something like "If I feel nothing, I cannot be threatened by the death all around me. . . . I am not responsible. . . ." And for those not present back then, it means the mind sees to it that the trauma becomes repressed, even "unimaginable."[59]

This numbing is a breakdown in the normal human symbolization process which in itself is a miniature "death in life," a symbolic death of the self, or "knowledge without feeling." In turn this only perpetuates the general malaise within a beleaguered society. "We can also speak of a profound symbolic gap characteristic of our age, a gap between the capacity for technological violence on the one hand, and our much more limited capacity for moral imagination on the other."[60] It is ironic that in repressing pictures of mass death, the mind instead—and in devious ways—"contracts" on the installment plan for an inward imitation of death.

A variant form of numbing, as a defense mechanism, is "denial." An unacceptable image is repressed by the mind until it actually disappears from the field of our perception. Nicholas Humphrey has given an early example of this striking self-deception.[61] Two hundred years ago, when Captain Cook's great sailing ship reached Australia and anchored in Botany Bay, it passed within a quarter of a mile of some Aborigines fishing offshore. But they showed no reaction whatever. Apparently they could not "see" a huge shape that was utterly without parallel in their experience. But they finally did take alarm when Cook put down some rowing boats, which presumably resembled dangers known from past experience.

In modern times we have more subtle forms of denial. Great assistance is given by inappropriate language that distorts perception, often with endearing or evasive labels. Lifton describes some examples of what has come to be known as "Nukespeak": the domesticating or "anesthetizing quality of the language of nuclear weapons."[62] The Hiroshima and Nagasaki bombs, for instance, were named "Little Boy" and "Fat Man," respectively. A "nuclear exchange" sounds like a party with mutual gift-giving, and so jargon obscures the grisly realities of carnage. There are, furthermore, many examples beyond those listed by Lifton. In the recent trial of the Plowshares Eight, Christian activists who were accused of damaging missile nosecones, the General Electric officials testifying insisted on calling the nosecone "the product," and warheads "the physics package."[63] "Doublespeak Awards" are given annually by the National Association of English Teachers to public officials using language that is "grossly deceptive, evasive, euphemistic, confusing, or self-contradictory"; a 1983 award went to the officer who described the Titan II missile and its nine-megaton warhead as a "potentially disruptive re-entry system."[64] Currently a renowned example of euphemism is the MX, our largest and most accurate offensive missile, which President Reagan has renamed "Peacekeeper"—possibly unaware that the cognate word "peacemaker" has a history as a humorous name for a gun or warship.[65]

Such affectations of language are not just happenstance. They have the effect of blocking images or of diverting intense emotion that would normally accompany any symbolization of mass destruction. The unthinkable is denied, the potential anguish benumbed, and all with a joyless intensity resembling religious fervor.

This avoidance by "linguistic detoxification," "*a way of talking about nuclear weapons without really talking about them*,"[66] is a prerequisite for the many illusions we cherish about the Bomb. Lifton lists, for instance, the illusion of limit and control (the supposition that thermonuclear warfare could be managed rationally and without escalating into global havoc), the illusions of effective foreknowledge, preparation, and protection, the illusion of stoic behavior while under nuclear attack, the illusion of recovery afterwards, and a more encompassing illusion of "systems rationality" that projects an aura of insane logic over the whole structure of nuclear strategy.[67] Self-deceptions of this kind depend upon "Nukespeak" and a habitual numbing against unspeakable images of holocaust. Moreover the entire process of denial is structurally reinforced and encouraged by the postwar growth of "chronic secrecy," as part of our government's mythic quest for national security.[68]

All these are consequences of nuclearism on the human psyche, which have been delineated by Lifton in his writings for two decades. Now, however, there is a much wider recognition of these effects. Attestation has been added by medical and psychiatric research by John E. Mack, Michael J. Carey, and Jerome D. Frank.[69] A still broader audience has been reached by Jonathan Schell's descriptions of living a double life (that is, by trying to ignore the peril we secretly know could at any time obliterate everything) and its pervasive effects on marriage, human relations, politics, and art.[70] In a nuclear age, explains another prominent writer, composing fiction is difficult now "that the story of any individual . . . may not be able to sustain an implication for the collective fate."[71] And in his Albert Einstein Peace Prize speech, former ambassador George F. Kennan characterizes our obsession with overkill:

> We have gone on piling weapon upon weapon, missile upon missile, new levels of destructiveness upon old ones. We have done this helplessly, almost involuntarily, like the victims of some sort of hypnotism, like men in a dream, like lemmings heading for the sea, like the children of Hamlin marching blindly along behind their Pied Piper. And the result is that today we have achieved, we and the Russians together, in the creation of these devices and their means of delivery, levels of redundancy of such grotesque dimensions as to defy rational understanding.[72]

So it defies rational understanding? But of course! Not because it is instinctual behavior, as supposedly is the case with lemmings heading to the sea, but because it is religious behavior. This is the point that is so often overlooked by antinuclear critics who shake their heads over the mindless futility of the arms race. Whether they realize it or not, they seriously overestimate the role of rationality in human nature. Here Lifton's depth psychology marks a great improvement. But more is needed. What is required finally is a religious diagnosis. For religion has always known that human beings will sacrifice reason and even life itself, if need be, for the sake of repressing chaos and securing cosmic meaning for their restless lives. Even suicide can be a last

ditch grasping at self-vindication and defiance! Instead of
puzzling over these lemming-like actions, we may gain more
understanding as well as improve our chances of averting
disaster if we address nuclearism at last as an appealing and
effective new religion.[73] And so we now move on to consider
what religious studies as a discipline may have to contribute.

Chaos and Nuclear Mythology

Lifton's analysis is carried further by a gifted young
scholar in the study of history of religions. Ira Chernus of the
University of Colorado at Boulder has been an inspiration to
many, including myself, in his pioneering work of applying
cross cultural studies and symbolisms to the hold which
nuclearism has on our inmost heart. Like Lifton he sees
religion as rooted in a profound hunger to experience
spiritual power and transcendence through images that
uphold the larger continuities of life.[74] He agrees that psychic
numbing is both cause and effect of the mind's inability to
produce culture-specific images that link death to these continuities. But he goes further than Lifton: our numbing
towards the nuclear threat cannot account for the lurid
fascination such themes nevertheless have for the public imagination. Popular culture returns again and again to such
pictures, and yet somehow the public never attains a concrete
understanding of what nuclear war would actually be like.
Why not? The answer lies in the role of myth.

> In thinking about nuclear war, we have largely set
> aside our rational, analytical faculties and our ca-
> pacity to think in realistic detail. The reality they
> depict has an elusive, blurred-at-the-edges quality,
> an open-endedness, a questionable mooring in
> everyday reality, and an emphasis on a few central,
> intensely concrete sensory images linked by un-
> predictable distortions of ordinary logic. For the
> student of religion, these characteristics remind one
> of nothing so much as that puzzlingly unreal reality
> found so often in myth. And the student of religion
> is well prepared to predict that constellations of im-
> ages relating to fundamental issues of life and death

will be likely to assume mythic forms.[75]

Analysis of mythic forms takes on a most practical function. "So psychic numbing is only half the story. It tells us why we fail to face the nuclear issue. The mythic approach tells us what happens when we do face the issue: We are fascinated, deeply moved, and somehow fulfilled in ways which we only dimly perceive or understand. Numbing and mythologizing thus reinforce each other, and the upshot of this secret alliance is political paralysis."[76]

Those knowledgeable in religion can fathom how this numbing emasculates traditional symbols of faith just when they are most needed while also impelling us to generate new mutations of mythic content. "The crisis of psychic numbing is, at its most fundamental level, a religious crisis."[77] Chernus describes several examples of cherished mythic images of nuclear war. One is the myth of the "heroic survivors" or the "big bang," so popular in science fiction plots: civilization is destroyed, but a band of people ("blond and beautiful and creative") survive the purgative fires and build a new society that is better than the past. We are beguiled with the promise of a fresh start after the traumas of rebirth. A second is the myth of "no survivors" or the "big whoosh." Here, instead of narratives, we are charmed by simple images of mushroom clouds and "the end" of everything, in a universally quick and painless death. Somehow the notions suggests a comforting regression to primal chaos and unity, a fantasy of "return to the womb." This gives expression to what Lifton calls the experience of transcendence, the Dionysian ecstasy of letting go one's self-consciousness and merging with cosmic nothingness.[78]

Together these two myths present a pair of attractive options as ways of maintaining sanity in the nuclear age: either I will survive and become a member of the heroic remnant, or I will be painlessly vaporized along with everyone else in an ecstatic "big whoosh." Both alternatives rest upon a third theme, the myth of "Destiny or Fate": the belief that one is powerless as the End approaches, and so under no obligation to make decisions. These mythic perceptions operate in reciprocity with numbing, shielding us from the concrete realities and the vast scale and chaos of what a holocaust would be. "When we face the immense, our minds revert to the modes of childhood and dream thinking—symbolism, fantasy, archetype, myth"[79]—and in direct proportion to the enormity of thermonuclear war. In effect these several myths "all share the common characteristic of making that war in some way acceptable or even attractive."[80]

However, Chernus points out, these and other nuclear myths betray us in two ways. First they are discredited when measured by the best knowledge available of what the likely results of nuclear war would be. The "big whoosh" view is refuted by statistical projections from the Office of Technology Assessment, which conclude that, although many tens of millions of Americans would die in the first thirty days after the initial blasts, even more would die thereafter.[81] Death for a majority would be neither instantaneous nor a rapturous release into what Freud called "oceanic feeling," but instead a slow process of agony. The "big bang" myth of new beginnings is hardly more credible. "The factors that make rapid recovery from a small-scale disaster possible . . . will almost certainly be absent following a nuclear attack. . . . Even the simplest requirements of survival will become major tasks."[82] Even if the ecological collapse predicted by recent studies on nuclear winter were somehow avoided, it is doubtful that the beleaguered bands of dazed survivors could ever produce enough surplus beyond their immediate physical needs to rebuild an economy. The same vicious circles that presently plague the Third World would become universal, and the greater the number of survivors, the more desperate and even violent may become the competition for scarce resources.

The second way nuclear myths betray us is that they fail even as myth. They lack the effective power which genuine symbols have that transmits depth of feeling, ennobling courage, and the rich texture of life. Although they retain remnants of older mythic narrative, such as purgation and rebirth or heroic warriors, they are but lifeless substitutes for the nurturing symbolism we desire so much. "Pseudomyths" though they be, we cling desperately to them because they seem to be the best available.[83] So the vicious circle of numbing and false myth goes on and on.

Thus Chernus offers a significant exposition of the specifically religious and yet self-deceptive role of myth for our crisis. Moreover — and in marked contrast to anti-nuclear critics such as Schell, Kaufman, and Lifton — Chernus does see a notable role as well for the church. Although making no claim to be a theologian, he points out that, "while the churches have a unique problem in the nuclear age, they also have a unique opportunity to illuminate our situation and respond creatively to it."[84]

Most anti-nuclear activity has come from a liberal ideological perspective. But there is a major failing which liberals share, whether they are within the church or outside the church. That failing is an overconfidence in human reason and its capacity to move people to realize and act upon their genuine self-interest. This prompts a liberal bent toward intellectualizing, if not moralizing as well — in effect a doom and gloom scolding about how incompatible the Bomb is to our survival or our morality. Then liberals puzzle over why their message has so little effect! The answer is, as we have seen, that nuclearism is itself an enticing covert religion. It arises because most people in their heart of hearts would prefer — and indeed demand — a sense of personal identity and cosmic purpose, over and above mere survival or morality. Even self-destruction, in the last analysis, is preferable to meaninglessness.[85] The role of the church, therefore, ought to be in redirecting anti-nuclear efforts towards deeper symbolic and even soteriological levels of communication.

Chernus goes on to apply the same critique of rationalism to both sides of the conventional debate over whether war has become incompatible with human survival. On the one hand there are the "defense intellectuals" in Washington who, since the Kennedy administration, seek both to identify rational purposes for nuclear weapons and to design rational ways of using such weapons for those purposes — a vicious circle between ends and means. "Abstract, technical, mathematical reason is the god at whose throne they worship — though the Bomb seems to be seated at this god's right hand."[86]

On the other hand, there are the anti-nuclear critics of

the defense intellectuals who claim that there can be no rational ends or means for weapons of mass destruction. They say that escalation would be inevitable, and so warfare by the Superpowers has become obsolete. Thereby, however, the critics admit that they share the same unspoken premise with their opponents: nuclear war is normally a *rational* activity! Still a further form of rationalism emerged when the Reagan administration sought to allay public fears about its steep buildup in nuclear forces. The result has been "the myth of rational balance,"[87] in other words, a professed support for arms control as well as deterrence, as a dual pressure on the Soviets to come to terms. We are asked simply to trust our experts, under whose benevolent and rational control the world can be kept in balanced tension indefinitely. In such a fashion, it is claimed, "the weapons will save us from themselves."[88]

All of these assertions about the rational function or dysfunction of war, says Chernus, only serve to ignore the realities of what is actually its religious function. He illustrates this from the works of three authors who have impressed him. James Aho,[89] first of all, says that in every religion, war has had the role of acting out some mythic scenario for the purpose of preserving a sense of "nomos" or cosmic order. This in turn holds back what humanity has always dreaded the most: "anomie," chaos, a final loss of orientation and sense of reality. In some cultures (especially Asian) war is an end in itself, a ritual combat that reenacts the structure of the cosmos. Thereby war is play, in the sense of drama and a game. In other cultures (especially Semitic or Protestant) war is a means to an end, a purification of the world from personified evil or anomie. Thereby war is work, in the sense of goal-oriented behavior with no limits on the means utilized to exterminate that evil. Thus, as Chernus likewise agrees, all wars, both ancient and modern, fulfill deep hungers for imposing anew a sense of orderliness on the stubborn irrationalities of life.

Another author cited by Chernus is J. Glenn Gray, who reports from his own battlefield experiences a mingling of awe in beholding spectacle, joy in comradely solidarity, ecstatic loss of self, and delight in destruction.[90] "War compresses the greatest opposites into the smallest place and the shortest time," Gray concludes.[91] This paradox Chernus proceeds to refer above all to the vast mingling of nomos and anomie, of structure side by side with destruction.

A third writer, Roger Caillois, in studying the role of festivals in traditional cultures, found the only analogue in modern times to be warfare. In both festival and war, says Caillois, "all excesses are permitted, for society expects to be regenerated as a result of excesses, waste, orgies, and violence. It hopes for new vigor to come out of explosion and exhaustion. . . ."[92] To return in ritual to primordial chaos is to touch a reservoir of potency that is thought to rejuvenate the world. Like celebration itself, warfare has always held an uncanny fascination. "The heart of war's secret attraction," Chernus concludes, "may lie in its ability to reflect all of our contradictory attitudes toward nomos, chaos, and their complex relationship,"[93] so that we can find a channel for the intensity of our ambivalences through a structured experience.

Therefore the analyses of these several writers, says Chernus, demonstrates why a rationalistic approach to either justifying or condemning nuclear weapons must miss the point. On the one hand, proponents of deterrence claim it protects us from the irrational power of the U.S.S.R. — but at a deeper level it, in fact, is irrationality itself which is feared. Unknowingly they wish to act out anew the timeless struggle to impose order upon primal chaos. It is in the last analysis a mythic struggle, and it is waged with a dauntless faith in technical reason and a literalistic, one-dimensional thinking that is only reinforced by what the mass media considers to be "news." On the other hand, this deadening rationalism is used also by mainstream liberalism in its opposition to the Bomb. That is a great mistake, insists Chernus, for even to enter the debate on the rationality of war or of nuclear weapons only "reinforces the potentially lethal paradigm we have been describing, regardless of the conclusions it attains."[94] It is instead at the level of religion and of symbol formation where the real issue must be decided.

This then is the advice offered by Chernus to the church and the disarmament movement. Human beings have an irrepressible need for life-sustaining symbols, and unfortunately at present it is nuclearism more than its critics which (albeit fraudulently) offers the more enticing mythology. It is tempting to try to "demythologize" nuclear war by publicizing the facts of what it would really be like. But this is ineffective unless accompanied by the difficult task of "remythologizing"—that is, selecting mythic themes from contemporary culture which give positive redirection to our quest for a nomos. Admittedly, the few examples Chernus gives are sketchy and somber, such as themes of the sufferings of the dead, of the existentialist antihero making forced choices, or myths of renewal such as a mundane heaven on a nuclear-free earth.[95]

In addition to calling for an indigenus new mythology to fill the vacuum, Chernus has more recently turned to the concept of "play" as a resource. If life ought not be a means to some end, but an end in itself, as occasion for joy and intrinsic satisfaction, then we can glimpse the freedom to extricate ourselves from technical reason and servitude to the Bomb. Life is a game in the best sense, "the human drama," but now nuclear weapons have made it possible for the entire theater to be destroyed! But that would hardly be in the best interest of the players, and so they ought to be awakened to that dire possibility. Therefore, instead of arguing that war is obsolete altogether, our cry should be "The show must go on!"[96] Chernus' appeal here comes down to a mixture of pragmatic and aesthetic motives: in some fashion deeper than that provided by rationality humans must be persuaded to be prudent enough to keep future warfare limited, because life itself is the ultimate value.

God, Reason, and Moral Response:

This brings us to the present moment. In this survey of how the implications of the nuclear threat have unfolded until we are brought up against the realization that a new religion is in our midst. Let us pause to review how this has become evident.

From 1945 until recently most responses to it by people of faith have been limited to an ethical level, comparable to other moral dilemmas of our time such as world hunger. A pioneering step was taken by Dale Aukerman, in offering a

provocative theological treatment of the Bomb. He vividly
sketches the idolatrous lure of limitless power, contrasting to
it the self-limiting God of Jesus the crucified. Yet some may
discount Aukerman's message because of his principled
pacifism, the intensity of his style, and the unreconstructed
biblical language to which he restricts himself.

For a wider audience it may have been Jonathan Schell
who first posed at least one aspect of the theological issue,
namely the finality and even nihilism of what extinction
would mean. One of those aroused by this grim specter, Gordon Kaufman, responded by reopening the ancient theodicy
question: how can a God who is both good and almighty permit undeserved suffering in the world? He is convinced the
nuclear age imposes on us a definitive if unconventional
answer: God must no longer be viewed as in charge of the
world. It is instead up to us — in our merely relative goodness
and might — to prevent the ultimate in undeserved suffering.
Kaufman urges the theological work of "imagination," but by
that he means less a re-envisioning of either God or the Bomb
as shapers of our perceived world, and more a Kantian boundary to the activity of the believing mind. Readers should appreciate Kaufman's warning against triumphalist tendencies
in conventional theism and its abuses by the bombmakers.
But in the austerity of his mission to demythologize our
language about God, he overlooks the already virulent
mythologizing surrounding the Bomb.

This, however, is precisely what must be understood, if
we are to account for the seductive fascination yet repressed
horror of our images of nuclear apocalypse. Here it is Robert
Jay Lifton who traces the quirks and quivers of the post-
Hiroshima mentality until the source is disclosed to be a
"secular religion," nuclearism. To be sure, it is the
psychological and behavioral consequences that interest Lifton, as a psychiatrist. But his trained observations over the
years corroborate the hypothesis that religion, functionally
defined, continues to thrive in our supposedly secular era.
The human drive for life-sustaining images of death and immortality, even when diverted into life-threatening folly, is irrepressible.

It remained for Ira Chernus to develop the religious

dimensions of nuclearism. He does so by delineating the uncanny yet compelling nature of myth, the corresponding
limitations of rational argumentation, and the special task of
the churches to reinvigorate traditional symbols of salvation
and blend them with new ones of an open future.

Thus the religious character of our crisis has at last been
displayed, and it will likely become still more apparent in the
months or years ahead. As a guidepost for our understanding
thus far, let us conclude this chapter by making some com-
parisons.

Of the authors discussed, the three who deal explicitly
with the theological challenge are Aukerman, Kaufman, and
Chernus. Coming from quite different backgrounds, they all
nevertheless recognize that the stark predicament of humanity in the nuclear age has unprecedented religious implications. Aukerman is true to the radical "peace church" tradition. His reflections on biblical themes conclude with a confidence that God not only will bring a final consummation,
but is already at work through obedient believers forming
shalom communities.

However, Kaufman and Chernus not only go beyond
Aukerman's biblical conceptuality, but also reject any longing for a supernatural rescue mission. A *deus ex machina*,
they claim, would only undercut the full responsibility which
humans must now assume for finding a path to survival.
They are alike in mistrusting classic theism, preferring instead
an organic evolutionary perspective on the human species.
This would include the relativity of cultures and of all
values — except of course for the overriding value of survival.
Their methodology differs from Aukerman's, for they
disclaim any reliance on revelation or any personal initiative
by God. For them, theology remains a human work, with emphasis on the imagination — although Chernus by implication
does allow that imagination far more scope and receptivity.

This latter point is the clue for the contrariety between
Kaufman and Chernus. The differences between these two
(we will return to Aukerman momentarily) are significant for
any attempts to understand nuclearism. On his own grounds
Kaufman seems unable to account for the baffling resiliency
of the arms race — a compulsive and Dionysian extravagance

which is potentially suicidal. However, Chernus, like Aukerman, recognizes the uncanny enticement of the Bomb in
meeting the human thirst for a sense of spiritual power, including both cosmic renewal and personal experiences of
transcendence. It is out of its fullness, not its immaturity,
that the mind demands such a rich medley of metaphor.
While Kaufman looks outward, so to speak, in a critical
"demythologizing" of theism as asymmetrical and alienating
to human value, Chernus looks inward to the human self and
its daily diet of symbols, seeking by remythologizing to improve that nourishment.

Kaufman's preferred theological method and heritage
stem from the Enlightenment and its critical rationalism. So
when he turns to consider nuclear holocaust he assumes that
after careful thought people must surely renounce such
supreme irrationality. But this procedure itself, Chernus
might reply, resembles that confidence in technical reason
and literal truth which actually sustains our mythic fascination with nuclear weapons. Perhaps a comparison of the two
writers in the last analysis must turn, not on their ideas about
God (for both are procedurally quite reticent to allow much
to be said here), but instead on their concepts of human
nature. Is the human self relatively univocal, a rational self-
consciousness that is only secondarily restricted by passion,
ambivalence, folly, or self-indulgence? Or is the human self a
bundle of complexities which depends on symbolization to
construct bridges within itself as well as to the outside world,
as it grapples with the tensions of finitude and self-
transcendence? Here I believe it is clearly Chernus who is
both more faithful to the Judeo-Christian vision, and more
capable of advancing our understanding of the nuclear dilemma.

There remains, however, one area to be addressed,
before we can begin to ask just how Christians ought to respond to this new secular religion. It has to do with the relationship of God and the human being. Here Aukerman may
return to help us. Both Kaufman and Chernus presume that
insofar as deity exists at all, God is—to say the least—passive.
Kaufman has very particular epistemological grounds for
asserting this, and he is right to call for a reformulation of

God-concepts. Our endangered generation does need to outgrow the crude notions of divine warrior or autocrat who exercises a coercive sovereignty. This is not the place, however, to enter the complex and far-ranging debate on recasting the language of theism. Suffice it to say that modern theology has heard a number of options for doing so, many of which do not entail Kaufman's outright abandonment of personal metaphoric language. Rather than the monarch/servant model, for instance, the biblical image of the vine and the branches (John 15) suggests models of connectedness and interpersonal relations.[97]

In any case, by assuming God's inactivity (and probably God's impersonality as well), both Kaufman and Chernus throw the entire weight of responsibility for solving the nuclear crisis on human shoulders. Quite apart from any unintended snub toward heavenly courts, this certainly results in a doctrine of humanity heavy with the freightage of a popularized Pelagianism. The ideas of Pelagius, the fifth century reformer criticized by Augustine, have sometimes been called "musty" religion: we *must* do what the urgency of the hour tells us we *ought* to, and so therefore we *can*. But—can we? It seems to me that the Pauline-Augustinian critique of the law, a religion of rules, or any salvation by human will power, has never been satisfactorily answered by musty activists, but only ignored. For the law or the cosmic "ought" condemns us to impotence and futility at the very time we try most desperately to fulfill it. We all know, for example, the experience of "freezing up" when we feel both singled out and overwhelmed with some enormous duty. Yet, on the other hand, we must grant that an extreme Augustinianism has overplayed this theme and thus legitimated human passivity before the status quo. So Kaufman's allergic reaction is understandable.

To put it rather too simply, the error in the traditional Pelagian-Augustinian quarrels through centuries of church history has been the inability to conceive the possibility that both the divine will and a human will might act concurrently—yet without curtailing the full and free responsibility of each. There is, however, precedence for this in the divine yet human will(s) of Jesus Christ, and in the New Testament experience of the Holy Spirit. It was not in benumbment, but at the height of his powers (even for lively polemic!) that Paul could insist, "it is no longer I who live, but Christ who lives in me" (Gal. 2:20a). Then there is a modern example in Dietrich Bonhoeffer, who from his prison cell in the closing months of World War II wrote movingly of "prayer and righteous action" in their integral unity.[98] In these prison letters there are famous words about living responsibly in a secular "world come of age," even "as if" there were no God, but those letters also contain a striking number of references to Providence! Bonhoeffer felt no sense of contradiction here, for the Lord of history summons human beings into partnership with the divine will to shape the course of events.[99]

In the crisis of the 1980s, as well as those faced by Bonhoeffer and by first century Christians, there should be no antithesis between Providence and human accountability. People of faith are called upon to act with conscious responsibility, but also to trust that God continues to work in the world—perhaps concurrently, and certainly in ways we only dimly comprehend. On this decisive point we return to Aukerman, for here his directly biblical perspective is also a surprisingly timely one. To the extent that more analytical methods are unable to move beyond a stalemate of two selves, the divine and the human, as self-contained entities, it is wiser to be content with the language of dialogue and personhood. Aukerman's meditations avoid that peculiar modern dichotomy, combining instead a confidence in God's faithfulness and providential care with a vision which can unlock human creativity and responsibility.

The confidence that we are not alone in the struggle to avert a humanly crafted Doomsday can give us the courage to turn to the hideous threat and face it squarely and calmly as one which in fact arises from a new religion, nuclearism. The moral challenge is grounded in a still deeper religious challenge. So we may return to the words of Luther and find that they take on a strangely modern ring: "Now, I say, whatever your heart clings to and confides in, that is really your God. . . ." But also the words of Richard Barnet may be read in a new light: "There was no way out of the race to destruction except somehow to transcend it."

We have long worhipped alien gods, and at this late date there are no short cuts to a "way out." But perhaps in the Providence of God, theology may yet assist us to transcend our numbed behavior and turn to face the menace looming before us.

2

Nuclearism as a Heresy

If nuclearism is an attractive and functioning religion, how then should the followers of Christ respond to it? We now turn to a consideration of how Christians may not only rise to this challenge, but do so on a theological level.

A cue may be taken from Stanley Hauerwas, a friendly critic of the anti-nuclear movement, and one of those faithful voices who remind us that the Bomb confronts us with far more than a moral dilemma. We have seen how he criticized Jonathan Schell for his "humanistic eschatology," which is in effect *no* eschatology at all since survivalism has no higher purpose than the sheer perpetuation of the human species.[1] Likewise the weakness he finds in so many proposals for world peace, from William James' "moral equivalent to war" to aspects of the Catholic bishops' pastoral letter on peace, is that they do not consistently offer "an alternative history," a broader vision of what is truly real. The following words refer to the nonviolent stance of New Testament Christianity, but could just as well instruct the modern church: "The Christian commitment to nonviolence is therefore not first of all an 'ethic' but a declaration of the reality of the new age."[2] For Christian ethics the first task is not to list the "Do's" and "Don't's," but rather "to help us rightly envision the world. . . . We can only act within the world we can envision, and we can envision the world rightly only as we are trained to see."[3] That new history or new reality has already begun through Jesus' life, death, and resurrection, and it will climax with God's kingdom. Until then, says Hauerwas, the church and not the nation-state is the bearer of this "true history" of the world. "Christians have been offered the possibility of a different history through participation in a community in which one learns to love the enemy."[4] Just as it is eschatology that shapes individual events into a new history, so it is in the church that individual Christians will find their identity.

The Church Amid Crisis:

To this we may add: in the confrontation with nuclearism (which is perhaps now the prime representative of the forces of the "old" world) it really ought to be the church that responds, and not just solitary Christians. Unfortunately the church is often divided, aimless, or unresponsive to the new history God has given. But in that case believers should not throw up their hands and drift off to individual peacework (which then is usually no more than piecework). They should instead throw themselves into the struggle for the renewed identity of the church. The reality of the Christian era ought to be reflected in as well as mediated by the corporate nature of the Body of Christ. If that new reality is contested by a virulent alternate religion such as nuclearism, it should require a response from the church as such. And the church will do so, even amid the ambiguities of a fallen world, insofar as it manages to be true to itself — that is, to its eschatological identity, to the gospel as such.

Concerning the nuclear arms race, most of the major Christian denominations have issued policy statements condemning its excesses and, to one degree or another, urging a renewed quest for non-military solutions to world tensions. The Catholic bishops' pastoral letter is but the most prominent of scores of similar pronouncements. "In many respects, the Christian churches stand singularly united on the issue of modern warfare. . . ."[5] Of course, as every church member knows, there are many voices in each denomination who object vigorously that such statements do not represent the majority of constituents, least of all themselves! They claim that such controversial positions only divide the church and blur (at least to the popular mind) its boundaries of identity. So, we wonder, just who and where is the church?

To those familiar with history, these complaints may

recall the great controversies that shook the churches in Germany in the 1930s, when the Nazi regime was consolidating its control over society. At that time there were not only severe outward pressures from the government in Berlin, but also internal pressures. These came from both the "Faith Movement of German Christians" (who were closely associated with the Nazi party) and the large middle ground, the avowedly neutral members of the church who commonly abhor controversy in any generation. Against these pressures arose the "confessing church" movement, which struggled to uphold the integrity of the gospel against the ideological encroachments of the Third Reich.[6]

In this politicized and acrimonious atmosphere of the 1930s. Dietrich Bonhoeffer spoke words which nowadays may guide us as well.

> The church has no control over the way in which unbelief marks itself off from the church. For this reason the establishment of the boundaries will always be a difficult one. Because *the knowledge of the extent of the church is never theoretically at the church's disposal* but must always be ascertained at any given time, there is no theoretical standard by which church membership could be measured. . . . This brings the element of living decision into the determination of the boundaries of the church for the Reformation concept of the church. The boundaries of the church are always decided only in the encounter between the church and unbelief; the act is a decision of the church.[7]

The true boundaries of the church remain hidden from it until, in obedience to its living Lord and in ever renewed acts of its confession of faith, those boundaries arise of themselves and are encountered afresh.

The same is true today, as we speak of the church responding to the nuclear menace. The term "church" represents neither an abstract ideal nor simply the empirical institution, but must necessarily refer to a God-given reality that emerges out of both in times of decision. It is no less the case now than in the 1930s that we find ourselves in "a struggle of the Church against itself for itself."[8]

We may now push the analogy a step further. The church in Bonhoeffer's day came to find it had no choice but to view Nazi ideology, both within and without its walls, to be a mortal threat to the gospel, that is, to the church's true identity. We have seen that in our own day the veneration and fascination with nuclear weapons comprise a functioning religion, nuclearism. By its pretensions to totalism and ultimacy it cannot in principle coexist with Christian monotheism. Moreover the content of its tacit belief system is antithetical to Christian faith, as we shall see later. Is there accordingly a mortal threat to the gospel and the church's identity? In other words, are we now—as in the 1930s—in a "confessional situation," a special crisis in which the church must reaffirm its identity by confessing anew its faith in Jesus Christ?

The Barmen Confession

In answering this question we will need to devote several pages to a review of some critical moments in the life of the twentieth-century church. In the case of the German church struggle, the high point was reached when a series of circumstances lead to the convening of the First Confessional Synod of the German Evangelical Church, held in the city of Barmen, May 29-31, 1934. The consensus it attained followed a series of preparations: many private statements (for instance some correspondence between Bonhoeffer and his theological mentor Karl Barth), declarations of the Pastors' Emergency League the preceding year, and then various provincial "free synods" in the spring of 1934. But the climax came at Barmen, in a remarkable gathering of Lutheran, Reformed, and United Churches in a (all too momentary) unity. But it was a unity that did not attempt to found a rival church to that of the "German Christians"—who by now dominated the state church apparatus. Rather its purpose was to call together the one true church of Christ in Germany.

Eventually, sad to say, schisms, compromises, and suppression did occur. Many confessing church pastors— including Bonhoeffer himself—died in Nazi prisons or as draftees on the Eastern Front. But the enduring achievement of Barmen was the composition of the most famous confession of faith of the twentieth century. Written largely under the influence of Barth, who recognized well the competing claims for totality and ultimacy that so agitated the atmosphere of the time, the statement opened with the cry, "Try the spirits whether they are of God!" (cf. 1 Thess. 5:19–21).[9] The most famous part of the Theological Declaration, Article One, which is prefaced by citations from John 14:6; 10:1, 9, is a stirring call to the church to reexamine the heart of its message. That means repulsing the infiltration of alien ideas — and indeed of any non-Christocentric criterion whatsoever: "Jesus Christ, as he is attested for us in Holy Scripture, is the one Word of God which we have to trust and obey in life and in death. We reject the false doctrine, as through the Church could and would have to acknowledge as a source of its proclamation, apart from and besides this one Word of God, still other events and powers, figures and truths, as God's revelation."[10]

Barmen has become a prototype for our times. The events of 1934 set the context for what is meant nowadays in talk about a "confessional situation." But the phrase has much older roots. In the early church *confessio* meant the profession of faith by a "confessor" or martyr who was put to the test during persecutions (see 1 Tim. 6:12–13; Heb. 4:14; 10:23). A time of great danger was also the occasion for clarity and courage in making a public declaration of the faith — not simply one's personal convictions (although facing mortal peril left no doubt about that), but the corporate faith of the Body of Christ. This is related to a second and more general meaning of the term: the biblical sense of praising God. Such praise thereby, as in the case of Peter at Caesarea Philippi (Matt. 16: 15-16), acknowledges Jesus as God's gift to us (2 Cor. 9:13; Phil. 2:11).

The sixteenth-century Reformation took over the term in both senses, gladly and publicly giving witness in particular situations to the justifying grace of God. Indeed this is one derivation of the word "Protestant," from *protestari*, to testify on behalf of. This is what dissenting Lutheran nobles did at the Diet of Speyer in 1529. Eventually the great Reformation statements of corporate faith emerged and accordingly were called confessions — from the Schleitheim Confession of Swiss Anabaptists (1527) to the Westminster Confession of English and Scottish Calvinists (1647).

There is, however, a more particular meaning to the phrase "confessional situation," or "a special case for confessing."[11] In his struggle with more radical reformers Luther was careful to distinguish between reforms that on the one hand were necessary and intrinsic to the gospel, and on the other hand what was only optional or *adiaphora* ("things indifferent"). The latter ought never to be imposed on the conscience. To mix these two, said Luther, would be to confuse grace with a salvation by works, and to transform gospel into law. But later, as polemic and armed coercion by various parties escalated, so did the selfconsciousness of defending the faith when under attack. In the late 1540s there was a politically enforced compromise that would have reintroduced many Roman Catholic practices under the guise of being indifferent things, *adiaphora* not worth fighting about. But some objected. In his resistance one defiant Lutheran of the second generation, Matthias Flacius Illyricus, is alleged to have said, "On the contrary, the truth is that nothing is an intermediate thing [*adiaphoron*] in the case confessing and scandal."[12]

That last phrase has taken on a historical importance. *In casu confessionis* ("in the case confessing") and, more recently, the related phrase *status confessionis*, have assumed a special significance in claiming that particular crises can transform even what Luther had called nonessentials into crucial matters of faith. The tenth article of the Formula of Concord, Lutheranism's definitive confessional statement of 1580, puts it this way: "In time of persecution, when a clearcut confession of faith is demanded of us, we dare not yield to the enemies in such indifferent things. . . . In such a case it is no longer a question of indifferent things, but a matter which has to do with the truth of the Gospel, Christian liberty, and the sanctioning of public idolatry. . . ."[13] Finally, observes one commentator, the completed body of Lutheran confessional writings may be summarized on this issue as giving direction in three sorts of circumstances, namely, under all conditions, to rightly distinguish what is indifferent from what is necessary; under normal conditions, to avoid offending the weak in faith by treating what is indifferent as though it were necessary or by imposing even what is necessary by force; and, in times of persecution, when the Gospel itself is at stake, to avoid compromise on any matters — whether necessary or not — where such a compromise would strengthen the enemies of the Gospel.[14]

The precise conditions of the "special case for confessing," as well as how to identify them, is not entirely clear.[15] They seem to include the following: persecution by enemies, the possibility of averting this by compromise on what some dismiss as nonessential matters, the threat thereby to the integrity of the gospel, and the risk and singular responsibility of decision which the church must therefore face — involuntarily and with no guarantees about the outcome. As Bonhoeffer said, it is only in encounter with unbelief that the church discovers its true boundaries. Certainly these qualifying conditions were present at Barmen, however. This is clear, even though technical expressions such as *in statu confessionis* or appeals to the Formula of Concord do not appear in its documents or records of proceedings.[16] Thus Barmen has become a prototype in our century of a time for confessing.

Dar es Salaam, Belhar, and Apartheid

Barmen in turn has formed the more immediate context for a surge of recent statements by official bodies as well as unofficial groups of Christians. In our generation the issue of racism has risen to special prominence, and especially with the Resolution on Southern Africa that was passed by the Sixth Assembly of the Lutheran World Federation in 1977. Meeting in Dar es Salaam, the assembly urged its member churches around the globe to make visible their common faith. This testimony should be not only through the doctrine they share, but "through their daily witness and service" and through welcoming at the unity of the Lord's Table everyone everywhere who accepts the same confession. Accordingly the assembly went so far as to condemn South African apartheid, using quite deliberately the formula expression that derived from the Sixteenth Century, *status confessionis.*

> Under normal circumstances Christians may have different opinions in political questions. However, political and social systems may become so perverted and oppressive that it is consistent with the confession to reject them and to work for changes. We especially appeal to our white member churches in Southern Africa to recognize that the situation in Southern Africa constitutes a *status confessionis.* This means that, on the basis of faith and in order to manifest the unity of the church, churches would publicly and unequivocally reject the existing apartheid system.[17]

It is of great significance that the error renounced by the invocation of this solemn formula is not, at least ostensibly, a theological doctrine per se, such as was the case in earlier centuries. Back then the disputes were over such sacred mysteries as the mode of Christ in *his* presence in the Lord's Supper. Here the issue is a socio-political system that divides Christians in *their* presence at the Lord's Supper — a folly which also of course has theological roots and legitimations supplied. Alternate belief systems which challenge the gospel can take on very tangible form. This is significant especially in the twentieth century, which prides itself on being secular and so the more easily falls prey to ideologies such as Nazism or apartheid.

Following the Dar es Salaam resolution by global representatives of the Lutheran tradition, South Africa's religio-social racism has several times been pronounced heretical by world ecumenical bodies. The World Alliance of Reformed Churches (WARC), meeting in Ottawa in 1982, suspended from membership two white Reformed churches in South Africa for neglecting past warnings, and declared apartheid to be "a sin, . . . a travesty of the Gospel and . . . a theological heresy." The conclusion follows: "Therefore, the General Council declares that this situation constitutes a *status confessionis* for our Churches, which means that we regard this as an issue on which it is not possible to differ without seriously jeopardizing the integrity of our common confession as Reformed Churches."[18] This was followed in the summer of 1984 by the Reformed Ecumenical Synod, a smaller body representing more conservative Reformed churches around the world. The synod condemned apartheid as "an ideology that is contrary to Scripture," and warned that "any teaching of the church that would defend this ideology would have to be regarded as heretical, that is, in conflict with the teaching of Scripture."[19]

Such pronouncements by international Christian bodies were not just paralleled but indeed preceded by movements of conscience in South Africa itself. Within that troubled land, in fact, there has been talk for decades of a confessing church movement, consciously modeled after the Barmen event.

It began after the infamous Sharpville massacre in 1960, in which 69 blacks were shot and killed by the police and 186 wounded, and after the failure of the subsequent Cottesloe Consultation. By 1965 the proposal was expressed publicly by Beyers Naudé, director of the Christian Institute, in the first of a series of articles, "The Time for a 'Confessing Church' Has Arrived." The parallels noted between the South African and the earlier German situations included "racism (i.e. anti-semitism in the case of Germany); a false unity between Church and *volk*; ideological pressure on, intimidation of, and an attack on the Church; and a sinful silence in the face of injustice."[20] Eberhard Bethge, the friend and biographer of Bonhoeffer, visited South Africa in 1973 and says that he found that this issue was raised "in almost every discussion I had in South Africa. . . . In many quarters the view is that a *status confessionis* now exists."[21] Moreover, the black delegates to a Consultation of Racism in 1980 raised the possibility that eventually they might have to disassociate themselves from the several denominations of the South African Council of Churches and become a confessing church. Since then the issue has been kept alive also by the Alliance of Black Reformed Christians in South Africa. The chair of this group is Allan Boesak, who in 1982 was elected president of the WARC at the same Ottawa gathering that condemned apartheid as a heresy.

Among whites, a young professor of theology at the University of Cape Town, John de Gruchy, has give valued leadership and has published widely in Europe and North America. It is no coincidence that he is very knowledgeable about Bonhoeffer; he often uses the latter's thought and the German church struggle to illuminate the effort against apartheid. For instance, in commenting on the World Alliance of Reformed Churches' declaration, his words echo those of Bonhoeffer about the boundary line between the church and unbelief: "This has not been done in an arbitrary manner. Indeed, *the boundaries have revealed themselves in the struggle for the truth of the Gospel*, and the WARC has finally been forced to acknowledge and articulate them."[22]

Finally there is the inspiring witness of that branch of the racially divided Dutch Reformed family of churches which is comprised of "colored" (that is, racially mixed) Christians, the Dutch Reformed Mission Church. At its 1982 Synod convening in Belhar, Cape Town, the delegates declared, "Because the secular gospel of apartheid most fundamentally *threatens the reconciliation in Jesus Christ and the very essence of the unity of the Church* of Jesus Christ, the DR Mission Church declares that it constitutes a *status confessionis* for the Church of Jesus Christ."[23] The synod went on to draft a confession of faith that is remarkable in its irenic spirit, its confident hope, and its balance of compassion and courage. It addresses directly the positive issues of the unity of the church, reconciliation in Christ, and the justice of God. Only then does it follow each affirmation with a brief negative corollary of ideas that must be rejected accordingly.[24] The Belhar Confession, as we will note later, should become a model for the wider church and what it means to confess Christ in the world today.

The Bomb and Status Confessionis

In addition to apartheid, various issues in recent years have prompted some to suggest that the church declare a special time of confessing.[25] But the only other major controversy to generate calls for a *status confessionis* has been the nuclear weapons debate in Western Europe. More especially this has been argued in the Federal Republic of Germany (West Germany), where the concentration of those weapons is probably higher than any comparable place on earth. Karl Barth in 1958 wrote a number of theses condemning the godless character of such weapons. A revised version was circulated by the Brotherhood Movement and presented to the synod of the EKD, the German federated Protestant church, where after debate it was rejected. The document asserted that "the church is now faced with the *status confessionis* on this question," and that a "contrary or neutral viewpoint on this question is not tenable on Christian grounds."[26] Ernst Wolf, one of Barth's foremost disciples, was a leader of this effort.

The issue would not go away, however. In 1981 the Society of Protestant Theology in that country passed its Declaration on Peace, strongly condemning the arms race. The next year the EKD was again set in an uproar. One of its component groups, the Reformed Alliance (comprising about ten percent of the membership) adopted a statement in 1982 condemning both the use and even the possession of nuclear arms as no passing matter of *adiaphora*, but indeed a "blasphemy destroying all life."[27] Again the phrase *status confessionis* was used, and again the wider state church turned it down. The following year the Reformed Alliance laid their report before the Ottawa meeting of the World Alliance of Reformed Churches, which responded with a strong statement on the issue but avoided the Latin catchphrase.

Outside Germany there has also been some effort to pose the Bomb as a special occasion for church confession. The General Synod of the Netherlands Reformed Church in 1979 stated that nuclear deterrence is "a modern form of idolatry" which endangers the church's oldest confession, "Christ is Lord."[28] Using less confessional language, the Sixth Assembly of the World Council of Churches (Vancouver, 1983) nevertheless condemned both the production and the use of nuclear weapons on theological as well as ethical grounds. The Central Canada Synod of the Lutheran Church in America in 1981 presented — unsuccessfully, as it turned out—their anti-nuclear Quinton Confession before the national LCA convention. In the United States, the Lutheran Peace Fellowship in 1983 made a formal statement that the very threat to use weapons of mass destruction was sufficient to precipitate an explicit time for confession. Similar calls for a *status confessionis* are voiced in this country by theologians such as Robert McAfee Brown, George Hunsinger, and Barthian scholar Arthur Cochrane, among others.[29]

Since the time of Barmen, therefore, and quite consciously in its shadow, we have seen that from various quarters the church has been urged to declare a special case for confessing. The focus in these decades has been on two grievous threats, apartheid and the Bomb. Not surprisingly, misgivings and even vehement opposition often have resulted.

Moreover, the use of the phrase *status confessionis* has been recognized as both an asset and a liability: an asset because it succeeded in focusing widespread attention on matters too long ignored, and a liability because of overuse and the ambiguity of its meaning. We have already noted some uncertainty about the origins of the phrase and those special conditions that should activate its declaration. The evolution of the term continued after the sixteenth-century Reformation. It accumulated new and not always consistent meanings, for instance, from eighteenth-century emphases on right doing (orthopraxis) as well as right doctrine (orthodoxy), from nineteenth century church law and the feelings provoked by enforced church merger in the western areas of the Prussian Union, and later by personal acts of conscience by individuals against Nazi tyranny.

Since such high moments of truth burst in upon us without prior announcement or calculation, probably we should not expect to attain a simple or clear cut definition of *status confessionis*. Nevertheless, critics such as Martin Schloemann become particularly irritated about this, warning of its "reckless use . . . without qualification as a shorthand term" or as "a catchword in party warfare" and an "increasingly hypostasized blanket concept."[30] Lutheran tradition holds dear the "two kingdoms" framework which has always acknowledged a major role to natural morality and the rightful autonomy of civil authorities, juxtaposing them to the realm of free grace. Like the principles of law and gospel, these two realms are to be kept strictly distinct in order to allow them to act reciprocally in the dialectic of salvation.

So it is especially from Lutheran quarters that voices are raised against any citation of confessional authority concerning matters of morality or socio-economic structures. To them such pronouncements appear to ignore Luther's magnificent insight into Christian liberty, and lapse instead into the fatal confusion between justification by faith and justification by works. In addition to the ambiguity of the phrase *status confessionis,* it is objected that such solemn authority can be invoked only when confession to Christ is seriously deformed or blocked. But, it is asserted, no socio-political policy can qualify for such formal condemnation, no matter how much it endangers human life, dignity, or even global survival. For politics and social systems occur in the realm of that freedom (and risk) of conscience granted by the gospel. In general conservatives and most Lutherans have resented the increasing usage of *status confessionis* for what they see as "only" ethical issues but with "the volume turned up" — even though a number of them would otherwise agree with anti-apartheid or anti-nuclear positions as such.

On the other hand, there are many defenders of these modern pronouncements of a confessional situation. They in turn can point to an action by no less than the German state church (the EKD) in 1970, which gave some indirect definition and sanction to the use of *status confessionis.* The 1970 "Memorandum on the Function and Limits of Church Statements on Social Questions" upholds unconditional church condemnation of "doctrines or actions" which gravely challenge the "freedom to confess with all its implications of the 'humanness' of humanity."[31] Here the scope of heresy is unmistakably widened to include actions as well as beliefs, with special attention to any ramifications on the humane quality of common life.

Another example comes from Louis Smith, a North American Lutheran, who reviewed four levels at which social evil can occur—in this case, racism and apartheid. It could take place 1) as a straightforward injustice, 2) as moreover an abuse of temporal authority, 3) as moreover legitimating that injustice and abuse by claiming it to be righteous according to civil standards, or 4) as elevating it still further by claiming it is righteous according to Christian teaching.[32] Smith says that the Dar es Salaam resolution was just as valid as the Barmen declaration, for they both recognized that the human system condemned was indeed a threat to the faith integrity of the church (level four), and not simply one of the lower three, over which the civil government would properly have jurisdiction.

Other writers point out that Barmen remains our best model. That 1934 synod, in which Calvinist (Reformed) predominated, was a healthy synthesis which succeeded in attaining a mutual balance of the Lutheran distinction of "the two kingdoms" with the Calvinist emphasis on "the sovereignty of God."[33] In the case of nuclearism, this Reformed theme is especially important. As we have seen, both Aukerman and Kaufman agree that the Bomb poses a conclusive challenge to the very concept that God rules the universe—even though these two authors draw opposite conclusions from that challenge. In any event the heritage of Calvin celebrates the lordship of Christ over every aspect of life, so it has always found easier the transition between confession and politics. "Not without reason it is often said that the Reformed way of thinking — with its always slumbering theocratic ideal — is the bloodbrother of Anabaptist radicalism."[34]

Also within official Lutheran circles there is at least a partial vindication of the Dar es Salaam decision. In response to the furor raised after 1977, the Commission on Studies of the Lutheran World Federation authorized a theological consultation to consider the issues raised. The event took place at Bossey, Switzerland, in early 1982. In its findings and recommendations the consultation presents serious qualms about the expression *status confessionis* as "an especially loaded term" in "inflationary use today."[35] However it did not shrink from using the word heretical. Concerning apartheid it stated flatly, "the Lutheran churches are called by God to confess their faith in face of an unjust political system that is based on an heretical perversion of ideology and a false reading of the Holy Scriptures."[36] Moreover it is ready to draw broader conclusions from this instance: "The resolution of Dar es Salaam has shown that under certain circumstances socio-political problems can provide the occasion for extraordinary confessional action."[37] Such circumstances include instances "when a church by its conduct or by its concessions to alien norms . . . so loses its credibility that it contradicts the gospel" or "when ideologies or worldviews infiltrate the church and dominate it by their power."[38] The upshot seems to be, regardless of whether and which technical terminology may be used, the church is accountable before God for exceptional times of confession of its faith, when confronted with whatever may jeopardize the gospel.

This is precisely what was done by the Dutch Reformed Mission Church in its 1982 Belhar Confession. Amid the pressures and personal dangers of the situation in South Africa, these gathered Christians have celebrated publicly the transforming power of the gospel for daily witness and service. Because it is the living Lord whom we acclaim in the world, says Japanese theologian Yoshinoba Kumazawa, confession cannot remain timeless or abstract: "Since the faith is to be confessed in relation to the historical acts of God, confessing the faith must bear an historical character. Specifically it should be *confession in loco et tempore:* confessing the faith in a certain place and time. We are not going to 'repeat' statically what was confessed in the past within a particular situation."[39]

Indeed, none other than Martin Luther can be cited in support of such an expansive yet specific evangelical duty: "If you preach the Gospel in all aspects with the exception of the issues which deal specifically with your time you are not preaching the Gospel at all."[40]

Nuclearism: A Special Time for Confessing?

Having thus reviewed some moments of high drama in recent church history, we can return to the question: does nuclearism pose a similar "confessional situation" to the church of our time and place?

To be sure, the nuclear situation differs from that presented by apartheid, which is a clear social policy of racial separation and disentitlement that is enforced quite openly by coercive state power. Nuclearism, by contrast, is a diffuse ideology that is at once more ambiguous in outline and more totalistic and ultimate in its thematic imagery. Because of these traits and also the psychic numbing and denial which invariably are evoked, it surely will be more difficult to attain such a broad consensus for the judgement that a *status confessionis*, or its semantic equivalent, does indeed exist. Nevertheless let us examine what this would mean, if such an effort were addressed to the nuclear threat.

    The early use of declarations of a special time of confessing in the sixteenth century was focused on church usage and ceremony. So we must ask if it is legitimate to broaden the scope of what is "necessary" for gospel integrity to include so-called "secular" matters beyond the walls of the church. The history we have reviewed shows this precedent has in fact already taken place, from the seventeenth-century emphasis on orthopraxis to the twentieth-century opposition to state-sponsored idolatries. That does not mean that just any grievance, injustice, or ideology ought to be an occasion for church confession. But, as we have noted, there are good reasons for designating nuclearism not only as the ultimate threat to "the 'humanness' of humanity" (EKD, 1970), but also as in itself a religion and thus no mere "secular" issue after all. The German church struggle against Nazism is a parallel, for certainly that was a case of ideological totalism which also infiltrated the church at every level. Does not the religion of the Bomb warrant equal vigilance?

    Also, however, a designation of *status confessionis* historically has been reserved for moments of extremity, a critical time of challenge which would call forth an equally critical time for confessing. Does that apply in our case?

    Normal times are the occasion for the more "ordinary" confession of Christians. That is, in the words of the Dar es Salaam resolution, Christians are "to show through their daily witness and service that the gospel has empowered them to live as the people of God."[41] But special cases arise whenever that daily witness entrusted to us by the gospel "is called into question by the very structure of our daily existence." In fact, comments Steven Schroeder, "That was the point of the Augsburg Confession, where 'ordinary' existence implied denial of the fundamental truth of justification by faith; it was the point of the Barmen Declaration, where 'ordinary' existence implied a limitation of God's sovereignty and a confusion of two kingdoms. Both confessions arose in situations where 'life as usual' put the Christian's acknowledgement of the Gospel on trial."[42] At such a critical occasion, a "moment of truth," dimensions of life formerly overlooked as discretionary or of no religious import suddenly take on a new coloration. "Precisely the abnormal situation itself causes viewpoints and arrangements which are adiaphora or neutral matters under normal circumstances to lose their innocence and neutrality."[43] Under these altered circumstances compromise is no longer a virtue (for instance, the citizen's duty to tolerate the opinions of fellow citizens), but a betrayal of principle.

Regarding nuclear weapons, therefore, do these conditions pertain? Admittedly the Bomb does not sponsor overt persecution of Christians, in the way the sixteenth-century Formula of Concord specified as a precondition for a special time of confessing. Yet it does press claims of ultimacy and totality, and it pervades the symbolic depths of the public consciousness in uncanny ways. If these effects be judged detrimental to Christian faith, as we shall argue, then surely the warped structures of our day to day existence, the very texture of "life as usual," must (in Schroeder's words) "put the Christian's acknowledgement of the Gospel on trial."

Attempting to read the signs of the times of course is in itself a speculative, even hazardous venture. There are no guarantees that individuals of conscience as well as church assemblies may not stake their lives on wrong judgments. Yet a full and sure knowledge of our historical situation is not possible for us mortals, and never will be until the glorious consummation. Each person from time to time must make judgments that are both momentous and irreversible. Likewise the church faces unavoidable risks in bearing witness at critical moments, if that witness is to be adequate as well as timely. Louis Smith states it well: "While hindsight sometimes produces clarity, confessing itself is always done before the results are in. Because *after* the results are in will be too late. Confession can only be made in the midst of ambiguity." Yet, he continues, this risk is to be faced courageously, since our assurance is in God and not our own wisdom or accurate perceptions: "In the act of confessing, the confessor trusts God to confirm their confession where it is right; and equally trusts God to undo the evil effects of their act where it has been wrong."[44]

A corollary to this risk is that confession should be no act of braggadocio or posturing, but is to be undertaken with modesty and awe. The focus instead is the contemporary events addressed, which are perceived as occasions for God acting in history. In a crisis "the congregation can never escape from the insecurity created by events over which it has no control. There is therefore nothing self-assertive about the confession, nothing of the overheroic. . . . "[45] Romanticized nineteenth century paintings of Luther defying the Imperial Diet at Worms manage to overlook the real anguish he felt in obeying the divine compulsion. *"Status confessionis* is no weapon in a private struggle, no handy 'stick to hit with'. . . , but the trembling acknowledgement that an hour has struck from on high in which something needs to be said."[46] Neither heroics nor defensiveness should intrude, since those who confess are thereby admitting openly that the situation as well as their compulsion to bear witness are both quite beyond their control.

This modesty moreover is rooted in a sense of shared humanity that refuses the temptation to scapegoat those who are in opposition. The cause for confession is a false idea, not false persons. Likewise it is the true gospel that is to be vindicated, not true believers. This entails an admission of shared guilt and an offer of reconciliation to opponents, which become genuine indicators of the Spirit of Christ at work. A beautiful example can be found in the 1982 Confession of the Dutch Reformed Mission Church at Belhar, which amply deserves to be quoted at length:

> This confession is not aimed at specific people or groups of people or a church or churches. We proclaim it against a false doctrine, against an ideological distortion which threatens the gospel itself in our church and our country. Our heartfelt longing is that no one will identify himself with this objec-

tionable doctrine and that all who have been wholly or partially blinded by it will turn themselves away from it. We are deeply aware of the deceiving nature of such a false doctrine and know that many who have been conditioned by it have to a greater or lesser extent learnt to take a half-truth for the whole. For this reason we do not doubt the Christian faith of many such people, their sincerity, honor, integrity, and good intentions and their, in many ways, estimable practice and conduct. However, it is precisely because we know the power of deception that we know we are not liberated by the seriousness, sincerity, or intensity of our certainties, but only by the truth in the Son. Our church and our land has an intense need of such liberation. Therefore it is that we speak pleadingly rather than accusingly. We plead for reconciliation, that true reconciliation which follows on conversion and change of attitudes and structures. And while we do so we are aware that an act of confession is a two-edged sword, that none of us can throw the first stone, and none is without a beam in his own eye. We know that the attitudes and conduct which work against the gospel are present in all of us and will continue to be so. Therefore this confession must be seen as a call to a continuous process of soul-searching together. . . . [47]

If a confessional movement is to be mobilized against nuclearism, it must likewise be acutely aware of these two requirements: the risk involved in declaring a given situation a threat to the gospel, and the humility and mutual accountability needed to keep self-righteousness in check. This brings us to a final characteristic required. Strictly speaking, the focus must be on idolatry, not ethics. Both are important, of course, and no sharp separation exists; but the idolatry takes precedence. If opponents as well as the large middle ground of the uncommitted are to be acknowledged as fellow Christians, however misled, then we must recognize that there is at least a range of diverse strategies which may still be held in

good conscience. The *status confessionis* position ought not
to be suspected as a way of selecting a particular means to attain a common end — whether that goal be a German church
free from Nazi ideology, an African nation free from racial
dehumanization, or a world free from the threat of nuclear
holocaust. In other words, a special time of confessing
focuses on the distinctively theological peril to the gospel. It
should be cautious about going beyhond that warning to ad-
judicate among the moral options which may remain, in living out one's obedience to the gospel in light of that peril.

This is illustrated by the wording of the 1982 Declaration
of the Reformed Alliance within the EKD, the state church in
West Germany: "Now as the possibility of atomic war is
becoming a probability, we come to this recognition: The
issue of peace is a confessional issue. In our opinion the
status confessionis is given to it because the attitude taken
toward mass destruction has to do with the affirmation or
denial of the gospel itself."[48] Note that the ban is not pronounced on nuclear weapons as such, but on our idolatrous
attitudes toward them. It is a matter of mindset more than
munitions!

Apparently there is room within the true church for not
only pacifists, but many holders of the just war tradition. (I
am assuming, of course, that just war theory can be genuinely
a means of seeking peace rather than somehow a ruse to lend
sanctity to national aggrandizement or even modern holy
wars!) In fact we are witnessing now a widening Christian vision of peacemaking that embraces both a chastened just war
perspective and the invaluable minority witness of historic
"peace church" pacifism. Most notably, the U.S. Catholic
bishops' pastoral letter on peace has recognized this shift. In
opening words that remind us of special times for confessing,
the bishops declare that "the 'new moment' in which we find
ourselves sees the Just-war teaching and nonviolence as
distinct but interdependent methods of evaluating warfare.
They diverge on some specific conclusions, but they share a
common presumption against the use of force as a means of
settling disputes. . . . We believe the two perspectives support
and complement one another, each preserving the other from
distortion," especially in their shared "opposition to methods

of . . . total warfare."[49]

In face of the nuclear threat, many theological ethicists are affirming the same thing. "Pacifists and proponents of just-war theories really need each other," says James Childress, a noted Protestant thinker.[50] David Hollenbach, a Jesuit ethicist, agrees. Prior to the eschatological New Age, he says, the historical tension between nonviolence and justice remains insurmountable; it should be therefore represented in the church by a pluralism of ethical stances.[51] Yet any conceivable use of nuclear weapons must be condemned.

This does not mean that the differences between these historic ethical alternatives have become negligible. Indeed they have not. Especially the clear and unmistakably nonviolent witness of New Testament Christianity and of the historic peace church tradition ought to be held high and uncompromised, for we know all too well how easily in past centuries an unchallenged just war tradition has been prostituted by nationalism. But the point is that a declaration of *status confessionis* ought not be considered a partisan device for suppressing one ethical choice in favor of another.

Instead such a declaration is directed at a level at once more broad and yet more narrow. It is broader, in that the Bomb puts in jeopardy everything which pacifists and just war theorists alike hold dear — any precondition for faithfulness to God, and even life itself. It is narrower, in that as a response to emergency, a confession confines itself to a specific menace to the gospel and the faith integrity of the church. Therefore the confrontation with nuclearism which I am proposing is not at the level of moral analysis — which would entail the enormous complexity of weighing what a responsible nuclear policy might be. Instead my argument will be at the theological level, an attempt to grapple with the idolatry which precedes and effectively prevents such moral clarity in the first place.

On Risking the Term Heresy: Four Objections

We have now examined what the characteristics of a special case of confession would be, as they pertain to the looming menace of the Bomb. At stake is not only human

survival but the vindication or discrediting of the New Age
which has been inaugurated by the life, death, and resurrection of Jesus Christ. Faithful Christians ought to be aroused
personally to meet this "awe-ful" challenge. But something
more is needed than individual responses. The Body of
Christ, the Christian faithful in their corporate life, should be
summoned to renew the witness to and embodiment of the
New Age. "The confessional response is confession, a communal account of faith in a time when that faith is questioned
by the very structure of everyday life, a communal acknowledgement of participation in that sinful structure, a communal account that relativizes false absolutes, a communal
account that for that reason is necessarily critical."[52] From
this point onward, therefore, let us turn our efforts to
assisting the growth of such a confessional movement within
and among our several churches. Let us pray and work for
recognition of a *status confessionis* concerning nuclearism
that will free the church at large to be the church.

In taking up this task, however, we must consider a pair
of terms which have not yet been utilized, but which are
bound to surface. "Heresy" and its correlate "orthodoxy"
have been historically part of the church's ongoing self-
examination and efforts to recover a faithful confession in
each generation. Yet these terms, and especially the former,
are freighted with offensive memories from the past. Even to
mention "heresy" is likely to conjure up lurid images of tor-
ture chambers and burnings at the stake, of bickering bishops
and meddling emperors, of witch hunts and of course the infamous Spanish Inquisition. If only we could discard the hor-
rid word once and for all! And yet it — or some synonym —
seems necessarily implied as the counterpart of a genuine confessing of faith.

Heresy (in Greek, *hairesis*) comes from a root meaning
"choice," and then sect or factional opinion. Already in the
New Testament it had acquired a negative sense (1 Cor. 11:19;
Gal. 5:20; 2 Pet. 2:1). In the second century Ignatius of An-
tioch and Irenaeus put the finishing touches on what we still
recognize as the caricature of the heretic: a self-seeking dissi-
dent who out of spite and ambition shatters the ancient unity
of the faith. This of course is a stereotype born from the pas-

sion of polemic, as the early church in its diversity struggled to formulate its true identity. Every great religion has co-existed with and tolerated an internal variety of ideas, shamans, and subgroups, and every religion at times has had to draw a line when some of this variety threatens to become too discordant. Heresies, before they are discerned as such, may have a long and even respectable prehistory. They are characterized, not by personal malice, but by a one-sided perspective on what comes to be accepted as truth in the wider community of faith. Moreover, as Karl Rahner admits, "even within the Church and for considerable periods of time there can be tendencies, attitudes, emphases, etc., perhaps in theory, but above all in spontaneous practice, which can only be characterized as latent, inarticulate but real heresies or as leanings to heresy."[53] This description is more accurate than the stereotypes, both historically and with reference to the modern idolatry of nuclearism.

Nevertheless, as is shown by the current controversy about whether apartheid in South Africa is a heresy or not, there are vigorous objections to using the term nowadays. So let us examine four of these misgivings.

1. It is objected that heresy is an antiquated term, conveying a self-righteous tone that is out of place in our modern age of pluralism and tolerance. In reply, we may grant that the word has connotations which render it difficult to rehabilitate. The imperious overtones can be diminished only by patient and careful explanation, combined with the personal humility of those daring to use the term. But we must not grant the assumption that pluralism levels all regard for truth into a plateau of indifference. As Bonhoeffer warned in 1938 in the German church struggle, "A church which no longer takes the rejection of false teaching seriously no longer takes truth, i.e., its salvation, seriously, and ultimately no longer takes the community seriously."[54] Tolerance towards a myriad of worldviews and faiths is mandated indeed by our admission that we and all humans are finite. Our knowledge is always partial. But no less mandated is the church's passion for the truth revealed in Christ, and therefore our unending struggle "for the integrity of the Gospel in the midst of, and for the sake of, a sceptical world."[55]

2. It is objected that heresy is a term wedded to an authoritarian hierarchy which claims a monopoly over revealed truth. Historically this has been linked with a closed society or a state church. This objection usually has in mind the context of Roman Catholic canon law and traditional moral theology. There heresy refers to "a sin of one who, having been baptized and retaining the name Christian, pertinaciously denies or doubts any of the truths that one is under obligation of divine and Catholic faith to believe."[56] The term is confined to baptized Christians who stubbornly choose to remain in error or doubt about a revealed truth. By implication, however, it further narrows the reference to isolated dissenters, mavericks who willfully oppose the hierarchy which is divinely authorized to stand guard over truth. And truth, in turn, is assumed to be a quantity of assured and timeless concepts. These latter constrictions are indeed authoritarian and are unacceptable to a Protestant understanding of what false teaching means.

Only with difficulty has such a notion of heresy been carried over into modern times at all. In fact, the Catholic hierarchy's bitter campaign against the "modernist movement" at the turn of the century may have been its last effective implementation.[57]

In any case these authoritarian traits are certainly not irrevocably wedded to a usage of the word heresy. This much has already been demonstrated by the twentieth century struggles in Germany and South Africa. In these instances we find a much less static understanding of true faith, and thereby a less constrictive prejudgment about the label of heresy. Here Karl Barth's criticism of unevangelical conservatism is appropriate, a warning against the church supposing itself to be the custodian of truth, with no further need of seeking to hear the living Word of God afresh in every situation.[58] "Confessing" the faith is more precarious and open ended than "confessionalism" permits. The tradition against which error is to be measured is less a static *traditum*, administered by a clergy elite and dispensed to the masses. Rather it is a dynamic act of *traditio* within which the boundaries of the true church disclose themselves anew and illuminate the darkness shared by all alike.[59] Heresy, accordingly, is no longer an accusation to be leveled at a defendant by some ecclesiastical court. Rather it is a collective dereliction, a lapse into the thought patterns of the Old Age now superseded in Christ's death and resurrection. It is a lapse to which the church as a whole or in part is prone at any time, and against which we can defend ourselves only by renewing our confession to God "in daily witness and service" (Dar es Salaam, 1977).

3. It is objected in our century that heresy designates false doctrine only, and must not be used to refer to political or ethical matters.[60] This may be answered on two levels. First, as we have noted, nuclearism itself is best described in terms of a functioning religion, a role that goes well beyond political or ethical considerations. This ideology need not masquerade as "Christian doctrine" to warrant being the object of a *status confessionis* against whatever threatens the "freedom to confess with all its implications of the 'humanness' of humanity" (to use the words of the 1970 statement of the German church)

Secondly, it is unfortunately true that nuclearism is also given quite explicit Christian sanction by some zealous religious groups. In these cases it would qualify as heretical under even the most strict doctrinal usage of the term. Such legitimation occurs most unequivocally from that quarter usually named the New Christian Right, or what Lifton calls "Nuclear Fundamentalism." We have noted several of the more exotic examples in the testimonials assembled in the preface of this book. It is possible that a beginning step in acknowledging the heretical status of such idolatry may have occurred in 1984. In that election year the New Christian Right was very active. In October, then, one hundred Christian and Jewish leaders found it necessary to call a news conference to warn against the strident voices championing what has come to be called a "theology of nuclear Armageddon."[61] Such beginnings have not been auspicious, however, for an accusatory tone too easily emerges. To summon to repentance and reconciliation those brothers and sisters in Christ who are in the grip of heresy will be among our most difficult tasks, as well as being one of the most important.

4. Finally, it can be objected that heresy implies a novel

departure from Christian consensus and so by definition must refer to minorities or even lone dissenters. Yet those who are now taking exception to nuclearism are themselves clearly a minority, while the majority of North American Christians either passively condone or actively support the veneration of the Bomb.

Admittedly this is a psychological obstacle in using the term. The word could even appear to be the verbal spasm of malcontents, frustrated by their powerlessness. However it need not be a theological obstacle. Orthodoxy is not a synonym for majority. Protestantism, for example, was born when a minority of voices called the greater church back to faithfulness. In our own century the confessing church movements in Germany and South Africa have always numbered a tiny fraction of Christians as their adherents. When measured by the gospel, all of us fall short, and certainly the majority of the church can be in error at a given time. "What we call 'normal' in psychology," Abraham Maslow observed, "is really a psychopathology of the average, so undramatic and widely spread that we don't even recognize it ordinarily."[62] If "normalcy" can be pathological in terms of mature ego development, so may it also in terms of mature faith development. Of course those who depart from the consensus of any community must take on special responsibility to examine their motives and guard against self-righteousness. But Christians are also and above all beholden to the Lordship of Christ and so, whether in the majority or the minority, they must devote themselves to the always unfinished task of renewing the church.

On Using the Term Heresy: a Reconsideration

Having noted these objections and granted the pitfalls to which they may point, let us now venture a redefinition of the two controversial terms from Christian history.

Let "orthodoxy" signify not a static deposit of timeless truth ("once for all delivered to the saints," in the words of Jude 3b), but rather an unceasing struggle to be true to the gospel. It is a struggle to recover the vision that founded and guided the early community of believers, and to articulate that vision afresh in ever-changing circumstances. The "tradi-

tioning" process is at the heart of the perennial tension between novelty and identity, as the church moves through the
centuries. Paul Ricoeur puts it this way: "tradition. . . , even
understood as the transmission of a *depositum*, remains a
dead tradition if it is not the continual interpretation of this
deposit: our 'heritage' is not a sealed package we pass from
hand to hand, without ever opening, but rather a treasure
from which we draw by the handful and which by this very
act is replenished. Every tradition lives by grace of interpretation, and it is at this price that it continues, that is, remains
living."[63] Orthodoxy thus is a direction more than it is a
resting place, a truthful vector more than a treasure vault.

Heresy, on the other hand, refers to what is disavowed
when the church is granted the ability to confess its faith
anew. It is a disclaimer, important only as a corollary to the
positive gift of confession. When the primal vision of the
community is regained, there is a realignment of perspective.
That means a fresh look at ideas formerly tolerated or even
unnoticed in the contextualized Christian message of a given
time and place.

Sometimes those renounced ideas were an integral part
of Christian belief at an earlier stage. By denouncing Arian-
ism, for example, the fourth-century church abandoned a
logical outgrowth of its own earlier Logos-Christology and
Angel-Christology. Sometimes, on the other hand, the ideas
renounced were of much more recent vintage, a product of
the ongoing process of Christian acculturation. Eighteenth-
century deism, for example, is usually held to be a graft of the
Age of Enlightenment on the rootstock of the gospel.

Of which type is nuclearism? I judge it to be of the latter
variety, an unwitting but disastrous compromise made by a
majority of church members in our society. In divesting itself
of this ideology, the church would be regaining its original vision of the New Age inaugurated by Jesus. Others, however,
may judge this alternative differently. Gordon Kaufman, for
instance, appears to trace the source of contamination back
to the earliest symbols of God as "father-lord-creator."[64] Or
some may view the prehistory of nuclearism as starting first
with the Age of Constantine, that is, when state power accen-
tuated those triumphalist tendencies already developing in the

church. Still others may be inclined toward the skepticism of Walter Bauer, the scholar who claimed that orthodoxy and heresy are meaningless labels awarded fortuitously throughout history, bestowed on winners and losers of church power struggles.[65]

However, in all these cases we should remember that many of those who hold that somehow nuclearism is a logical offspring of the church, at some stage of its development, may still be potential allies in the coming church struggle. The important thing is to work toward an ever wider recognition that nuclearism is both a covert religion and a powerful challenge to the gospel. That is, regardless of the past, nuclearism is now a heresy.

To use that term does remain a risk. At best it may still prompt misunderstanding among bystanders, or smugness among allies. Possibly the term is beyond any useful recovery. But whatever the language selected, those who recognize nuclearism for what it is must work for a renewal of the church, in a special time of confessing. This is no time for self-righteousness or Star Chamber proceedings. Instead we need self-examination and prayer. We need mutual penance concerning habits of thought and numbness in which we all share some grievous complicity.

In short, orthodoxy is a never-ending process. So the renunciation of heresy should be a mutual and ongoing struggle. Here the gentle but steadfast spirit of the confessing church movement in South Africa is a better model for us than the bombast and coercion of the fourth and sixteenth centuries. When the church is true to itself and to its Lord, as the Reformed heritage in particular reminds us, it is a church always in the process of reformation: *ecclesia semper reformanda*. May we now resume that process!

3

Deterrence as Sacred Doctrine

Before we proceed to consider how best to take up the emerging church struggle of our time, let us pause. Perhaps the specifically theological challenge of nuclearism as a covert religion may be clarified if we can discover in it some counterpart to doctrine as such. Traditionally heresy has been defined as a grave threat to the gospel by wrong belief, rather than wrong morality, worship, or church practices. Yet we have seen that nuclearism functions largely at a preconceptual level, by its peculiar combination of fragmentary images, fantasy, numbing, and denial. From this blend it draws the mythic power it holds over us. Christianity on the other hand has become a highly conceptualized religion; it has an elaborate belief system — which is the very trait that might seem lacking in nuclearism. Therefore Christians who assume any religious rival or subversion must be similarly configured are liable to overlook the possibility that nuclearism might be a religion after all — much less a heretical one as well!

As a heresy nuclearism threatens the gospel on many levels, some of them by means of ritualized behavior or vivid images with the meanings unarticulated. Nevertheless, it does have also its "theologians," as the Pentagon indeed calls them. These are grand nuclear strategists who by arguing their schools of thought do contribute to targeting policy and refinements on the master plan for the ultimate in warfare. Herman Kahn, for instance, in the early 1960s wrote a trilogy of books in which he tried to make nuclear war more "thinkable" and thus controllable and even (as theologians often like to do) rational.[1]

In the 1980s these "theological" treatises are back in style, since many of our nation's leaders are now true believers in the notion of manageable nuclear war. So the theologians of nuclearism have been busy. In the documents of research institutes, in Washington interoffice memos, and on university blackboards their doctrines are propounded and argued with all the religious seriousness which in past centuries was accorded the Queen of Sciences.

Deterrence: Defined and Ill-defined

The preeminent dogma of nuclearism has been "the theory of deterrence, the main canon of U. S. nuclear doctrine for nearly 40 years."[2] In general, deterrence means using threats to manipulate another's behavior. Since it is widely believed to be a description of how the superpowers have averted global holocaust for these four decades, it serves broadly as the chief legitimating concept for the arms race in all its phases. Alan Geyer describes it well:

> Nuclear deterrence, after all, is a quasi-theology. It has a dogmatic character and an elaborate theoretic superstructure. It is prone to absolute claims about the deepest springs of human motivation and conduct — although, like too many churchly theologies, nuclear deterrence lacks a fully rounded view of human experience. While it may or may not name the name of God, deterrence deals in the most ultimate weapons and the most ultimate threats. Deterrence is thus a penultimate eschatology.[3]

An official definition of deterrence comes from the Joint Chiefs of Staff and their *Dictionary of Military and Associated Terms* is "The prevention from action by fear of the consequences. Deterrence is a state of mind brought about by the existence of a credible threat of unacceptable counter action."[4] In a sense such a concept has always been part of military defensive measures, where bluff and posturing have historically served a function. But only in the nuclear age has deterrence risen to dominate strategic planning. It was made thinkable by the dreadful precedent of extermination bombing by the R.A.F. and the U.S.A.F. in World War II.[5] And it was made necessary by the stark certitude that nothing can "defend" against a nuclear attack once begun, so the only recourse is to dissuade by any means possible the potential attacker.

Since deterrence is a "state of mind" that is generated by "credible" action, it is clear that we are already in the realm of religious discourse. In its broad strokes and generalizations, the doctrine seems curiously removed from daily life. Indeed, as a state of mind, only a would-be attacker could say whether deterrence even exists or not! From our side the theory must remain a grand array of conjecture, of second-guessing what is beyond the limits of human knowledge and yet what is believed to be of ultimate concern for our survival. In short, it becomes a grisly parody of medieval theology. "Strategic analysis is a dream world," comments a defense analyst. "It is the realm of data-free analysis. There is no test data, no combat data."[6] In fact, the concept of deterrence has been called "a gift to strategists in that its nature and workings remain so elusive and so imperfectly understood as to permit endless speculation with little danger of empirical refutation, and justifying the maintenance of almost any military capability on the grounds that it might be doing good and we could well·be worse off without it."[7] Yet, as in the case of scholastic theology, such rarefied mental constructs routinely deal with supreme matters of life or death—including ours.

From the beginning of the nuclear age, the paradoxical nature of the concept of deterrence has been recognized. In a speech on March 1, 1955, Winston Churchill anticipated an age of mutual deterrence, a time when by a "process of sublime irony, safety will be the sturdy child of terror, and survival the twin brother of annihilation."[8] A disinterested onlooker must be struck with a sense of absurdity and surrealism at the thought of threatening unlimited devastation in the name of peace. Yet ironically it is only with the advent of weapons of mass destruction that the idea of deterrence has become really workable. Its subjectivity and ambiguity kept it of secondary significance in the pre-Hiroshima era of conventional weapons. But nuclear arms are so devastating that they impose, in the words of strategist Bernard Brodie, a "marvelous clarity of choice between nonwar and destruction"; instead of fine-tuning calculations we have a "bludgeon."[9] "The idea," adds another analyst, "is to make the threat so stark and so obvious that it swamps all misperceptions."[10]

And so the nuclear bludgeon has come of age, wreathed in paradox. The unthinkable has presented itself as the only key to the unattainable, peace. Or as a perceptive student of mine put it one day, "the threat of war is the deterrent to war; the deterrent to peace is the threat of war."[11]

Recently, however, the tension of that paradox has been slipping, degenerating into formlessness. Deterrence, or Mutual Assured Destruction (MAD), remains in public as the U.S. "declaratory policy." But increasingly several types of nuclear warfighting policies are replacing it as our actual or "operational policy."[12] These innovations effectively undermine those conditions which seem to promise a stable deterrent: to preserve rational control by leaders in a crisis, to avoid any miscalculations by potential aggressors, to avert accidents that would trigger a wider war, and so on. Furthermore, events of the 1970s had already suggested that our strategic forces in fact have a major purpose other than direct confrontation with the U.S.S.R. "These weapons," says Daniel Ellsberg, "are designed to strengthen the ability of American expeditionary forces to avert, or defeat, nonnuclear challenges to U.S. and allied interests far from our shores. They are to do this by enhancing the credibility of U.S. threats to initiate 'limited' nuclear war."[13]

Yet the public still believes in old style deterrence, a term which evokes comforting images of the nuclear umbrella shielding our homeland. Most people are reluctant to recognize the fact that the ephemeral promise has begun to dissipate altogether.

> Thus the concept of deterrence retains its value as an emotive word, sparking feelings of security and safety, but has lost any precise meaning. This is clear even in the authoritative study of nuclear deterrence by a pro-nuclear strategic theorist,

> Laurence Freedman, when he concluded (rather
> strangely) that "the Emperor Deterrence may have
> no clothes, but he is still Emperor." The loss cannot
> . be restored through word-playing ("extended deter-
> rence," etc.). Nuclear deterrence today means what-
> ever the speaker wishes it to mean. It is a blank
> check.[14]

So the "umbrella" metaphor could better be replaced by the
metaphor of the "blank check"—a truly exorbitant voucher,
by the way, which we are all requested to sign. Alan Geyer
details some of the contents which seem to have crept in:
"Nuclear deterrence no longer defines a coherent strategy or
ethic, if it ever did. If deterrence can mean possession but not
use, or no first use, or a first use option, or a second strike, or
massive retaliation, or counterforce superiority, or certain intention, or uncertain intention, it is time for much more
discriminating ethical typologies on nuclear issues."[15] A
preferred term in official circles, by the way, has become "extended deterrence." Apparently the umbrella has been
stretched beyond all limits, and the blank check made an
elastic one.

But let us put aside, for the moment, this current
unravelling of the concept of deterrence. Let us instead address it as a doctrine in the strength of its heyday years ago. If
the most venerable of all dogmas of nuclearism can be challenged, even on its own favored ground, then we will have
begun to illustrate the classical approach of Christian
argumentation against a heresy, namely by direct refutation
of a false idea. The approach will be twofold: First we will
survey a secular critique of deterrence, both as internally inconsistent and also as dubious when compared to empirical
studies of human behavior. Secondly, a more explicitly
theological critique will follow.

Four Questions

A pretheological critique of deterrence would analyze
the ambiguity of the concept, even in its days of prime health,
and it would compare this with relevant summaries of social
science research. Such a survey is provided in an excellent

book by Patrick Morgan: *Deterrence: A Conceptual Analysis*. To manipulate another's behavior by threat is a primitive form of conduct, Morgan observes, and to the degree it has worked, it relies less on human rationality or wisdom than on human caution. His analysis is even-handed and fair. For our purposes it may be summarized by four questions which proponents of deterrence have not sufficiently pondered.

1. Which kind of deterrence situation is foreseen?[16] The term does not refer to just any act of coercion or bravado, but to forestalling a military assault. "Immediate deterrence," on the one hand, is that quite rare occasion when one nation is directly planning an attack (a blow at Pearl Harbor, for instance), which then is cancelled because the would-be victim nation makes an explicit threat of retaliation. "General deterrence," on the other hand, is a long term rivalry between hostile nations, in which each makes vague threats as a part of its military "preparedness." The problem is that governments confuse these two types, habitually using the scare language of the former (infrequent) scenario to justify the latter condition. The result is a confusion of long-term realities in international affairs, a neglect of all the normal factors influencing an adversary's government, and acquiescence to a perpetual arms race.

2. How may we in fact influence the plans of a hostile government?[17] To do so, we would need to know how that particular regime makes decisions, so our actions could be tailored accordingly. In the case of a closed and enigmatic society such as the U.S.S.R. This knowledge is difficult at best. Yet as other writers have noted, there is in America a shocking lack of interest in Soviet or Russian studies of every kind. Furthermore the few Kremlinologists we have are usually self-selected by their zeal for a prior ideological position. How then can we expect to actually exert a deterring effect on the Politburo?

Quite different notions of deterrence flow from different models of government decision making. The trick is to find threats that effectively deter, but do not go so far as to incite a preemptive attack instead! One such model is an individualist one, which assumes decisions are made by a key governmental figure, and then seeks whatever would impress that leader's personality. Deterrence would become "*a fortunate conjunction between the personal characteristics of two sets of leaders.*"[18] However, not only is personal diplomacy notoriously unstable, but it often neglects the findings of social science research about the nature of misperception, how communication is regularly filtered and misjudged by decision makers.

Another model believes that decisions emerge from shifting factions within bureaucratic groups. Here the aberrations stem from what is called "groupthink," which includes a series of group illusions about invulnerability, moral purpose, and unanimity, combined with the stereotyping of enemy leaders, and a persistent self-censorship that ignores deviations from the team's consensus. The problem here is that external threats only weaken the influences of any "dovish" factions and strengthen the hand of the most militant members of the group. Again, it is uncertain which kinds of threats toward a given government might work — or which are least counterproductive, at any rate!

3. In what kind of situation is deterrence likely to succeed or to fail?[19] This must remain unclear under general deterrence, of course, which is so amorphous a condition. But when a case of immediate deterrence is thought to exist, the focus usually is on individual decision makers — their propensity for risk and other such personality traits. Those who have come to office through normal social channels are usually moderate, flexible, and reluctant to make sudden gambles. But leaders who rise to power by a coup, revolution, or amid social disorder are likely to be so self-confident and inexperienced that little may be able to deter them.

Most important, the experience of crisis in itself may either help or hinder the effectiveness of retaliatory threats. Deterrence is strengthened if a crisis increases a government's caution, by either prompting a bureaucracy to seek consensus or a leader to "keep his options open." But an emergency situation may also have the opposite result. On the one hand a sudden crisis may promote a leader's excessive confidence in managing the situation or even hopes of a quick, cheap victory. A team mentality tempts a group to take bigger risks than any single member would venture, especially when accompanied by fatigue and the psychological process of "bolstering." And on the other hand in a prolonged crisis, "all the various forces that sustain incrementalist behavior in leaders, and thereby enhance deterrence in the sudden crisis, now work in the same way but have the opposite effect. This encourages an illusion of crisis management — because both sides are cautious and have time to consider their moves — while setting the stage for the two sides to gradually perceive the approaching war as probably inevitable."[20]

Such a war of nerves may well reach the point of reversing the effects of deterrence. It may instead impel a first strike, in hopes of fighting an unavoidable war on the most favorable terms. Emotions may finally reach such a pitch that caution is thrown to the winds and the urge to destroy the enemy becomes greater than the desire to survive oneself. "Even if we are bled to death," the Kaiser is reported to have said in 1914, "England will at least lose India."[21] Thus any attempt to deter must rest on quite fragile judgments of the specific situation at the moment.

4. On what kind of rationality does deterrence depend?[22] With this question raised by Morgan, we now approach the transition from a secular to a theological critique — and of course each may supplement the other. To threaten an opponent both credibly and effectively requires some reasoning powers on both sides. But of what sort? There is much confusion on this premise among nuclear theorists. Of course a perfect rationality cannot be assumed — for in such a case threats would be obsolete! Only in a world of uncertainty, where misjudgments exist and minds can be changed, is deterrence either possible or needed. So a less-than-perfect reason must characterize our world.

But even a more chastened view of rationality would raise some question about deterrence theory. Any imbalance between two nations will stir the weaker to try to catch up, and the stronger to consider forestalling this by a preemptive strike. Even when there is no imbalance, each side may have some incentive to strike first — unless, that is, both have a capacity of overkill so vast that "*the costs of accepting retaliation or attacking first are the same — virtually total destruction.*"[23] But then the logic of overkill produces its own set of problems, its own climate of anxiety and crisis.

Moreover, most rational people cannot help noticing that deterrence functions only in a prewar situation. Once aversion by threat fails and war actually begins, it becomes irrational to retaliate against a nation that has nuclear weapons. That would only assure still greater devastation. So deterrence collapses just when it would most be needed! Jonathan Schell also comments on this inner contradiction: "Once the action begins, the whole doctrine is self-cancelling. In sum the doctrine is based on a monumental logical mistake: one cannot credibly deter a first strike with a second strike whose *raison d'être* dissolves the moment the first strike arrives."[24]

The enthusiasm for deterrence theory seems to "deter" too close an inspection, then, lest the insanity of actual retaliation be uncovered. The so-called theologians of nuclearism sense this and have sought to restore its credibility in various ways. Herman Kahn described the possibility of a literal doomsday machine which would eliminate any doubt about retaliation by making it fully automatic — and thereby destroying the world. Others suggest deliberately cultivating the appearance of irrationality, to intimidate an enemy. One example arises from Richard Nixon's determination to force North Vietnam to negotiate an end to the Vietnam war. Confiding to his chief of staff, H. R. Haldeman, he said, "I call it the Madman Theory, Bob. I want the North Vietnamese to believe I've reached the point where I might do *anything* to stop the war. We'll just slip the word to them that, for God's sake, you know Nixon is obsessed about Communism. We can't restrain him when he's angry — and he has his hand on the nuclear button. . . ."[25] In this instance, of course, the enemy had no strategic weapons to use against our homeland. But in a case involving nuclear superpowers, it becomes even more irrational to try to make credible threats of retaliation.

Therefore, Morgan urges a still further reduced estimate of rationality in our nuclear policy: the model of reason viewed as "sensible decision making."[26] Here the emphasis is on human limits, impulses, error, and cautious common sense. "Sensible" decision makers are aware of their limitations and uncertainties; typically they defer making choices before it is necessary, and even then they try to make them piecemeal and incrementally. Pragmatic in temperament, they adapt to the complexities of global affairs. Their chief aim is to avoid disasters, and in return they seek a cautious progress toward national goals. With such leaders deterrence "works" to the extent that it reminds humans, not of their powers of reason, but of their fallibility — and of the emotional excitability of their opponent. In fact, "deterrence results from a combination of the uncertainty facing the aggressor and the irrationality present in the deterrer"[27] Those who are "sensible" become aware both of the threatener's capacity for foolhardy response, as the potential victim of attack, and also the necessity of caution, even fear, by the nation contemplating attack.

Of course even this model of rationality contains the inner contradiction common to all deterrence theory: "There is no obvious way for governments to appear appropriately irrational for making threats without at the same time appearing too irrational to be deterred"[28] — or, for that matter, appearing to prepare for a first strike! But at least the model of sensible decision making does avoid the excesses of rationalism found in classic deterrence theory, an overconfidence in "crisis management" which has now also spawned the reckless innovations of the Reagan administration. As Morgan puts it, if automobile accidents are an unavoidable possibility, does it make sense then to rationalize having even more and faster cars, and ever greater self-confidence?[29] And in the case of nuclear policies, we should add, even *one* "accident" is more than the world can afford.

Rationality and Terror

Now we turn to a critique of deterrence more directly from the perspective of Christian faith. And here, "rationality," the most reputable doctrine within nuclearism, is likewise found to be lacking. Patrick Morgan's analysis in several ways parallels such a theological critique. In the best humanist tradition he has a healthy mistrust of any intellectual pride that fancies itself to be disinterested and able to control the precarious events of history. He prefers to speak of human "sensibility" rather than rationality, and his sense of human limitation and fallibility echoes the clear-sightedness of the biblical prophets. However, sin and salvation are not in Morgan's vocabulary. The depths of human lust for power, as well as the human hunger for satisfying public symbols of our continuity and identity, are beyond his grasp. The final critique of deterrence, therefore, must be theological.

Alan Geyer aptly sums it up: "If deterrence theorists' absolute presumption of rationality seems to exalt cerebral powers to superhuman levels, their punitive preoccupation with threats seems to degrade *homo sapiens* to subhuman levels. This lack of a coherent and credible portrait of human nature is perhaps the most fundamental flaw in the whole body of deterrence dogma."[30] The theologians of nuclearism first propose "that we should frustrate our opponents by frightening them very badly and that we should then rely on their cool-headed rationality for our survival."[31] What is theologically objectionable, however, is not just the absurdity of this juxtaposition, but also the polar extremes in and of themselves. Let us examine each of the two in turn.

On the one hand we have seen the doctrine of deterrence rests on a rationalist premise, which in turn serves to disguise both irrationality and rationalizations. If there is no logic or sense in retaliating after being hit by a first strike, well then, it seems that other reasons must be contrived. Examples include a show of credibility and national resolve, war-fighting plans for victory, damage limitation, and so forth. The ambiguity of deterrence as a "state of mind," a "realm of data-free analysis," and "a blank check" must surely invite a carnival of rationalizations in its train!

"How much," for instance, it would take to deter the Soviets is an estimate that increases closely in tandem with our own growing ability to inflict destruction. Yet it is unthinkable for us to admit the converse, that *we* would be deterred only if the U.S.S.R. could do just as much damage to us as we can to them![32] "What's crucial," Theodore Draper observes, "is not how many weapons a nuclear power has but how few it needs."[33] The underlying issue, however, seems to be that our technological age is especially susceptible to an oversimplified view of human nature. It is popularly assumed that the human being is a self-contained monad, rational and unequivocal, that one is fully in command of oneself and therefore fit to command similarly over one's environment.

This however is a false doctrine of what is human. Christian faith knows human nature is instead a bundle of opposites, a self that is ever in tension between finitude and freedom, depravity and grandeur. In our hearts we discover we are less an exclamation mark over the world, and more a question mark to ourselves. At the burning bush Moses asked, "Who am I. . . ?" He obtained no direct reply to that question—nor do any of us—but instead received the promise, "I will be with you" (Ex. 3:11–12), and this became eventually the self-giving of Immanuel, "God with us."[34] We receive our selfhood, including our genuine powers—and genuine limits—of reason, only in unceasing relationship with the Self who is ever faithful. The human "'essence,' and that means his identity and continuity, is determined by the call of God, by his being called to a partnership in the covenant, by the event of justification."[35] In the reciprocity of that covenant, humans find their true being as "promise-making, promise-keeping, promise-breaking being."[36] That human identity comes as a gift from the God of promise, who rescued Israel and raised Jesus up—and who offers that promise also in a nuclear age.

The other pole of deterrence doctrine rests upon a premise of terror. Geyer notes that this aspect, in contrast to the superhuman confidence in reason, suddenly plummets human nature to a subhuman level. Now other persons are seen as objects to be manipulated, to be terrorized by threatening an annihilation which would engulf us all. Indeed, ever since the invention of the crossbow, history has witnessed a perpetual search for the ultimate weapon, one that would be so horrific that warfare would be obsolete. Alfred Nobel, inventor of dynamite and founder of the famed peace prize, said, "I wish I could produce a substance or invent a machine of such frightful efficiency for wholesale destruction that wars should thereby become altogether impossible."[37] Apparently the hope is to scare people into rationality—or at least into seeing things our way!

But the logic of terror is self-defeating. Fear does not

produce clarity but confusion, and manipulation cannot turn compulsion into consensus. The analyses by Robert Jay Lifton and Ira Chernus have shown that after a certain anxiety threshold is passed, our minds shut down, go blank, or revert to childhood fantasy and dream thinking. Varieties of numbing and denial spring up in profusion, and their resiliency is increased by the accompanying guise of rationality. The same fallacy is at work on a higher level with the common assumption that peacemaking is only a version of war thinking, an armed truce. "Because we accept war as a seemingly inevitable part of human experience we think that peace can be kept by mastering the techniques of war."[38] Or as someone recently suggested in the Pentagon, perhaps in jest or perhaps not, peace might better be redefined as "permanent prehostility."

This too is false doctrine. The degradation of human nature to a subhuman level by threat of brute force is no less repugnant to Christian faith than is the inflation of humanity to sublime competence in mastering the forces of life and death. To mistake war preparation for peacemaking, or intimidation for security is to dehumanize all humanity — ourselves included. When human subjects are perceived so relentlessly as inhuman objects then it is no wonder they often internalize that expectation and behave accordingly.

"Who is my neighbor?" is the lawyer-question with which something in each of us seeks to evade the twin commandments to love God and each other (Luke 10:29–37). We would prefer to pigeonhole someone as "enemy," perhaps as a hated Samaritan — that way they are easier to hold at a distance, to bend to our purposes. Somehow a known hostility is more comfortable to our darkened minds than those unknown requirements which love at any time might spring upon us. But despite this preference for prejudice there is often a divine interruption of our self-serving busyness — travel plans, say, from Jerusalem to Jericho, or from Hiroshima to Armageddon. The neighbor question can not be deferred, for our convenience, to some indefinite future when the world has been "made safe" for our way of life. As Jesus' parable shows, for those who receive the kingdom of God the neighbor may not after all be a fellow countryman, one of "us" (over against "them"). Instead the neighbor is disclosed at unexpected and even inopportune times as "the one who showed . . . kindness" and (correspondingly) the one who needed it. Degradation through terror is to be replaced by exaltation through tenderness. For the Jesus who spoke to the wily lawyer is himself the Neighbor who comes into hostile territory and enables our inhospitable hearts to open doors to strangers.

In sum, the doctrine of deterrence should be rejected by the church as false doctrine, resting upon distorted perceptions of what it means to be human. It fuses together excessive estimates of rationality and self-serving notions of depravity. These merge to become a grotesque parody of the Christian doctrine of the human being as both the image of God and fallen creature, as simultaneously justified and sinner. Cold War dichotomies then complicate matters still further. There is the inflated rationality that affects both superpowers: the crisis managers on our side are supposedly clever enough to make suitable threats, while theirs are reasonable enough to respond properly. But also there is the principle of intimidation which degrades both sides: the Soviets because they are said to deserve to be threatened, as monsters who "don't understand anything but force," and the U.S. because we must convince the world we are irrational enough to carry out suicidal threats. Double standards and wishful thinking, therefore, give deterrence a complexity which has often been mistaken for "realism" in a rough and tumble world.

But Christian faith knows a higher realism, derived from what we are convinced is the overriding reality of God's new creation. First God's original creative act established humankind as the *imago dei*, the commission to represent God in and for God's creation, and to display that vocation through our co-humanity. Then the further creative act, through Jesus' death and resurrection, reestablished that lapsed vocation and confirmed our co-humanity as founded on the Body of Christ in the world. Our essential humanness rests not upon a fixed human essence or invariable traits, but upon our ever renewed summons to interpersonal relationships, to mutuality—or, as Martin Buber and his followers put it, "the capacity to say Thou."[39] And this "Thou" must be addressed both to God and to the neighbor—including the global neighborhood—if our humanity is to be confirmed daily and replenished.

It is precisely this dimension of mutuality, or what Eric Erikson calls "generativity," which is corroded by the deterrence doctrine. It affects both aspects of this interpersonal existence, the vertical, so to speak, as well as the horizontal. The covenant bond with God, the One who initiates by divine promise and who responds in faithfulness, is warped by a concept of the human being as self-sufficient and rational, the omnicompetent manager of global crises and technological innovations. And the covenant bond with fellow humans, who daily receive and bestow upon one another the gift of personhood, is prostituted by a doctrine that fosters demonization of opponents and manipulation by terror. The everyday conversation that reconstitutes our humanness, not to mention any Samaritan-like deeds of neighborliness, are effectively aborted when the world is prescribed as two divided camps, "us" vs. "them," those who threaten and those to be intimidated.

The very ties that hold God and collective humanity in their reciprocal and ever renewed identities are dissolved by this doctrine, this mental act that redefines reality. Indeed, the fragmenting effect evoked symbolically by deterrence is a prefiguration of the physical fragmentation to which it eventually must lead: the splitting of atoms into global chaos. On both levels there is—or will be—a rupture of those bonds which mercifully hold together our fragile existence amid God's creation.

Deterrence, then, is not an intellectually more respectable mollification of nuclearism. While plausible at first glance, it is actually a dubious expression in doctrinal form of deeper and more sinister notions. The latent images of potency, chaos, and infinity betray the presence of a virulent and concealed religion. That is why both the explicit doctrine of deterrence and the implicit religion of nuclearism which undergirds it should be discerned and denounced as heretical. Their beguiling power reaches everywhere and manages to affect us all, in some degree. At a time of confessing faith, therefore, each and all of us need to pray for deliverance from this artful temptation. Lord, have mercy. . .

4

Coping with Heresies

If nuclearism is a functioning religion, it is more than simply a false idea. In fact it has become a heretical challenge to the Christian faith. What then is to be done? The question quickly becomes even more pointed: how to cope with a heresy?

How indeed! Even the term has an embarrassingly archaic sound in a society known for its tolerance and pluralism. Ordinarily and in most company it may be wise to avoid altogether the word heresy, with its tarnished connotations from the past. But perhaps in the presence of those who have recognized that a special time for confessing is at hand, as we confront a powerful mythology of terror and chaos, even this term may be brought into the open.

The problem, after all, is not with the word, but with its reality. Any popular belief system, whether judged as false or true, has a resiliency, a self-perpetuating hardiness which is not easily uprooted. If a religion endures at all, it has somehow provided a satisfying connection between the unseen sacred order of the cosmos and the depths of emotion, imagery, and uncertainty experienced by us mortals. Such a connection appears to be found in nuclearism by masses of people today. As a religion, it "works." That is, it *seems* to work, at least temporarily—a momentary pause before Doomsday that has been extended, by God's providential mercy, far longer than we had any reason or merit to expect.

We may protest that false faith cannot deliver on its

promises, that it is fraudulent in its appeal, or even that its sanctified self-indulgence will actually encourage a final orgy of self-destruction. But for now the short-term satisfactions do give nuclearism a wide credibility. Ira Chernus correctly names its images "pseudomyths." "They are built of mythic themes and structures, but they fail to communicate the rich multi-dimensional truths and depths of feeling that genuine myths embody. For a society bereft of all other myths, however, these myths have immense appeal because they are the best we have."[1] Of course, we might add, a society with a Judaeo-Christian heritage actually *does* have other and better "myths" and symbols. But regrettably they often have been laid aside, worn thin, or actively perverted by generations of misuse.

So the virulent appeal of Bomb worship has propelled it to dominance in our culture, including the minds of many who are church members. The heretical threat it poses assails us from the surrounding culture as well as from within the walls of the church. When recognized as such, the church must no longer overlook the moment of truth. The crisis now calls for a special act of confessing.

Let us then begin working to found a confessing church movement against the heresy of nuclearism. In committing ourselves to such a venture in faith, of course, many practical questions remain to be answered. What shape would such a movement take, for instance? We should leave it to the Spirit to lead on such matters. But if we will learn from the historical experience of believers' churches (free churches), we may expect a beginning at the "grass roots" of faith communities. Already the Spirit is stirring some action/reflection groups within local congregations or in community ecumenical groups. Proceeding up the "grass stem," so to speak, surely this movement must ascend also through lower and upper levels of church judicatories, synods, dioceses, and assemblies. Perhaps there may even be a national convocation for an ecumenical act of confession. Or perhaps the movement will remain decentralized but with informal collegiality among its components. But in any case the reformation must find its own shape and process, and structures.

The Limits of Official Action

Division and acrimony can hardly be avoided, however. This will present two dangers to a confessing movement against nuclearism. First, the turmoil will offer serious temptations to self-righteousness, counter polemic, or a despairing withdrawal into enclaves of true believers. Polarization too often hardens hearts as well as closes minds. To guard against this it would be wise to return often to the experience of the confessing church movements against Nazism and apartheid, both to learn from their lapses and be fortified by their example. Especially within the Body of Christ those who are familiar with history should be less likely to repeat its mistakes.

Secondly, even if factions of confessing Christians should attain some leverage or even dominance within church governing bodies, there is the problem of spiritual coercion. That is, the exercise of ecclesiastical authority brings along with it a partially self-cancelling backlash. The results attained are always less than those desired, if not actually contrary. To read the history of Western Christianity can be a depressing exercise, as one notes the succession of quarrels and bitterness, the sects and schisms, and the mixture of good intentions with less than good results in coping with these divisions. Just to name some of the more flagrant factions— Arians and Manichaeans, Cathari and Socinians, for instance—is to evoke memories of struggles in which the remedy was sometimes worse than the malady. No one today would condone anything remotely resembling the inquisitions, even if such were possible and for even the best of causes.

More to the point, however, in the event that spiritual coercion were used for defending the gospel, it would still be counterproductive. We already know that in the case of truth, repression only stimulates its growth. The Confessing Church in Germany, for instance, was nurtured by the blood of its martyrs. But we should also recall that repression of error brings a comparable stimulus. Imagine for a moment: if the tables had been turned in the 1930s and the confessing Christians somehow had controlled the levers of power and applied the same pressures used in fact against them—would the "German Christian" heresy then have dwindled away? Not likely! Nor is nuclearism likely to diminish, in the improbable event that its opponents should attain ecclesiastical power.

A milder parallel to official action is theological debate, as a means of refuting error. But debate is enmeshed in a similar quandary. Even in an open forum, free from the muscle of ecclesiastical power, there often remains a whiff of coercion because of differentials, say, in social status or group leverage. Defensiveness against verbal attack serves to further entrench opinion, and to an extent only slightly less than in the case of physical attack. Historically, in the face of debate, pamphleteering, and recrimination, dissenting pieties have often been unexpectedly resilient. For example, the sixteenth-century Reformation coincided with the development of the printing press, unleashing a torrent of highly charged words about the proper interpretation of the faith. But unless accompanied by other plausibility factors (such as the satisfactions of group identity or socio-economic advancement), sheer polemic was probably no more effective then than it is now.

Likewise in our century the church has witnessed heated debates over such classic topics as the inspiration or inerrancy of Scripture, creationism and evolution, the virgin birth, or the timing and prefatory signs of the Millennium. But there is little evidence that argument as such wins many people over. More recently the lines of division have fallen on fresh areas: pro-life or pro-choice, support or dissent from U.S. foreign policies, or church involvement in racial and economic issues. Again the impassioned flow of words seems to fall on reciprocally deaf ears. Now the leadership of almost every denomination has turned its attention to the Bomb; the Catholic bishops' letter is a major case in point. A profusion of warnings about the arms race issues forth from church ruling bodies and corporate offices — but, sad to say, with little enough effect on local congregations.

In all these instances, the volume of words expended doubtless is far in excess of any change of opinion effected. Perhaps there is even an immunizing effect at work, whereby contention produces its own antibodies. In short — and this is painful for a teacher or theologian to admit — conceptual argument is largely ineffective as a means of altering someone's religious persuasion. That was true in those past eras when classic theological topics were viewed as supremely important. And it is true today when it is a covert religion that both grips and numbs the restless human heart.

Of course in every age there are striking instances of conversion, and sometimes in a wave of spiritual fervor it reaches massive proportions. But when deeply rooted religious symbol systems are abandoned or exchanged, it is primarily the result of a fresh vision, a revitalizing new pattern of reordering familiar data. Argumentation can support or explain such a flash of insight, but it is unlikely to produce it. "The Spirit blows where it wills. . ." (John 3:8), and we mortals do not direct its "whence" or "whither." It depends rather on the providence of the triune God. Accordingly our century has seen every great confession of faith, from Barmen to Belhar, rest its appeal on God's living presence: the workings of the risen Christ or the mysterious faithfulness of the Holy Spirit. Our words can only follow.

Word and Spirit

How then to cope with heresy? Certainly not through coercion by state or ecclesiastical officialdom. Even conceptual argument has its limits, as we have noted. However this is not inconsistent with the fact that a life-giving confession of faith must utilize concepts. Issues of truth vs. falsehood are not spurious issues; they do matter. "Orthodoxy" means not only right praise, but right thinking, whereas heresy is declared detrimental to both. While the clash of ideas is not a very effective way of encouraging a transfer from false faith to true faith, that true faith does include sound doctrine. Accordingly, some ideas must be excluded. In short, even in our age of narcissism and an indifference towards ideas that verges on outright solipsism, the truth question cannot be repressed.

Nuclearism is to be rejected not only because it is immoral, even suicidally dangerous, but also because it is profoundly untrue. To call it a heresy does assume, therefore, some confidence about orthodoxy, some consensus about

Christian norms. This must be so, even if it be granted that at the moment truth seems strangely obscured to a majority of believers. A call to confession is a struggle of the church to be true to itself and to the gospel which bestows on it its identity. Nuclearism, if it is a heresy, must be demonstrated to contradict and gravely endanger that identity, that truthfulness.

The location of the truth question, moreover, is important. It is to be sought in the Scriptures as they are illuminated by the Spirit. Either by itself seems unable to guide our darkened minds. But together they open the heart to a fresh inbreaking of truth in the immediate here and now. Alone, either could be and all too often has been misused by various sectarians or false prophets. But in their mutual ministering they offer us fresh hope of a faithful confession, even in a nuclear age.

Scripture by itself is impotent, a dead letter. In fact it may even assail the conscience; Luther recognized this as the onslaught of "the law" which may drive one to despair. At the very least each of us sometimes has the experience of opening the Bible and finding it lifeless. Moreover, heretics themselves make ready use of it for their own purposes. Marcion was devoted to Paul's writings, the Cathari to John's gospel, and twentieth-century racists or Nazi sympathizers favor certain Old Testament texts of militant exclusivism.

On the other hand we know the words of Scripture can unexpectedly leap into life, with overpowering conviction. Often this happens when the listeners or readers are in crisis situations. It is reported that in the dark years of the war and persecution, congregations of the German Confessing Church heard soul-stirring meaning even in conventional and apolitical sermons or prescribed lectionary readings. Similarly in their Bible studies, the persecuted "base Christian communities" in Latin America uncover a rich wisdom which the rest of us miss on the very same pages.[2] A given biblical passage read in a sick room, a peace demonstration, a prison cell, or to casual church-goers in well padded pews simply does not mean the same thing! In an uncanny way, "something new" seems to be added to the written word through the immediate circumstances. Each of us has experienced the thrill of hearing read a text, formerly considered insignificant or perhaps trite, which becomes utterly radiant through the voice of, say, a William Stringfellow or some unheralded local saint.

What makes the difference? We all share the same Bible. Yet most texts remain inconsequential in our eyes, and almost as many seem pliable in the hands of dissenters or heretics of every stripe. How may a "true" meaning of Scripture be recovered by mortal minds? This has become particularly difficult in modern times. As Lifton and others have pointed out, the process of symbol formation in the psyche has largely been blocked, the imagination stultified or trivialized as "daydreaming" or "just" entertainment. Unfortunately at the same time that the unconscious is avenging itself on us, resulting in images of death, invasion, or world annihilation, the consciousness has fenced itself in by a narrow rationalism.

This mental constriction has been developing for a long time, as Western society became more and more oriented toward technology. Almost two centuries ago it was described by William Blake as "single vision," a surface gaze which lacks the symbolic depth of "twofold vision."[3] In our time it has been designated variously as "instrumental reason" (Max Weber, Jürgen Habermas), "calculative thought" (Martin Heidegger), and "technical reason" (Paul Tillich). "Technology is the theology of our generation,"[4] says Alan Geyer, and so perhaps the best term for us to use is "technological reason."

By emphasizing problem solving and material productivity, our society increasingly forfeits a reflection on final goals, value judgments, or deeper insight of every sort. Naturally the Bible would then be read with literalist eyeglasses which flatten a rich landscape of symbols into a dreary chain of axioms and alleged facts. Such literalism has generated many a false problem, as would-be lawyers and technicians swarm over its pages, seeking to "prove" or "disprove" this or that detail. The sad result is that as we lose access to the preconscious depths of meaning in Scripture, it becomes both intractable to our commonplace reading and malleable to those who would impose their prejudgments. So the Bible degenerates into a happy hunting ground for heretical prooftexting.

If, however, Scripture is to manifest its lively truth again at this crucial time for confessing, it must be read with the assistance of the Spirit. But since the Spirit is hardly subject to our beck and call, perhaps we should state this for the moment in less theological terms: Scripture must be read and it must be read with new vision. Somehow a fresh imagination must be acquired, what Blake called the "twofold vision," so that the profound symbols of the Bible may once again satisfy our hunger for images that nourish the foundations of our being. For decades theologians have entitled this a search for a new "hermeneutic" (principle of Scripture interpretation), and much intellectual effort has been expended upon it. This quest on a theological level coincides closely with the post-Hiroshima warnings by Einstein and so many others that we desperately need "a substantially new manner of thinking" if humankind is to survive. That parallel is no coincidence. For the same reasoning that has blocked our access to biblical truth has also prompted us, as an incurably religious species, to unlock the primal energies of the universe and then unknowingly to enshrine the awesome result deep within our hearts. Benumbed against the Spirit, we still harbor spiritual thirsts which we no longer know how to satisfy.

But if the Spirit is to illumine our reading of Scripture, we must allow the Spirit first to touch the deepest part of the self—the very part which a high technological society has spurned. That means, as Carl Jung pointed out in his reflections on a lifetime of analytical psychology, "We can no longer afford to be so God-Almighty-like as to set ourselves up as judges of the merits or demerits of natural phenomena. We do not base our botany upon the old-fashioned division into useful and useless plants, or our zoology upon the naive distinction between harmless and dangerous animals. But we still complacently assume that consciousness is sense and the unconscious is nonsense."[5] Indeed it is the unconscious mind which is the seedbed of the images and rich symbolism we crave so much, and thus also the contact point for the stirrings of the Spirit. It is there that we must seek the mysterious reservoirs of revitalization for the self and its surrounding society.

In response to the common complaint that God no longer seems to speak clearly to our generation, Jung recalls the story of "the rabbi who was asked how it could be that God often showed himself to people in the olden days while nowadays nobody ever sees him. The rabbi replied, 'Nowadays there is no longer anybody who can bow low enough.'"[6]

To "bow" in quietness and humility so that we can gaze along the inward path will no doubt appear as folly to a people that prefers to "stand tall" and look towards the stars as our next stepping stone. But the insights of Carl Jung and of the school of psychology which derives from him are proving to be the framework for some of the most creative movements today in rediscovering the living and lively voice of Scripture. Examples include the "transforming Bible study" method of Walter Wink,[7] which has indeed had transforming effects on many who attend his workshops, and also the prolific studies in biblical thought of Walter Brueggemann,[8] which are remarkable in their ability to stir the hearts of lay people as well as fellow scholars.

As the creative labors of Wink and Brueggemann demonstrate, however, it is essential that the fruitfulness of the Spirit and the luxuriant store of symbols in our unconscious mind be linked to the Word of the biblical text. Otherwise the unbridled power of the psyche may run rampant, generating images in such profusion and incoherent energy that the conscious mind will feel under siege. This easily leads to surrealistic fantasies which lose touch with daily life, or charismatic excesses which lose touch with Christian faith. Recent years have witnessed an abundance of evidences of just such aimless attempts to tap the repressed forces of the psyche. There are ever new extravagances in fads and cults, from theatrical rock concerts to underground societies, for instance, and from MTV fantasies to drug dependencies.

We have noted that literalism is the problem in reading Scripture when one is in a culture dominated by technological reason. But there is an equivalent problem in seeking new spiritual power when one lives in an age of the individual and the consumer. In the latter case the temptation is spiritualism. I do not mean spiritualism in the older sense of believing that mediums can communicate with the dead, but rather a newer sense: a shopping list of options (how appropriate for a market economy!) for freehand exploration of the psyche. In a society that has long lost its acquaintance with the unconscious, those options range from the trite to the bizarre. But in most cases they resemble the proverbial individual, cut off from communication with the rest of history, who labors to reinvent the wheel. The new spiritualism is sadly unaware of the bountiful heritage of Christian spirituality. Moreover, in its intense individualism it is easily seduced by self-indulgences or private excess.

So it appears that neither the Bible by itself nor the Spirit alone (insofar as our mortal minds can receive it though the unconscious) can answer the truth question in our time. But together — that is a different matter! When Scripture and the Holy Spirit mutually test and attest one another, then it is that the truth can stand forth. "The Spirit goes before the church to enlighten her in understanding the Word," John Calvin said, "while the Word itself is like the Lydian stone, by which she tests all doctrines."[9] When that occurs, reformation is ready to happen — whether in the sixteenth century or in any generation.

This is no simple process, of course. In fact the mysterious interaction of Word and Spirit cannot be prejudged or packaged into neat doctrines — even when a heresy brings upon us a desperate need for truth and a wish for fast answers. But in special times of confessing in the past, this conjunction of biblical word and God's Word has again and again brought the church into new life. And so today we must attune our minds and hearts to await a new deliverance.

If Scripture is to differ from a flat Biblicism and have genuine authority today, it must be newly read by *receptive* visionaries — those with a "twofold" vision that goes beyond technological reason and plumbs our precognitive depths. It must rekindle the imagination so that our hearts can respond freely and our creativity interpret faithfully the Word for each new concrete situation. And, on the other hand, if the Spirit is to differ from spiritualism and any number of ecstatic self-indulgences or contrived artifices, it must be awaited by *disciplined* visionaries — those who are also trained and diligent in the study of Scripture. It also calls for sufficient nonconformity to the world so that the popular is not so easily confused with the prophetic.

Finally, in this time of global peril, we need nothing less than a new reformation by the Holy Spirit. It is the Spirit, after all, that will make the final difference if Scripture is to be revivified to clarity, the church restored to fidelity, and the world recalled from the nuclear abyss. Of course by definition the Spirit is beyond human control, and we can have no assurances about the outcome of our crisis. But, as the rabbi in Jung's anecdote implicitly suggested, we can practice bowing low enough to behold God. Much the same suggestion is offered by the sociologist Peter Berger, at the close of his recent study of religion and modernity: "It is not given to men to make God speak. It is only given to them to live and to think in such a way that, if God's thunder should come, they will not have stopped their ears."[10]

How then may we begin to unstop our all too human ears? At this point, having reviewed the limits of official action and yet the persistence of the truth question even in an age of pluralism, we should begin to construct a strategy. Since it is to the preconceptual level that theology must now turn its attention, if we are to open ourselves for a new birth through the Holy Spirit, the remainder of this study will be devoted to two proposals towards such a strategy. Furthermore, since in Berger's words, we are "to live and to think in such a way" that we will not miss God's thunder, one proposal is directed toward our way of thinking and the other towards our way of living.

The former of the two tasks will be to seek to challenge and replace those root assumptions about reality, those unspoken hunches about "the way things are," which undergird the worldview of nuclearism. These will be discussed in chapters five through nine. The latter task is to cultivate a new lifestyle, one which by individual example and eventually (let us hope!) by collective momentum could help to "delegitimize" the social credibility of nuclearism. Chapter ten will be devoted to this urgent task. Actually, these two proposals are intimately related. For on the one hand, our mindset inevitably overflows into patterns of behavior and, on the other, the actions we take and the social groupings we live in do inspire and reinforce the way we think.

Either or both of these projects will require a monumental collaboration. For nuclearism has so captured the allegiance of most modern Christians that it appears incontestable, looming over us much as does the proverbial mushroom cloud that has become its awful icon and emblem. But as God is faithful, so heresy can and must be challenged. The cloud can be dissipated and its fateful attraction broken. There are already prophetic voices and communities in our time which may coalesce into a wider movement of renewal. If we fix our vision, not towards the uncanny writhing of the clouds, but towards the light on the horizon, we may be blessed by finding that it is not the twilight of the planet after all. Perhaps it is instead the dawning of a new day. . . .

PART II
Preparing for Reformation: A Paradigm Shift

5

Belief, Models, and Holy Midwifery

If we "bow low enough" and no longer have "stopped . . . ears," perhaps a new vision can possess our minds. "The human race is governed by its imagination," Napoleon Bonaparte is reported to have said. And so it is. The first preconceptual project, then, for the reformation against nuclear heresy must be to make room for the Spirit's renewal by discerning and then contending against those root metaphors which lend to nuclearism its cloak (or shroud?) of credibility. In contesting this or any belief system, such devout undermining may well be the most effective approach!

The Power of Paradigms

After all, why does any theory or worldview become widely believed, while others decline in public acceptance? The history of science offers examples of this. Since the revolution of Copernicus in astronomy, why do most people take for granted that the earth goes around the sun — when for centuries common opinion had held the reverse? Why did Newtonian physics replace the long venerated views of Aristotle and the scholastics about how the world worked? And since Einstein, Newtonian theory in its turn has given way to quantum mechanics and relativity theory.

Here is the clue: the credibility of such explanations owes more to frameworks than to facts. It is not just a matter of additional or improved data, although that of course was also important. But primarily what made the difference was a seismic shift in the basic ways of fitting the data together, an alternate patterning of perceptions. In a sense, then, the world changed because first our vision of it changed, and not vice versa. That certainly is true for the public at large, but it can be argued that it applies also to the scientists themselves. Thomas S. Kuhn's famous book, *The Structure of Scientific Revolutions,*[1] illuminates how from time to time a "gestalt switch" has unexpectedly happened in the history of science. That is, a sudden shift in mental maps, perceptual models, allowed accumulated anomalies in data to be explained and opened the way for new discoveries to be made. Apparently, even in the physical sciences, the disciplined scrutiny of so-called hard facts, there is what we may call a faith dimension. If that is so, then how much more so in other fields of knowledge, or in general public expectations and shifting moods — or in a national idolatry such as nuclearism!

Why is this? We mortals are finite, with limited powers of comprehension. The mind can at best perceive only fragmentary aspects of the truth. Experimental psychology suggests that human beings are unable to keep more than seven or so disparate items in mental focus at one time, so they reduce the complexities by abstracting or "chunking"[2] similar qualities into patterns or models. However, different cultures or generations will do this differently. We all know of the proverbial blind men feeling diverse parts of the elephant. This partiality is unmistakable, for instance, when we read the unfolding history of philosophy. It strikes us in the amazing diversity of cultures, which every tourist remarks about, or even when we page through *The National Geographic.*

But not until recent times has it been really understood just how fragile and malleable is the link between our minds and the rest of the universe. The realization accumulated from a number of factors: the fragmentation of the medieval world, the rise of critical philosophy and its self-conscious modes of analysis, the secularization of values and frames of reference, the expansion of the industrial and technological revolutions into every nook and cranny of life, the resulting complexity and impersonality of our societies, and now the bewildering pace of modern social change. All of these, and more, have greatly influenced what we "know" about reality, and how we come to know it. Subjective factors, therefore, have subtle and pervasive effects on human perception as well as thinking. The debut of the discipline of sociology of knowledge has clarified many of these factors. But really this should come as no surprise to people of faith. Down through the ages, virtually every religion has insisted that genuine knowledge comes only through belief. In other words, to "understand" requires the humility and trust to "stand under" that which is to be known. That means bowing low enough to receive the vision.

Overall there has long been a continuing struggle of faith to determine just how it may come to terms with modernity. That vast and complex topic cannot be explored here. It is sufficient for us to observe, however, that both the sociology of knowledge and Christian faith agree that nonrational factors have enormous influence on what people hold to be "common sense," the taken-for-granted framework of what we perceive daily life to be all about. That sense is "common" by virtue of the fact that anyone who "knows" something is also one who "lives" in a social matrix and shares its collective assumptions. Science, for instance, is a group activity. If this holds true for schools of thought among scientists, it all the more applies to public notions of the "real world" around us. In every case, belief systems gain their credibility not simply through tests of reason and repeatable experience. They also win acceptance to the degree they articulate a group's "crucial shared examples,"[3] primal hunches, and submerged metaphors of perceived reality.

Since the publication of Kuhn's book, the term "paradigm" has been widely used in referring to those preconscious models or patterns that both shape what we "know" and filter out what we disregard. In the history of science there have been long periods of contentment with a dominant paradigm — for instance, the geocentric model of the solar system, the phlogiston theory of gases, and so on. But then momentous changes sometimes happen quickly. Often it occurs when young researchers arrive on the scene, less encumbered by commitments to the conventional wisdom, who puzzle over inconsistencies in the data.[4] But sooner or later, when reality is envisioned by a new model, older evidence suddenly falls into place somehow and new findings may be predicted with some accuracy. When such amazing spurts happen in science we usually speak of "progress," even when perhaps not a single new object has materialized under a microscope.

Other areas of life are likewise altered—whether for good or for ill—by paradigm shifts. Sometimes the change is drastic and sudden, and other times not. Yet in any case the new pattern is soon regarded as so normal that it becomes difficult to imagine how people "back in the old days" could have believed differently! Compare, for instance, the child-rearing practices of today with those of one or two centuries ago in which the toddler was regarded both as "embryo angel" and "infant fiend" (Samuel Davies), and parental duty was summarized by John Wesley's words, "Break their wills that you may save their souls."[5] Other examples could easily be found in modern male/female roles in family or work place, in dating customs, or in the expansionary ethos of consumer credit and spending—all of which are at sharp variance with the ways our parents or grandparents assumed were "natural."

The Atom and Our Ways of Thinking

Now comes one of the greatest upheavals of all: the arrival of the power of the split atom, and its immediate application in 1945 to weaponry. Many voices tell us that in matters of war and peace, a perceptual revolution of no less magnitude will be needed, if global disaster is to be averted.[6] The foremost of this series of warnings, of course, is that classic quotation from Albert Einstein, "The unleashed power of the atom has changed everything except our ways of thinking. Thus we are drifting towards a catastrophe beyond comparison. We shall require a substantially new manner of thinking, if mankind is to survive."[7] Concerning this matter, above all else, a paradigm shift is needed in our generation—if there are to be later generations . . . .

As we have noted, the response since 1945 to this world-shaking event has been what Robert Jay Lifton has termed "nuclearism." It refers to more than simply an uncritical embrace of nuclear weapons, their possession and threatened use; that represents only the tip of the iceberg, so to speak, signaling the massive presence of a partly submerged worldview. The mythic tenacity and enticing power of this secular religion have been remarkable during the forty wilderness years of the Cold War. In that period there have been several surges of public debate about the Bomb, but then it all subsides with little having been accomplished. Conceptual argument seems strangely ineffective. Richard Barnet helps us see why:

> There has been no disarmament because the assumptions of the arms race have been almost universally accepted. Most people, including most people who favor disarmament, accept the premise that more weapons mean more security, that alternative systems of security not based on making hostages of hundreds of millions of people are utopian, and that the survival of the United States as a sovereign actor in the world justifies mass murder, poisoning of the earth, and the hideous mutation of the human species. We do not seem to be able to generate the moral passion to rid the world of arms, because we ourselves are psychologically dependent upon them.[8]

Because of such assumptions the nuclearist belief system lives on, with a durability which reminds us of that of the atoms themselves. Consequently in the late 1970s, a time of stagflation, low morale, and resentment of perceived foreign policy setbacks for the U.S., there seemed little that could restrain the public from rallying, with a fervor that often resembled relief, to the clarion calls for a renewed Cold War. So a new and ominous phase of the postwar arms race between the two superpowers has begun.[9]

The new nuclear militancy has been demanded in the name of "realism." But what is reality, in the 1980s? As political scientist Paul N. Goldstene notes, entrenched institutions cultivate "a view of the world which controls perceptions of what is, and limits the possibilities of what might be," and they do so behind a screen so that the public lives in "a condition where the effects of power are pervasive, but where its identity is lost."[10] This explains the unusual anger which government officials often show toward alternative journalists and investigative reporters. A former C.I.A. employee put it flatly: "true power consists of being able to require others to accept your reality. . . . It's frightening. . . . When you put forward an alternative to that, they get very angry because you are breaking an essential monopoly."[11]

No wonder that in discussing politics or any peace issue, we find that labels such as "realism" or charges of "being unrealistic" quickly lapse into fruitless circularity. They serve in effect as rallying cries, as tags that merely designate someone else's model of experience as either congruent or not with one's own — or with the prevailing national consensus. Words like realism and its synonyms threaten to become meaningless when it is worldviews that are in controversy; worse yet, they effectively beg the faith-question of what after all *is* reality. To the wary, however, these labels may have some usefulness. They resemble buoys in a Maine harbor that signal the presence of submerged lobster traps — traps which, like paradigms, can be examined only if they are first retrieved.

So it is at the preconceptual level, at last, where the worldview of nuclearism must be challenged. Here theology must take up the patient role of midwifery. That is the sort of patience that is needed, because the task at hand must seem overwhelming. For to all who share it, a belief system or worldview is present with a closeness, and yet a strange elusiveness, that parallels the very forces of nature itself. This is all the more so if, as Gibson Winter maintains, nuclearism turns out to be no simple cultural aberration, but "the logical, if not inevitable, consequence of Western technological and industrial development" at a terminal stage.[12] Furthermore, an effective pattern shift is not something that is subject to human manipulation. It can occur only when the time is ripe. In our case that means an imponderable complex of cultural and historical factors, among which (also and primarily) the Holy Spirit begins to move.

We can at best serve, then, as midwives for a new vision's birthing that is already underway. Of course, to dredge up the murky underpinnings of nuclearism into the light of day cannot of itself refute or annul them. To do so, however, does constitute a first step, the necessary but not yet sufficient means of confronting their powers of mystification and dispelling their aura of inviolability. In venturing this step, we may take courage from Kuhn's observations that it is only in periods of crisis and paradigm breakdown that realignments occur and new models gain ascendancy. Certainly we live in such a crisis. "Nothing can save us that is possible: We who must die demand a miracle," mused W. H. Auden.[13] Somber words — except that they appear within a Christmas oratorio! So the birthing time may now be at hand.

Whether that time of gestalt shift is indeed here or not is, of course, something that will become clear only in retrospect. On the one hand there are some hopeful signs. Michael MccGwire, analyst in naval and Soviet affairs at the Brookings Institution, offers an example:

> I suspect that the breakdown in the consensus on foreign policy and defense reflects something much more fundamental, namely the accumulation of counter-instances of the kind that precedes a paradigm shift in the world of scientific theory, and we may be coming up to an equivalent shift in our perceptions of national and international security. . . . Should there be a possibility of moving from the "Ptolemaic" stage of international relations to some new "Copernican" stage whose paradigm has yet to be discerned, its actualization will depend on our capacity to identify and challenge the assumptions underlying our present policies and postures, and our ability to perceive the world in all its human diversity.[14]

On the other hand there are enough discouraging signs so that they need no enumeration here. In any case, Christians have always lived in uncertainty about what the future holds, but they also live joyfully because they know Who holds the future! Moreover, faithful midwives do not wait until all the facts are quite clear; they begin with the task at hand. And so must we.

Concerning nuclear heresy, therefore, the calling of the church is twofold: 1) It should strive to become a catalyst in the global village, assisting the coming to birth of a new and more wholesome vision of reality for the whole human family. 2) It should therefore first of all purge itself of the enticements of nuclearism, recognizing it as a covert ideology which, when ingested into the Body of Christ, should also be identified as a heresy and renounced as such. It is this second point, actually the prior task, which will occupy us for the remainder of these pages. Only when the church has struggled for its own identity, responded to a special time for confessing, and attained a renewed faithfulness (i.e., orthodoxy) can it then hope to address or serve effectively the rest of humankind in a nuclear age.

A Procedure for Demystification

So a fresh imagination must first of all possess our minds. Accordingly we begin our labors in the hope that the Holy Spirit already is orchestrating a time of new reformation, preparing human ears to become "unstopped" so that they may "hear new things"(Isa. 48:6).

We start by recognizing that the reason nuclearism thus far has remained so credible is that it rests on a network of preconscious models which themselves are widely taken for granted. Of these models, four have been selected here as test cases in the following pages, chapters six through nine. If these paradigms are to be stripped of their aura of self-evidence and unmasked as mere postulates, as human constructs rather than any direct window into "the way things are," they must first be raised to the conscious level. Only then can they be examined and demystified.

Here then is our procedure: in each case the process of demystification will focus on three dimensions for the paradigm being studied. 1) Its ontology—that is, what is the broader notion implied about being as such, the underlying primal hunches about "the way things are" and the very cosmos itself? 2) Its societal expressions—what are some typical manifestations of this notion of being which we can recognize in our social and international behavior? 3) Its interpersonal expressions—what are some representative examples of this mental model from the more individual levels of daily life?

There is a very practical purpose in noting the ramifications of each paradigm in our common everyday experience. So much of the official ideology and justification of public nuclearism is presented by both its adherents and its benefactors in technical jargon, that most of us hardly know how to grapple with it. The temptation is to sit back and let the experts handle it, the shamans who seem privy to the sacred mysteries. But if we can recognize the societal and interpersonal expressions of nuclearist paradigms, this may have several beneficial effects. First, the demystification may help average citizens to realize just how thoroughly these same thought models have pervaded everyday life. Secondly, it should raise questions, even misgivings, about whether such commanding responsibility over actual nuclear issues in national policy ought to be altogether relinquished by ordinary people, simply turned over to the reputed experts. Thirdly, since these paradigms are found at virtually every level of modern existence, these analogies may help to break through the psychic numbing, the paralyzing sense of helplessness that so afflicts us. It may even encourage more of us to take on the role of mindset midwives, in the conviction that those changes we make around us, at the everyday, microcosmic level, may indeed affect the global macrocosmic level as well.

After demystification, there is a remaining step in our procedure. In each case we need to reexamine briefly what at least the mainstream of the Bible would portray about the paradigm under consideration. An alternate model, more directly rooted in the scriptural vision of reality, will be sketched—admittedly without the elaboration or nuancing which biblical theologians would want to add. Nor is this the place to make proposals for hermeneutical methods, even though new approaches in biblical interpretation will certainly have to be developed—if ancient thoughtforms are to be creatively appropriated today, and not imposed by fiat. After all we cannot simply replicate a first century worldview or command ourselves to think in ancient Jewish patterns, as if modernity no longer existed. Instead of "Back to the Bible!," our watchword should be "From the Bible forward!"

For purposes here, however, the sheer juxtaposition of the biblical vision next to its nuclearist counterpart (or counterfeit, should one say!) ought to be sufficiently suggestive of how and where the church should begin its obligatory struggle in these matters for sound doctrine. Whether or not the terminology of "orthodoxy/heresy" is even used at all is an issue which can be decided later. What cannot be postponed, however, is the church's need to confess its faith and reclaim the biblical vision. This must happen before it can confront and exorcise the uncanny spell of nuclearism within as well as outside its walls, and certainly before it can then hope to mediate new thoughtforms to a world bewitched and toying with nuclear suicide. Let us begin, then, with the prayer, *veni creator spiritus*! Come creator spirit!

6

The Paradigm of Power as Violence

In order for the church to prepare for a new reformation through the Spirit, it must first of all criticize and modify the conventional paradigm of power. Power is usually defined as the ability to do or act, with the implication that it makes actual (or else prevents) that which was previously latent in the very nature of things. So power is related to reality, at its deeper levels. "To exist is the most universal and primordial form of power; what is, in proportion as it is, is powerful. . . . Power is both identical with being and an intensification of being."[1] Theologically stated, "the understanding of human power is derived from the God-situation in which one lives."[2] This latter comment adds the clue to why our current predicament can be called idolatrous. In other words, how power is conceptualized in any given society depends largely on that society's primal hunches of whatever is most real, that is, divine.

That is why the exercise of power usually elicits from the bystanders a numinous awe. Who among us has not felt a twinge verging on worship while standing close to the cascades of a hydroelectric dam, to a screaming jet engine, or to a hulking steam locomotive? We moderns are not all that far removed from the preoccupation of early religion and traditional cultures with *mana*, impersonal supernatural power, and their elaborate etiquette for its usage. Indeed, a rough but serviceable definition of human religion as such could be something like this: the quest for the ultimate qualities of power.

Because of the affinity between potency and reverence, it was inevitable that the advent of nuclear power would arouse an array of emotions and mythic images. For centuries humans in the West have been enamored with the possibilities of reordering their environment through the study and application of the laws, first of mechanics, then of chemistry. No Aladdin could search more avidly for some new genie, willing to bring to pass more and more of his master's bidding. So in modern times, when science finally unlocked the atom, unleashing what physicists tell us is the strongest of the basic four forces of the universe, we mortals of course could not fail to perceive the results "religiously."

Unfortunately that dramatic series of events in nuclear physics also reinforced in the public mind the reductionist notion of power as physical force and, ultimately, as violence. From that point on, nuclearism as a surrogate religion was to become an irrepressible temptation. As Lifton sees it, *"nuclearism is a general twentieth-century disease of power, a form of totalism of thought and consequence particularly if paradoxically tempting to contemporary man as another of his technological replacements for his waning sense of the reliability and continuity of life"*[3]

Legacies from Hobbes and Phinehas

Any paradigm, resting as it does on partial and idiosyncratic perceptions, likely contains some truth. Such is the case here, as well. Power does have religious implications. No one doubts, furthermore, that conflict and struggle have been part of the human experience from the beginning. Conflict is universal in one form or another. It originates in the mysteries of a basic disjunction within the human self (especially the results of what Christians know as "original sin") and also between the self and its environment (symbolized as the consequences of "the Fall"). Indeed, every religion develops ways of explaining and dealing with this primordial tension, even recognizing that some types of it are therapeutic, or may at least bring opportunities for revelation or salvation.

But the problem arises when human struggle and power are narrowly perceived in terms of violence. Through such reductionism the tensions in human nature are taken as evidence that the human race is innately violent, that (to use a phrase from Thomas Merton) "man is a gorilla with a gun."[4] The corollary becomes that bloodshed and warfare are inevitable and to be expected; from there it is a very short step to legitimate them. Thus power comes to be viewed as domination, as that coercion which is sufficient to forestall or else prevail over the bloodlust of others. This so-called "jungle" imagery has been around for a long time, and nowadays we find continually updated versions of it forming a crucial underpinning for nuclearism.

What this thought model overlooks, however, is that there are other, more wholistic ways of envisioning this elemental human restlessness, and thus of depicting the sort of power appropriate to meet it. According to the classification framework used by the Group for the Advancement of Psychiatry, for instance, conflict in its broadest form would be "mastery," a wide range of human efforts to cope with the environment, while "force" is a narrower word applied to influencing or restraining an object. "Violence," then, is a still narrower term, "a specific physical form of force, the purpose of which is to injure or destroy the object."[5]

The point is that, in our imperfect world, there is not one, but many forms of conflict, some more benign than others. Nuclearism, however, simply assumes that conflict and violence are synonymous and also that both are universal, "natural," and thus somehow justifiable. All too quickly this assumption slides from the general to the specific, mistaking only one set of examples for the principle, or a part for the whole. It is like stereotyping all Chicago residents as gangsters because of the legendary exploits of a few, or generalizing from one rock concert what modern music must be like.

There is a long and varied ancestry to this discordant vision. The classic summary goes back centuries ago to the philosopher Thomas Hobbes, whose famed definition of the original human situation is "that condition which is called *war*; and such a war as is of every man against every man."[6] Out of this background, the truncated model of power as violence is bound to offer itself as the "normal" way humans interact. To curb the excesses, Hobbes went on to say, humans contrive and willingly submit to autocratic systems of rule. This also hints at the modern link between the violence of an absolute weapon and of absolutist government.

Unfortunately, religion has often compounded the problem, from time to time recklessly bestowing legitimation on this violent paradigm. One theme that has recurred in Western religion is the mystique of redemptive violence, which effectively immunizes the Hobbsian view of existence against any moral restraint. A prototype in the Old Testament is the righteous indignation of Phinehas the priest (Num. 25), who took a spear and skewered the cohabiting couple that presumably brought contamination to Israel's purity.[7] With a dreadful directness, human wrath thus was identified with divine vengeance. Consequently the traditions of holy war and blood purge have entered our heritage and continue to surface periodically.

A similar godly fervor possessed the Puritans, who responded to the breakup of the late medieval world by internalizing the chaos and then externalizing it in an apocalyptic activism, a perpetual warfare against Satan in the world. The seventeenth century rallying cry of John Knox is typical: "Our captain Christ Jesus and Satan his adversary are now at plain defiance. Their banners be displayed and the trumpets blow upon either party, for assembling of their armies."[8] There must be an all-out attack on evil, with no noncombatants allowed. Out of this same mental pattern, Puritans in North America both evangelized and slaughtered the native peoples of this continent with impartial missionary zeal. Since the 1840s, moreover, our nation has continued to plunge through periodic fits of apocalyptic passion which did not flinch at mass bloodshed, as long as it seemed a necessary burning out of the dross. For that purging was a prerequisite to our messianic role to save the world.[9]

Over the years the religious stridency has become more refined. But redemptive violence in sublimated form can still be detected in, for example, the militant rhythms and martial imagery of the "old fashioned" gospel songs so fiercely beloved in almost every congregation. Other examples may be found in crusade after crusade launched through the TV tube by the electronic church. The language may be softer, but the world is still perceived by many faithful to be a holy battle-field. Accordingly, it is easier to understand why nowadays "those who regard themselves as strict followers of the Christian faith are more inclined to an attitude approving war than are those of a more liberal attitude." This is the sad conclusion, at any rate, of a twenty-year study of attitudes towards war in the U.S., Canada, and West Germany, by professor Richard Friedli of the University of Fribourg. It is atheists, he found, who are the least likely to support nuclear war![10]

Predictably, of course, such holy militancy will flare up in periods of cultural turmoil and transition. No wonder, then, that the twentieth century, with its random massacres, terrorist attacks, and international arms races, would seem to validate the pessimism of Thomas Hobbes. The human self, when beleaguered and struggling to secure its identity, often imposes rigid dichotomies on the buzzing confusion of its inner experience. This regimented world within is then externalized onto the screen of public life. Anxieties are displaced upon "them," the latest enemy, and the conflict pursued by power of the sort that inclines towards violence. If then the strife is also legitimated by religious zealotry, the last moral restraints crumble.

No wonder that in recent years militant fundamentalist groups are setting up a fierce clamor within all three major Western religions: Judaism, Christianity, and Islam. In America the New Christian Right exploits our dread of chaos. It offers a God defined primarily in terms of authoritarian power, and a faith defined primarily as compliance to law and submission to the cosmic Law-giver. But in any case, whether in explicitly religious or allegedly secular guises, we are seeing now a global resurgence of this holy wrath against disorder and uncertainty. Such zeal smolders in the politics of the Near East, middle America, and the far right. The end result, both the most subtle and yet the most extravagant in its sacred claims, is some form of the religion of nuclearism.

To begin the process of exposing and demystifying this paradigm of power as violence, we should first of all explore the ontological assumptions which lie behind it. That is, what *is* the really real? If power is reducible to injurious and physically destructive acts, then despite any supernaturalist language applied by the sons of the zealots, it actually is a restrictive sort of naturalism that dominates. Not Phinehas but Hobbes is in control. In other words, here is a materialist vision of what is finally real: self-existent units of matter in motion, both mindless and valueless, which are altogether reducible to explanation by the physical sciences.

Moreover the materialism appears to be of a mechanistic type. All this follows the tradition of Thomas Hobbes, who was much impressed by Galileo's celestial mechanics and Descartes's aim to transform philosophy into a universal mathematics. If the geometric method is seen as the only source of certitude, then the cosmos, society — and you and I as well! — become no more than immensely complex machines. Like its modern offspring, positivism, this classic mechanism is even more restrictive than other forms of materialism. That is, it overlooks the organic ebb and flow of nature's dynamism. Instead it fixates upon the cruder patterns of action and reaction, of straightforward pleasure seeking and pain avoidance.

Not only materialism and mechanism, but also atomism characterizes this ontology. If violence is the essence of power, it implies that the cosmos must be a jumble of isolated entities, ever colliding at random. In that case it would seem only "natural" that discord supplants harmony, that adversarial relations subsume any reciprocity, and that little alternative remains to the Hobbsian view of humanity in perpetual warfare.

If this be the nature of reality — materialist, mechanistic, and atomistic — then the nature of power will be envisioned accordingly. As the ability to do or act, the goal of power in such a bleak setting must be to dominate — or to ward off domination. The resulting struggle for power becomes what Malcolm Muggeridge called "a pornography of the will."[11] And the means chosen will likely be violent. So the vicious circle continues, until a destructive and belligerent polarity has imprinted itself on human perception at every level — whether one is studying a slide under a microscope or carnage on a battlefield. In this sense, our notions of power have been preparing us for centuries to welcome nuclearism, once technology cleared the way for it.

A Society of Guns and Fantasy

There are numerous societal expressions of this paradigm of power as violence. Among the nations of the world the United States often has been noted for having a poor reputation in this regard. Americans are known for unusually high rates of handgun possession, homicide, and crimes of violence. One estimate for a recent year is that handguns killed 10,728 people in the United States. This number is fifty times the combined total of all those killed by such guns in Japan, Great Britain, Switzerland, Canada, Israel, Sweden, and West Germany. Nowadays we are witnessing, moreover, an unabashed popularity of explicitly survivalist or weapons magazines, various kinds of war gaming, and toys and clothing styles that are right out of the battlefield.

Furthermore our everyday language is colorful largely because of its extravagances in martial or violent metaphor. We "combat" a vice and "fight" for a cause. We "target" a market or audience and "bombard" it with data. We "mobilize" our members to "crush" the opposition or "trounce" the visiting team, and every worthwhile plan of operation becomes a "campaign," "plan of attack," or even a "crusade." Looking backwards in history, then, it is not surprising that "vigilante" and "lynch " are words that were coined in this country; it reflects a distinctive and ominous notion of justice. In fact this reaches beyond the human level to the cosmic, with disturbing implications about ultimate reality. After all justice must look beyond everyday events; its purpose is to depict how cosmic order, unbalanced by human folly, is to be returned to its proper equilibrium.

These social manifestations do have religious implications, whether or not they be accompanied by the traditional zealot language of divine wrath. More often nowadays, indeed, they are framed in some secular guise. Apart from the rhetoric of the New Christian Right, in the 1980s this violent tradition is carried on most notably in our pop culture and mass entertainment. Probably this began as far back as the early Puritan tales of being captured by Indians. At that time the wild rigors of the North American frontier generated a lurid but enduring taste for mythic narratives about regeneration through violence.[12] And ever since then, that enticing theme has evolved through popular literature.

It attained a special prominence in the 1930s, during the Great Depression, when public morale received a welcome boost from the back pages of newspapers and pulp paper magazines. This was the innovation of adventure comic strips, which offered a beguiling portrayal of how to solve virtually any problem: daring, plus brute force! Although the sale of comic books seems to have peaked in the late 1940s, their model of power remains. Indeed, the influence seems to be growing. Overdrawn heroes continue to invite us, the readers, to imitate their excesses, yet all in good conscience and at no cost of guilt to ourselves. Superman and Spiderman, after all, serve only the cause of justice — which eventually, remember, becomes synonymous with reality. A line from the Dick Tracy strip makes quite explicit this remarkable message: "Violence is golden when it's used to put evil down."[13]

This vision of power and its self-deceiving legitimation is only a few steps short of nuclearism. The line just quoted from Dick Tracy is not far removed from the famous motto in the 1964 presidential campaign, "Extremism in the defense of liberty is no vice." Senator Barry Goldwater, who first used these words in his 1964 acceptance speech, was candid enough to reintroduce them in his address to the 1984 Republican National Convention. The theme lives on and is still applauded. Mythic peacekeepers such as the Lone Ranger prepared the way for President Reagan's giant "Peacekeeper," the MX. The pulp paper heroes prepare and invite a godly nation to embrace the doctrine of nuclear deterrence, a rationale which, with cheery confidence, likewise claims that overwhelming fire power is needed to solve conflicts quickly and cleanly. Supremacy (by whatever name we cloak it) means that the villains are disarmed, with minimum fuss or injury. In effect, the bad boys are scolded and sent home. Even the imagery is parallel: for both the Lone Ranger and Uncle Sam it is "magical silver missiles" that deter the diabolical foes of civilization, and yet do so innocently, without incurring any moral blame on the unselfish redeemer figure.[14]

Some object to this criticism, of course, insisting this is all coincidental, and that popular entertainments and fantasy are harmless. They claim it is merely a refreshing diversion, like Musak or "bubblegum" for the mind,[15] after which normal people go back and live responsibly in what is the "real world." But ought this disclaimer go unchallenged? How should we reply?

First of all, let us recall that the familiar phrase, the "real world," only begs the question. Exactly what is at issue throughout this discussion is the contested perception of final reality! Along with that goes the indispensable role of faith (including paradigm thinking) in discerning what *is* real — what, in other words, for Christians ought to be confessed as orthodox (i.e., true), rather than heretical (i.e., false). The "real world" for us mortals is a social construct, as we have seen, including many components that are less than rational and which in some sense are matters of faith.

Secondly, in response to the "bubblegum" objection, we should point out that these leisure time diversions ought not to be so lightly dismissed. Within the controversies about mass media and pop culture, there is a growing body of research data that our after-hours side trips into fantasy do after all affect our workaday notions of reality. George Gerbner and his associates at the University of Pennsylvania, for instance, report increasing evidence corroborating a significant correlation between television watching and preoccupation in real life with violence.[16] That is, heavy viewers of TV tend to have exaggerated estimates of violence and danger in the "real world," and they are more likely than light viewers or nonviewers to be fearful and expect to be victims of crime themselves. The conclusion, we may infer, is that our perceptual worlds are not so easily compartmentalized after all. The boundary lines we draw are often deceptively porous.

Whereas the role of inducting the younger generation into a society's worldview used to be dominated by religious institutions, for us much of that function has now been taken over by mass entertainment. Many unwanted lessons may be taught the young through the arts, in a beguiling fashion — as

elders since the time of Plato have warned. The model of
power as violence is but one of several. In the mid-1980s, the
electronic media have become a particularly effective means
of socialization. Concerning modern films, for instance,
parents for this very reason ought to take an interest in
whatever stirs the collective psyche enough to become a box
office hit. Perhaps this is especially true of those films that
purport to be fantasy, since to a greater degree they are ab-
solved of normal restraints and responsibility, and more freely give expression to subconscious patterns and urges. We
ought to think twice, for instance, about the paradigms of
power (and thereby the alleged reality to be actualized) that
are both offered and made a bit more acceptable by the
popular "Star Wars" series, or the swashbuckling and gory
exploits of Conan, Rambo, or Indiana Jones.

Another example of the effects on youth is the current
passion for video games. It has been reported that armed
forces recruitment officers find fertile ground around video
game arcades. The images of battleground and playground
are so blurred as to merge, in our public fantasies. There is
great irony in the words of a so-called "Pac-Man Junkie," a
teenager who gave an interview that ended up affirming just
what he began by denying: "People say these games make
kids more violent, but come on, it's just a game. If anything,
it kind of shows you what it's really like out in the world.
You've got to know what's out there. And you *know* it's all
out there."[17] No mere bubblegum, this! If such an unguarded
statement is at all typical, then a worldview is at stake — and
Thomas Hobbes would be pleased at the prognosis so far.

Not only at the level of society, but also in more personal
dimensions of everyday life the effect of this paradigm is felt.
As individuals we have grown accustomed to the distorted
notion that violence somehow is the only real form of power.
On the interpersonal level, of course, this is not easily admitted, for we sense how disruptive the effects must be. So instead it is arranged that, concerning this personal level at
least, our culture transmit mixed signals. This means both a
veiled admiration for symbols of personal violence (especially
expressions of machismo as a means of consolidating a fraz-
zled masculine identity), and yet also a selective suppression

of the exercise of such power, lest it get out of hand.

The ambiguity runs very deep in a patriarchal culture. For those of us who are relatively well socialized, nurtured by a web of warm relationships, it may be possible to maintain an uneasy balance. We do this by sublimating dangerous emotion and by projecting into safe abstractions the belief that true power is violent. Often there may be only a few clues surfacing about the deeper paradigm, such as the rifle on display on the den wall or the truck's gunrack, or perhaps a bumpersticker about "God, guns, and guts" being the core of our nation's values. But then there are much grimmer evidences: the high incidents of rape, personal assault, and abortion as a first rather than a last resort. Domestic violence affects two million families in our society, and three out of five households have experienced battering of spouses or abuse of children at least once. In 1983, for instance, over 1.7 million children were maltreated, 3.4 percent of them suffering major injury. In Pennsylvania, for example, where I live, one of every two women will be beaten at least once during her marriage, and every year one in five is beaten by a husband or boyfriend.[18]

These sad facts point not to simply individual aberrations from the law and social standards—which of course they are. But at the same time these episodes of personal violence are enactments of a deep cultural paradigm that is only partly disavowed. Then there are those cases where individuals are less well socialized, less nurtured by human relationships. For such marginalized persons the enactments may take a highly visible form, such as an airplane hijacking, or an attempted assassination of a public figure. In any case the model of violence as effective power is a part of our transmitted culture, a mindset linked to patriarchy and received by each of us, regardless of how directly we may respond to it. Like a dry creek bed in drought, the channel remains there, waiting and ready to direct the flood of impulse at the next opportunity. And now in our generation, nuclearist piety both reflects that fatal pattern and encourages the final flood.

However at the personal level we do have qualms about this form of power. That is why a high premium is awarded to ways that appear to reconcile it with our moral sensibilities. The popular religion of zealous nationalism, the legacy of Phinehas which we have noted, is one approach. Another is the recent wave of nostalgia which allows, even promotes, this happy inconsistency. There is a longing for what is believed to have been the cherished virtues of a bygone day in North America: the current watchwords include "family," "neighborhood," "work," and so on. Insofar as these words express the covenantal bonds which constitute our very humanity, of course, they remind us of values that indeed ought to be conserved. But the context as well as the content of these catchwords often suggest something else: romanticized, even fictionalized memories. Images are evoked of the family hearthside and Grandma's kitchen, of neighborhood picnics in Small Town U.S.A., and of country artisans laboring with pride over their handmade products.

At best these nostalgic images function partly to obscure the past, the very real structural violence of turn-of-the-century Main Street America, and how much the country was built on the exploitation of women, slaves or former slaves, newer immigrant groups, and unorganized labor. At worst they function to obscure the present as well, masking the hidden anger behind happy faces, and justifying new and often more subtle indignities today. In either case nostalgia projects a fantasy of Hometown America, bygone days when women and racial minorities knew their place, neighbors were convivial and kept the noise down, schoolmarms used the switch freely, and parents were unhindered in "disciplining" their kids—by which is usually meant no better than a slap, spanking, or beating. *That*, we secretly assume, is the kind of power that gets things done!

Such fantasies masquerading as memory provide a ready tool—a tool by which the powerful may suppress inhibitions about using compulsion or promoting an authoritarian mentality. This has been a favorite tactic of right-wing ideologues, for instance, in monarchial periods of Europe, in the Germany of the 1930s, and in both North and South America today. Nostalgia can have a very political function. Like an anesthesia, it can quiet moral qualms. A heroic past has often proved useful in driving home the lesson that physical coercion, after all, is the effective and final arbiter in human relations.

The Violence Paradigm Critiqued

However, there is a fatal inconsistency in this power as violence model. The homey relationships that we long for cannot be sustained in the mechanistic universe that is presupposed by violence. This paradigm of power promises what it cannot deliver, for violence can only degrade the quality of life — whether in the bygone days of a mythic Dodge City or in real life today. Battering and bettering a child are mutually exclusive actions, and neighborhoods are not improved by posted warnings and handguns. Instead, the actual consequences are as Simone Weil has memorably portrayed them: "Force has a 'petrifactive quality.' It changes a person into inert matter, a corpse or into an abject slave or suppliant completely subject to the determinations of force; or it changes the wielder of force into an unfeeling, driven entity. Everyone who falls under the dominion of force undergoes the death of the soul, the change into a thing, a stone."[19]

There is, in fact, a flat contradiction between power, which is the ability to do and actualize, and violence, which is physical force applied for injury or destruction. Actualization and the "petrifactive quality" cannot be combined. This is true, moreover, not just at the personal level but also at every other level. This insight is firmly embedded in the gospel, and thus the earliest Christian orthodoxy. So a confessing church movement ought to proclaim vigorously that, across the board, there is an *intrinsic incompatibility between power and violence.* For I am convinced that the root metaphors of any given worldview pertain to the macrocosmic and the microcosmic levels alike, and therefore that to defend or to alter key paradigms at any juncture will also influence the other dimensions of that belief system.

Indeed, one of the sharpest examples of this is the nuclear dilemma itself. Arthur Koestler, back in 1963, put the problem graphically: "A policeman, armed with an atom bomb and nothing else, could not prevent the escape of a couple of house breakers without blowing the whole town to glory, himself included. We are faced with a new paradox: the superior power of a weapon may reduce its bearer to helplessness."[20]

On the global level this has usually been recognized — at least until the recent phase of the Cold War — as "the trap of nuclearism," or "the paradox of security." "It is an inverse relationship: the more that people and states seek to increase their own security by the old methods, but with the new atomic power, the less security they have; and the more that heightened insecurity is sensed, the faster the arms race becomes, the heavier its economic burden, and the more hateful, aggressive, expansionist and devious the enemy appears."[21] Furthermore, as Henry Kissinger observed years ago, "the more powerful the weapon . . . the greater becomes the reluctance to use them."[22]

Of course it has always been true that "military power . . . . is a key that fits only certain locks,"[23] a brittle strength which time and again has shown itself unable to go far towards settling most political problems. But since nuclear weapons have become an added factor, the whole paradox of power is shoved to a new and apocalyptic extremity. That realization is what prompted Dwight D. Eisenhower, at the mid-point of his presidency, to write, "The true security problem . . . is not merely man against man or nation against nation. It is man against war."[24] George W. Ball, former Undersecretary of State, reminds us that in earlier times it was accepted that "a weapon is an instrument that can be used to achieve a political objective in the Clausewitzian sense of war as an extension of diplomacy. But the public knows that nuclear weapons are not usable for that purpose; they can only facilitate mutual suicide."[25] That is why, as former Secretary of Defense Robert S. McNamara put it bluntly, "nuclear weapons serve no military purpose whatsoever."[26] They can merely threaten, in an effort to avert military action. It is this function of prevention which our declared doctrine of nuclear deterrence has been officially assigned to clarify.

Recently, however, even this function has been undermined by a new strategic idea. The trap of nuclearism and the paradox of power and security are being obscured in the public mind by more and more national leaders, especially since the later years of the Carter administration. A new situation has begun, with the arrival of "counterforce" (striking an enemy's military capacity) as a targeting doctrine, which was first publicly acknowledged in August, 1980, in Presidential Directive 59. Counterforce, in turn, is supported by a new generation of missiles with "first strike" capability, such as the MX, the Pershing II, and the Trident II or D-5.

Both these developments rest on the amazing presumption that nuclear wars are not necessarily to be deterred, but may in fact be fought and perhaps won. The clearest admission of this new doctrine came from Secretary of Defense Caspar Weinberger's congressional testimony in September, 1981, and in the Department of Defense *Fiscal 1984-1988 Defense Guidance*:

> United States nuclear capabilities must prevail even under the condition of a prolonged war. . . . and be able to force the Soviet Union to seek earliest termination of hostilities on terms favorable to the United States. . . . US strategic nuclear forces and their command and communications links should be capable of supporting controlled ´ nuclear counterattacks over a protracted period while maintaining a reserve of nuclear forces sufficient for trans- and post-attack protection and coercion.[27]

This frightening development marks an explicit move away from Mutual Assured Destruction (deterrence) as an operating strategy—even though public alarm prompted the Reagan administration to deny that this is the case. A shift has indeed taken place, regardless of public disclaimers to the contrary. What is euphemistically called "modernization" of our strategic forces, however, turns out to be another yearning for yesteryear, one more exercise in nostalgia. It is an attempt to turn the clock back to the illusions of bygone days in Hometown U.S.A., before the internal contradictions between power and violence had become quite so evident. This is one more example of how moving the effect of a paradigm is on human thinking, even when it seriously endangers human wellbeing. We are witnessing, indeed, the attempt by

national leaders to do away with the paradox of power/
powerlessness, especially in its heightened nuclear form, by
simply defining it out of existence.

A Biblical Vision of Power

But is there another way? If power as effective violence
is the metaphor that is dominant today, what may we find as
an alternative? More particularly within the churches, what
notion of power should win recognition as "orthodox" and
thereupon be attested to the wider world? We turn now from
an internal to an external crituque, that is, a judgment made
through comparison to a model of power presented in the
Bible.

Thomas Hobbes thought ideas of the supernatural were
superstitious, reflecting defective ideas of nature. It is all the
more ironic, therefore, that Hobbsian views of a materialist,
fragmented, and warring biosphere are so widely accepted
within the very communities of faith that claim the Bible as
scripture! For one thing, theism and its doctrine of creation
can hardly be harmonized with such a model. Indeed *creatio
ex nihilo* (creation out of nothing) requires the belief that
the world is neither a self-contained mechanism nor self-
explanatory, but that it relies on the Creator as the uncondi-
tioned source of its origin, as well as its daily preservation. It
requires also the belief that the world is neither illusory nor
intrinsically evil, but — even though grievously defaced in its
fallenness — all creatureliness is undergirded and upheld as
indelibly good.[28] Already, therefore, the presuppositions
behind the reduction of power to violence are put in question.

Beyond simple theism, however, Christianity also views
creation Christocentrically — which makes it even less susceptible to the mechanistic ontology needed by nuclearism. The
cosmos is regarded as the handiwork of that triune One
whom faith first recognizes in Jesus Christ. The imprint of
redemption is already on the creation, and all of life is founded on a trinitarian faithfulness. "All things were created
through him and for him. He is before all things, and in him
all things hold together" (Col. 1:16b-17). If the creation be
"through him and for him," it cannot be purposeless. And if
"in him all things hold together," then its parts (atoms,

amoebae, or selves) cannot finally be in incessant strife — as Hobbes put it, "such a war as is of every man against every man." If Christ be "before all things," as well as their goal, then the very cosmos is opened up into a call to freedom and fulfillment in the glorification of God. The fundamental *nature* of the world, then, is established by its instrumental *nurture*. Christologically viewed, that nurture means preparation for the incarnation, reconciliation by the atonement, and transfiguration by the resurrection.

Nor can this process be comprehended apart from its eschatological culmination. "For the creation waits with eager longing for the revealing of the sons of God . . . the creation itself will be set free from its bondage to decay and obtain the glorious liberty of the children of God" (Rom. 8:19, 21). The violence and mechanistic processes which admittedly do exist in nature cannot constitute the final word. Jesus embodies both the Alpha and the Omega. Through hope we know him both in the light of the resurrection of the Crucified and in the light of the cross of the Risen One. From this standpoint, then, we turn our gaze anew to the creation, in its present fallenness and its promised glorification, its bitter divisions and its reconciliation. When we are able at last to envision it as the New Creation, we can also act within it accordingly. This, then, is the model of "reality" which is brought us by Scripture, and which the church in the nuclear age should strive to confess.

To revitalize this vision, of course, is no easy undertaking. Actually, the main obstacle to it may not be science after all, its methods and postulates, as has been claimed since the Age of Enlightenment. But the "laws" of science should be recognized as, in part, social constructs too, the disciplined "common sense" (i.e., views held in *common*) of the community of scientists. And in physics now, matter is interpreted less as autonomous particles than as a network of relationships.[29] This is not to deny, however, that complex problems remain to be worked out if a more biblical paradigm of Christocentric creation is to be attained in a high technology society — that is, without lapsing into a biblical literalism by fiat, a crude represtination of a worldview from antiquity.

But instead of science, the main obstacle may well be

socio-political. That is, there have long been ideological benefits rendered by the Hobbsian model to the Western world. These have included several centuries of expropriating the natural resources of other lands and the unskilled labor of other races, as well as the self-serving explanations of why some members of society prosper or find advancement while others cannot. Understandably, the biblical vision of reality under the Lordship of Christ is not found congenial by a belligerent and bitterly divided world. It has been and will be resisted.

Public acceptance of such a vision thus will require a conversion, a massive paradigm shift in our world no less drastic than that accomplished by Einstein in the realm of physics. In urging "peace as a paradigm shift," in fact, Michael Nagler makes that same comparison. He then goes on to quote words of Einstein himself which happen to offer suggestive parallels to the biblical paradigm. "A human being is part of the whole, called by us the 'universe,'" he said, so the conventional notion that each person is "something separate from the rest" is really "a kind of optical delusion of his consciousness. . . . Our task must be to free ourselves from this prison by widening our circle of compassion to embrace all living creatures and the whole nature in its beauty."[30]

How does all this affect the paradigms of violent conflict and power which nuclearism utilizes? If reality is envisioned differently, then so must be the power which overcomes conflict and which actualizes that reality.

Of course conflict and antagonisms are a part of our actual existence. The world is fallen and its eschatological renewal is not a natural extension *of* the present, but a promise *to* the present. However even now, conflict is not the same as bloodshed or aggression, and certainly it does not justify the hasty conclusion that war somehow must be innate to human nature. In fact, says Gibson Winter, "conflict seems regulative rather than constitutive of the relational processes of species life. Interdependent play and support of species life are prior, else there could not have been a development of culture. Where relative independence is violated by excess of power or domination, conflict is a regulative struggle to reestablish fundamental rhythms."[31] This struggle accordingly defined, in both its character and its moderation, by the broader life forces which it sustains.

Christians, moreover, should view this broader context eschatologically. The "fundamental rhythms" of life are not a closed system, deflecting all of nature's unfolding into a vast and futile circularity, a cycle in the eternal return of all being unto itself. Instead the biblical vision discerns in these tensions a majestic sweep of interrelated movement. "We know that the whole creation has been groaning in travail together until now" (Rom. 8:22). The biblical metaphor of labor pangs as an anticipated part of the birth of the New Age casts a different light on the experience of conflict. This alternate paradigm certainly acknowledges the pain and risk of struggles at every level of the biosphere. But it is careful nevertheless to define them through hope in a wider purpose, the consummation of the New Creation.

If this be a more biblical view of conflict than nuclearism permits, then the paradigm of power likewise must be quite different than violence. Power, the ability to do and actualize in a conflictual world, must have many modes and subtleties. On a quite practical level, for instance, which the world outside the church should already recognize, this is demonstrated by the emerging discipline of conflict resolution. Many hostages of terrorist attack and victims of hijackings and domestic violence are alive today, thanks to the skilled intervention of negotiators. Such techniques are often effective, even in a fallen world and by pragmatic standards.

Social scientists, recognizing the many forms power can take, have classified them in various ways. That of Rollo May is an example: power can be 1) exploitative, 2) manipulative (both of which are power *over* another person), 3) competitive (power *against* another), 4) nutrient (power *for* the care of others), and finally 5) integrative (power *with* the others).[32] The latter, so-called higher forms of power support personhood and are more stable, for they sustain that intricate yet vital reciprocity between love and the ability to act. These higher forms are, in this sense, more "real."

At a deeper level, the grounds for this distinctive paradigm of power are depicted in Scripture. That is, the source of power is God alone, and so the characteristics of power must be recast accordingly. Power does not define itself in isolation, but is closely blended with the other attributes of the triune One (for example, righteousness, mercy, glory), indeed with the very contents of God's will. "The power of God constitutes the inner energy of holiness . . . "[33] That power is in fact saving power, to which the proper response (by mortals and even the cosmos itself) is praise, doxology. This is true even in the Old Testament, which admittedly also describes holy wars and massacres. But in the Old Testament God's strength is displayed, not so much in the awesome inauguration of the heavens and the earth, or the rout of enemy armies, but in God's power to save. And that power may as well happen within captivity as in victories, and with a "still small voice" rather than a hurricane, earthquake, and fire (1 Kings 19:11–12).

This paradigm of saving power is continued and refined in the New Testament where, like other concepts, "the concept of power is given its decisive impress by the fact of Christ."[34] The mode of resurrection life shared by the risen Lord and by the faithful community was the daily experience of this power. Therefore, with few exceptions, the New Testament clearly renounces military force and other coercive shortcuts to a "solution" at any level of life. Instead *agape,* steadfast and nonviolent love, is the way of the "real world" revealed through Jesus, and was clearly understood as such by the early church.[35] This quality of power was new — a foretaste of the Messianic banquet, the eschatological jubilation in which both sinners and the (realtively) righteous sit down together. Yet it also was as old as "the first born of all creation," in whom "all things were created, in heaven and on earth" (Col. 1:15–16). Finally, on a certain Friday long ago, it came to a hitherto unimagined focus. There, on a hillside outside Jerusalem, that power was disclosed by which "all things, whether on earth or in heaven" are reconciled, namely, "by the blood of his cross" (Col. 1:20).

Now if this event testifies to the real world, as Christians claim to believe, then surely the word "realism" must take on a definition radically contrary to its conventional usage nowadays. For reality is not so amenable after all to violence and rough-handed manipulations. Power must be seen less as a domination — or for that matter as invlunerability to domination — by antagonists in an alienated time and space. Rather, power is congruent with a Christ-formed cosmos, and so ought to be perceived as relational and reconciling, as wholistic instead of partisan, and even as artistic.[36]

Biblically speaking, in short, the paradigm of power is better viewed as nonviolent love than as violence. The term "nonviolence" ought to be rehabilitated in Christian circles, for it is actually more orthodox than the compromising alternatives explored by a thousand years of church history. It does not mean inaction or sectarian withdrawal, as its detractors often allege, but instead a positive response to conflict. That means a response that underscores those humanizing commonalities that bind and encompass those who for the moment find themselves as antagonists. By evoking the very ideals held by the adversary, it blocks dehumanizing projections and their "petrifactive quality," thereby breaking the vicious cycle of domination and defensiveness. In doing so it opens up the future for everyone.

Modern tyrannies, by contrast, build their power on the irreversibility of evil, on the notion that some evil is so clearcut and unforgivable that society must be mobilized to exterminate it. But nonviolence knows that humans are unfinished, that society is in a state of becoming, and so forgiveness and change are possible. "Nonviolence takes account precisely of this dynamic and non-final state of all relationships among men, for nonviolence seeks to change relationships that are evil into others that are good."[37]

Of course this summons forth an altogether broader paradigm of power. As Thomas Merton elsewhere wrote, "Nonviolence is not for power [that is, as conventionally understood] but for truth. It is not aimed at immediate political results, but at the manifestation of fundamental and crucially important truth."[38] Instead of the reductionist model of violence or a "fetishism of immediate visible results,"[39] power can be envisioned more broadly as "nutrient and integrative" (May), as "truth force" (Gandhi) or "life force."[40] True power invites artistic integration into a higher purposefulness. Even the forces of nature respond better to the farmer who forgoes the disruptive "quick fix" of harsh technologies, hot-wiring the agricultural system, but practices instead a gentle enhancement of existing harmonies in the biosphere.

Likewise on the societal level, amid conflicting social forces, the active nonviolence of a Gandhi or a Martin Luther King, Jr., has already shown itself to be an explicit and usable alternative. More recently in the nuclear age, discussion has begun concerning the possibilities of nonviolent forms of "civilian based defense," for countering even the most extreme of possible dangers, namely an invation by hostile armies.[41]

A new pardigm of power may be no panacea in our complex and troubled world, no short cut to the ability to do and act. But it can open up transforming new possibilities. Again, the words of Thomas Merton:

> Nonviolence must be realistic and concrete. Like ordinary political action, it is no more than the "art of the possible" But precisely the advantage of nonviolence is that it has a *more Christian and more humane notion of what is possible.* When the powerful believe that only power is efficacious, the nonviolent resister is persuaded of the superior efficacy of love, openness, peaceful negotiation and above all of truth.[42]

As faithful midwives of the New Creation have come to know, that kind of power is closer to the heart of reality than is the alleged power of the Sword — or the Bomb.

7

Life Together: a Zero-sum Game

The human being is an intensely social being. From a physiological standpoint, no other creature is so vulnerable for such a long period of post-natal development. By contrast, other animal life is born with a virtually complete set of instinctual behaviors already embedded in their neural networks. Even among the social insects or a herd of deer, for instance, each member is genetically programed to develop into a fixed identity. But humans at birth are incomplete and for at least a year afterwards live in what is essentially an extended fetal period outside the womb. Even thereafter the biological drives of our species are highly unspecialized and undirected.

In short, our nature requires nurture! That is, our physiological substructures are so open-ended and adaptable that we require a sustaining community. From this source we receive the complex of learned ways of living transmitted from previous generations which is called "culture." As communal creatures, then, we depend upon our sociality, our life together. Even Robinson Crusoe or the most antisocial hermit could hardly exist without the benefit of earlier years of formative group nurture.

However nuclearism represents, among other things, the culmination of quite a different notion of sociality. Human life together is constricted into a hardened antagonism which resembles what has been lately called "zero sum" game theory.

Of course there is a background to this. Western culture

has long fostered an intense competitiveness, which has depended upon the presumption that the resources needed to sustain life are always in short supply. This sense of contrariety has been further articulated by a new branch of mathematics: game theory. The model is of a contest that involves strategy, bargaining, rewards and threats. It offers a way of analyzing the results of various combinations of decisions by the contestants, whether the "game" be international diplomacy, war, an election, a contract negotiation, or just children's games.

The "zero sum" game is a new term for an old and familiar pattern; examples include chess, poker, and most other parlor and board games. What defines this category is that the total of gains and losses must add up to zero. So the only way to get ahead is to take something away from your opponent — or vice versa. The assumption again is that basic resources are in short supply, so a contest must be waged in order to redistribute those scarce goods. The distribution is regulated precisely by an inverse correlation: any gain by one player requires a corresponding loss from the other(s). Whatever harms my opponent, therefore, must benefit me. Likewise any loss to me is automatically my enemy's gain.

Of course many games are not like that — frisbee throwing, for instance, or a friendly game of catch. And it is quite possible to devise contests that are not so rigidly symmetrical. In parlor games, charades would be an example — that is, when players are not divided into teams. In a "variable sum" or nonzero-sum game players may still try to win the most points, but often each can do better if the others are also doing better. Moreover in real life, many of the conflicts we experience do not require that winnings be balanced by losses. The best resolutions of conflict, in fact, are those in which all participants leave the bargaining table with a sense of satisfaction. Conflict is not thereby abolished in, say, labor/management or marital disputes, but would be channeled to a level that manages to enhance all sides.

Unfortunately, our society is strongly predisposed toward a directly zero-sum mentality, and imposes this rigidity upon many situations that do not actually require it. "One-upmanship" seems to demand that someone else be "put down" correspondingly. From childhood on we are taught that competition is the way to survival, that in order not to be a loser one must aspire continually to be a winner. This is accompanied by the silent assumption that others must be made into losers, shouldering unwillingly the cost of the victor's triumphs. Conflict situations which could just as well spur an individual to a higher level of development, or challenge a community to a more equitable distribution of goods and services, are instead transformed into a contest, a direct face-off between contenders for an indivisible prize. Newspapers often find that sales increase when headlines feature such emotion-laden words as "win," "defeat," "rout," or "avenge"—even when the story deals with commonplace matters: the session of a legislature, for instance, or a family quarrel, or the budget of a city library.

Those who chose to view life in this manner may be slow to recognize the price it exacts upon all would-be contestants, losers and winners alike. One's security and self-esteem are ever in doubt and in need of renewed victories. Envy towards others poisons relationships and blocks self-esteem. Anxiety about future provisions prevents contentment with the nourishment of daily bread. The smallest incidents can be magnified by vigilance and fear into huge proportions. Elation one day over some symbolic victory may be followed by despondency the next. In the rush to displace or even eliminate our rivals of the moment, we forfeit the creativity instead to surmount long-lived dilemmas.

A World of Scarcity

The ontological assumptions of this model build upon those already noted in the case of power as violence—but they also move beyond. A "zero sum" universe is not only a cosmic container for colliding atoms, inhospitable to anything beyond physical matter. It is in addition a finite world and, so to speak, becoming even more so. The basic resources needed to sustain life—food, clean air, potable water, accessible minerals, and so on—are limited and even diminishing in supply. This concept seizes upon entropy and the Second Law of Thermodynamics, which hold that motion is becoming ever more randomized and matter is slowly unraveling, and it applies such concepts to the basic economic goods we all need. Before us is raised the specter of a shrinking habitable world, at the very time our demands upon it are expanding. The implicit message: we'd better get ours now, and fast! Faster, that is, than "they" can — whether such competitors be defined as rival superpowers or future generations.

A world so conceived does not merely incline human beings to violence, but drives them to it. If we are living atop a pile of melting resources, then we must scramble just to maintain our present position and ward off any intruders, not to mention hopes for expanding our advantage. The fight for survival is then as impersonal as it is ferocious. For the focus is not upon any special iniquity of one's hungry rivals, but on the alarming and irreversible shrinkage of those commodities essential to life itself.

The basic way in which humans relate to one another, accordingly, must be as adversaries, contestants in an unremitting struggle in which only the fittest may survive. With this notion of reality in the background, no explicit argument for a desperate competitiveness is even needed. For it is seen as only natural that a frenzied rivalry be now pursued over what will eventually be only glowing embers of our planet's life-warming energies. From this ontology, zero-sum gaming must come to be perceived as normal, as a direct reflection — whether in sport and games or in high diplomacy — of the way things are.

A Society of Confrontations

The zero-sum paradigm expresses itself quite explicitly in the way we live together, our patterns of sociality. Again it is an extension of the heretical model of power, which supports the view that humans are innately violent. Now there is the added specification that such violence is most naturally directed toward confrontation between adversaries.

As children we are taught this expectation at an early age. It is true that every culture supplies its young with adventurous stories of some sort, to offer role models and guide their rites of passage into adulthood. But in the stories of our society there is a difference: confrontations are portrayed as both violent and normal. Most of the stories served to our young, in fiction and film, are an endless series of variations on quite a narrow theme: some apocalyptic showdown between the good guys and the bad guys. A study some years ago calculated that over a span of seventeen years the average teenager will have watched at least 15,000 hours of television, including 350,000 commercials and 18,000 murders.[1] Such repeated exposure, even if casual or of low intensity, must surely influence the prevailing assumptions about human life together. There is a relentless cavalcade of caricatures across the small screen, "us" vs. "them" — and Dodge City (or planet earth), we are told, "ain't big enough fer the two of us."

By the time one reaches adulthood, these instructional entertainments have had their effect and one is prepared to carry on the unremitting duties of rivalry. The scarcity of what we have come to desire is what spurs us on, if our zeal should falter. We are duly warned that true romance with "the" (only) right person is not for everyone, but is won by those who select the right toiletries and blue jeans or gulp the correct cola. Moreover, "the man who wants your job is reading Forbes," or your volume of sales is jeopardized by the competitor who has just installed the right telecommunications system.

In a shrinking pool of necessities, it seems, survival will demand ever greater exertion and ruthlessness. Or, to vary the image, in a lifeboat cast adrift with diminishing supplies and prospectively increased claims, such qualities as compassion and cooperation are accounted absurd luxuries. The debate of a decade ago about "lifeboat ethics" reflects simply an extreme form of that zero-sum thinking.[2] So adults take their place in a society pervaded by an uneasy gamesmanship, a calculus of threat and bargaining.

The readiness for confrontation naturally bubbles up as well to the international level. It is very widely assumed, in the words of R. Buckminster Fuller, that "wars have always occurred because of the underlying inadequacy of vital supplies. We will always have war until there is enough to support all humanity."[3] Certainly this is one of the major reasons for warfare down through the ages. But such a statement should not pass unchallenged, for it offers convenient shelter for two self-serving rationalizations.

First, the level of vital supplies which is deemed "enough" turns out to be a highly subjective judgment. The rising level of expectations is not just a Third World phenomenon, but even more a characteristic of the affluent First World. The steady climb of our living standards and our imports of basic materials from around the globe imposes a staggering burden on the rest of the planet. As a result, the gap between the wealthier nations and the poorer ones is widening at a faster rate than ever.

This brings us to the second problem. There would be little "inadequacy of vital supplies" even today, if they were more equitably distributed. In recent years global grain production has averaged 2.2 pounds per person per day, which is enough to provide ample protein and more than 3000 calories daily to everyone on earth.[4] But since a third or more of that grain is fed to livestock, so some of us can enjoy meat, and much land is devoted to cash crops for export to gain hard currency, hundreds of millions go malnourished — or worse.

In other words, the scarcity scare we have heard so much about is often a matter of subjective judgment and of social justice. We do indeed need to be faithful stewards of the earth's resources. But it is plainly unfair for the steward at the same time to be feasting and hoarding at the expense of others.

But the image of scarcity, whether accurate or misconstrued, continues to sharpen our eagerness for confrontation on the world scene. We have observed, for instance, how the Olympic games, supposedly a (nonzero-sum) celebration of human prowess and international presence, have been trivialized into a crass enumeration of how many gold medals were netted this time by our side. That popular mindset is then confirmed when *Time* magazine in its 1984 Man of the Year cover story, acclaimed the Olympics as "Darwinian theater."

Foreign policy is likewise treated as a global poker game, for stakes that have become virtually limitless. The rule is, reports Richard Barnet from his own experience in the U.S. State Department, that "all the world is the playing field. There are no spectators. Every nation, no matter how small, insular, or neutralist in outlook, is a potential member of somebody's team."[5] In the Cold War tally sheet governments are rudely categorized as either allies or evil empires, with no middle ground permitted. Neutrality or urgent local issues are brushed aside as a mere charade.

Instead our foreign policy is possessed by eagerness for confrontation and the tokens of victory. In preliminary negotiations for ending the Vietnam war, for instance, when the Vietnamese agreed to meet in Paris instead of Warsaw, an official from the U.S. State Department gloated, "There we were right off the bat — eyeball to eyeball on a question of prestige as well as procedure. And they're the ones who blinked. Now we're one up."[6] For the United States this polarized worldview was first given a doctrinal basis, so to speak, in 1950 with the National Security Council Document No. 68. NSC-68 pioneered in portraying the entire world as an arena of competition between the U.S. and the Soviet Union. It warned that American global interests would collapse like those of previous empires if we accept "disorder" in the world at large. Instead we must use "any means, covert or overt, violent or nonviolent," to attain our international objectives — including to "foster a fundamental change in the nature of the Soviet system."[7]

The zero-sum model thrives in this confrontational climate, demanding elaborate ledger books on gains and losses. Any misfortune suffered by an opponent — such as bad crops, a faltering economy, or unruly allies — is construed as a credit in our column simply because it is a debit in theirs. Likewise any sort of setback for our side is doubly alarming, as a threat to national security and quite possibly an enemy plot as well. In the spirit of NSC-68 presidential candidate Ronald Reagan said thirty years later, "The Soviet Union underlies all the unrest that is going on. If they weren't engaged in this game of dominoes, there wouldn't be any hot spots in the world."[8] The reference to a zero-sum game, dominoes, is significant. Indeed the metaphor of "domino theory" all too often has dominated U.S. outlook on the rest of the world.

A better metaphor, however, might be a geopolitical Superbowl. To the coaches and fans of nuclearism, everything appears at stake in the showdown of the two top teams. With the aid of what has come to be named "linkage," the team managers survey local conflicts strictly in the light of a global ledger book. Linkage means that serious talks about superpower disarmament are deferred until the rest of the world scene is tidied up to our satisfaction.[9] In fact, however, there are numerous "unlinked" issues in our world, such as Soviet Jewish emigration or repression and revolution in Latin America. When such problems are forced onto the overall zero-sum score board, they become both insoluble on their own terms and inflammable in global terms. In the passion of the ultimate game, there arises a risk of losing all perspective in a suicidal mania just to harm the opponent. We recall the boast of Kaiser Wilhelm in 1914, mentioned in an earlier chapter: "Even if we are bled to death, England will at least lose India."[10] But can a nuclear age afford this sort of fervor?

A Life of One-upmanship

If we view the life support systems of the cosmos as contracting, so that both society and the globe conceal adversaries ever lurking in wait and ready to snatch away our share, this must in turn infect our attitudes at every level. In daily life one finds open minds and hands becoming cramped, and the sight of another human face before one's eyes is blurred through adversarial frenzy. Interpersonal relationships, as well, are warped and constricted along team lines that are ever shifting.

In the home, for instance, learning to share ought to be one of the most important lessons for everyone. A wholesome family life should dispel the illusion that another's gain means my deprivation. But far too many houses along an average residential street are just containers for unresolved rivalry, depriving their occupants of a lifelong blessing of learning mutuality. Parents may compete for their children's affections (or vice versa), taking for granted that more love for Mom, say, must mean less for Dad. Grandparents, household guests, or relatives may be unwelcome if it is assumed that family happiness is a limited resource — a commodity which cannot be multiplied but only drained away by hospitality. A world of anxious scarcity often lies behind the old slogan about one's home being one's "castle," since fortifications are designed to gather in and protect whatever is of value from outside marauders. A fortress mentality, however, can fossilize a home and subvert the very family values which it hopes to safeguard.

Outside the household, our personal lives are likewise affected by the zero-sum model. In the office or workplace, one person's advancement or reward is often perceived to be at the expense of another's. Indeed the rest of the crew or staff may feel depressed, and individuals may note in themselves a deepened sense of failure and self-recrimination. A joyless if not ruthless professionalism becomes part of pursuing a career. It may be that a vague hope for "better luck next time," the next round or inning of the so-called game, is the only consolation for those who "also ran" in what is by common consent a race with few prizes. For jobs that may in themselves hold little intrinsic satisfaction, competition may add spice — but at a later cost to the digestive systems of the inner self.

The drive to be "Number One" pervades our leisure hours as well. At those infrequent moments of elation when we are the ones at the pinnacle, it seems to matter little that by definition others must lose. After all, they can console themselves with hopes for "next time," can't they? The North American fascination with competitive sports embodies much that is wholesome. But in a zero-sum climate it does invite degradation of sportsmanship. When news reports arrive about riots at European soccer matches, indeed, they carry also a grim reminder of the potential for obsessive violence that accompanies the lust for victory and its gratifications.

Another example, as we have noted elsewhere, is television programing. "The tube" both satisfies and stimulates the need to rehearse ever again the timeless battle of evil vs. good, so that the latter's triumph may once more calm our inner fears. Then there is the favorite indoor sport of all: gossip. Here one's age or physique is no barrier; we are all contenders, if not potential superstars! In personal sarcasm or innuendo about a third party there is a special satisfaction. Just as in the playground seesaws of our childhood, so as adults one's own ego seems to ascend in direct proportion to the lowering of another's. On a broader scale, racism, sexism, and lesser forms of ethnic prejudice have always bolstered the uncertain self by offering a "contrast concept," against which one can always compare oneself favorably. We seem convinced that human dignity is a scarce commodity, and our gain is from the other's loss.

But to be Number One is a lonely and insecure position, requiring constant reassurance against the normal erosions of circumstance. Like many popular devotional practices it can become an obsessive ritual, supported by repeated reenactments and draining psychic energy away from a normal development of other parts of the personality. Even short of such extremes, a zero-sum mentality does take its toll on all of us, and our life together is misshapen by its dictates. The model is summed up in some famous words often attributed to football coach Vince Lombardi: "Winning is not everything but it is the *only* thing."[11]

An Intrinsic Critique

Before contrasting this paradigm of life together with a more biblical perspective, let us note that it suffers from internal flaws even from a secular standpoint. The pictures of a physical universe winding down like a spent watchspring or of a shrinking pile of critical resources have indeed, in some respects, a mass of scientific support. Therefore ecological ethics and distributive justice are issues that must continue to be of grave concern in the decades to come. But that does not necessarily mean human life in essence is a jungle warfare for survival. In fact the biological history of the planet appears to be the reverse of its physical decline: the evolution of ever more centralized and cooperative life-forms. "I now see that the major shift in human evolution," said the famous Dr. Jonas Salk, "is from behaving like an animal struggling to survive to behaving like an animal choosing to evolve. . . . And to evolve we need a new kind of thinking and a new kind of behavior. . . . the evolution of everyone rather than the survival of the fittest."[12]

But long before the arrival of humanity, the earliest life forms on earth had already found cooperation and ecological interdependence to be just as important as competition. Biologist Lynn Margulis of Boston University, for instance, is currently studying vast communities of microorganisms which dominated the planet three billion years ago. Known as microbial mats, they thrived because of a powerful interdependence between those bacteria and organisms that used sunlight to produce only food, and those that used sunlight to produce oxygen as well as food. From this interchange, most textbooks now agree, arose those cells containing nuclei and chromosomes which opened the way for the higher life forms — including ourselves. In fact, "all beings from sperm to sperm whales are simply extensions, demonstrations of the profound bacterial penchant for forming tightly knit, controlled symbiotic communities." Margulis's views, which are gaining a wider acceptance among biologists, quite reverse the zero-sum notion of a battle in which only the fittest survive. Rather, "it appears the most adept and adapted organisms are those that have combined into cell cooperatives. Bargain making invaders, forming consortia, have inherited the earth."[13]

Not only the biological sciences, but also game theory itself can offer evidence which challenges the zero-sum model as an adequate guide for human life together. With the aid of computer simulations, a political scientist at the University of Michigan, Robert Axelrod, finds that in long term relationships a simple strategy of cooperation turns out to be the most successful.[14] He started with a classic game known as the Prisoner's Dilemma: two convicted criminals are given a one-time chance to betray each other in exchange for lighter sentences. The catch is that if they *both* do so, each will instead get an even longer sentence than if both had kept quiet. The scenario pits the self-interest of each against the other — unless of course they both respond in a zero-sum fashion, in which case they are both worse off. Experience shows that in a one-time only situation, one might risk defecting, in hopes that the other is not doing likewise. But most human relationships involve repeated contacts. Indeed relations among nations always do — since we are co-tenants on this planet indefinitely.

Axelrod's experiment found that those repeated contacts

made all the difference. In two successive computer tournaments of 200 moves each, the rules for each pair of contestants rewarded betrayal or defection if only one side did it; only a moderate score was given, then, for concurrent cooperation. It was interesting that the simplest computer program submitted won in both tournaments. Called TIT FOR TAT, its strategy was to cooperate on the first move, and thereafter do whatever the opponent did on the previous move. Its virtue was its clarity and absolutely predictable response, in a situation where each partner knows there will be another round. It thereby removed the incentive for a stab in the back and assured that in the long run each side will be better off by cooperating. In such cases, the logic of the game dictates that, in fact, "nice guys finish first."

This experiment matches the common sense experience of those who are not already inflamed by the zero-sum model. Neighbors, for instance, usually know that friendliness and mutual assistance benefit everyone. It is easier to be predatory toward passing strangers, since then there is no durable relationship, no future to be shared. Another example is found in the practice of diamond dealers who conduct millions of dollars of business with a simple handshake and a verbal agreement. Legal contracts are usually unnecessary for those who know they will be dealing with each other again and again. Axelrod's conclusion is that the nurture of cooperation does not even require trust, friendship, or formal agreements. But it does need an enduring relationship within a common framework of time and space.

That latter stipulation, in the case of the arms race and its fondness for zero-sum thinking, should remind us that the U.S. and the Soviet Union already share such a common framework, namely, the future and this planet. They ignore that fact only at their own peril. Mutual survival is to everyone's benefit. Or to state it conversely, in the words of Michael MccGwire, it may be "hard to determine exactly what is *in* a country's interest (even one's own), but it is much easier to see what is *against* a country's interest. The concept of negative interests is important in avoiding the pitfall of assuming that what is bad for us must be good for our opponents, and a moment's reflection shows that Russia and the

West share a broad span of negative interests."[15] In short, nobody wants a nuclear war. Moreover, such a moment's reflection should also recognize that the zero-sum game paradigm is a human construct. It is not inevitable, but only one of several possible ways of envisioning human life together.

The Biblical Promise

Scripture, however, opens up a horizon of new insights into human sociality, in God's gracious purpose. It does so in part by describing the disastrous results of zero-sum thinking. The earliest example was Cain, who blamed his lack of blessing from God on the comparable favor shown to his brother Abel. The first murder resulted from the first brooding suspicion that God's blessing was somehow indivisible, that it was awarded to one at the expense of another.

Admittedly there is much in the "chosenness" motif of the Old Testament which can be used to justify this dichotomy — as Jacob displaces Esau, and eventually the Israelites displace the indigenous peoples of Canaan. Yet even in those ruthless early years there was a vision of the immeasurable bounty of God (Deut. 33:13-16; Psa. 65:9-13), and the resulting duty for all within the covenant community to transcend their differences in mutual acceptance (Psa. 133). From this came Israel's code of laws on tithing, commerce, gleaning, the sabbatical year, the Jubilee principle of periodic property redistribution, and the prophets' descriptions of social justice.[16]

Within the community of Jesus and his followers, then, this redefinition of social existence emerged with new clarity. The abundance of God's goodness and providential provision for human needs is seen in unnumbered healings, exorcisms, hours of teaching in Galilean villages, and the astounding feeding of multitudes. Relying on this providential bounty, the disciples found the power to lead lives of voluntary simplicity, share their goods communally (John 12:6b), and even travel far from home without benefit of baggage (Mark 6:7-13). Jesus rebuked a disputatious attitude towards property ("who made me a judge or divider over you?" Luke 12:14) and went on to link that mindset to the fatal greed and self-satisfaction of the rich fool (vss. 15-21). Both the anxiety over scarcity and its divisive effects upon life together, so familiar in our own time, are thus reprimanded.

Furthermore, the gospels portray a living alternative to all this, in the community that formed around Jesus, sharing all things in common. There the insatiable hunger to be Number One was explicitly condemned and dramatically reversed in Jesus' pronouncement that lording it over others is superceded by service to others (Mark 10:35–45; cf. 1 Cor. 9). The remarkable table fellowship of Jesus with his own, both before and after the resurrection, embodies quite literally this new life together.

From the Lord's Table the early church carried forth this new paradigm. Any lapse into what we now call zero-sum gaming was expressly reproved to those who are entering the community of the New Covenant. Among such death-ridden qualities of the Old Age are the very contentiousness and factional thinking (1 Cor. 1:10–13; 11:18–20; Eph. 4:1–24; Tit. 3:2–9) which in our market economy are widely acclaimed as essential. They are said to be needed to motivate what is called a dynamic and productive society. Of such, however, is *not* the kingdom of God. Apparently early Christians knew that better than we do, even though they too needed continual admonition on the subject! Indeed, to modern readers familiar with the strategic doctrine of Mutual Assured Destruction, the New English Bible translation of Gal. 5:15 must confront us with an ominous warning: "But if you go on fighting one another, tooth and nail, all you can expect is mutual destruction."

In his study of early Christianity, John Gager comments from a sociological perspective on why this faith became preeminent among the many religions of the Roman world. On the historical scene there were several external reasons for Christianity's success. But there was also "a single, overriding *internal* factor, the radical sense of Christian community — open to all, insistent on absolute and exclusive loyalty, and concerned for every aspect of the believer's life. From the very beginning, the one distinctive gift of Christianity was this sense of community."[17]

That outstanding trait was possible, not because the ancient world was blessed with high living standards and stockpiles of life's necessities. Quite the contrary! It was made possible in even a comparatively poor society by the New Testament vision of reality. That vision was of the righteousness of God which had bestowed manna in the wilderness, as well as bread and fish aplenty to the five thousand, and was now about to reconstitute creation in its primal bounty — and more. Therefore even now, "God is able to provide you with every blessing in abundance, so that you may always have enough of everything and may provide in abundance for every good work " (2 Cor. 9:8; cf. Rom. 8:32; Phil. 4:19).

Here and now, within poverty-stricken but sharing and caring communities of the New Age, the irrepressible fullness and richness of the Holy Spirit was granting a foretaste of that age.[18] Each member of the Body of Christ was better off, not at the expense of others, but precisely because of the wellbeing of others — and thus the edifying or "upbuilding" of the whole Body (1 Cor. 12-14). From this vision flowed quite naturally Paul's exhortations on economic *koinonia* (fellowship, participation), both within a congregation and among them all (2 Cor. 8-9). The sufficiency of God's provision and promise establishes directly as its corollary the "unlimited liability and total availability"[19] of Christians, one for another. Thus is love incarnated.

So the popular zero-sum pattern ought not to remain plausible today for a confessing church. By the proclamation of Jesus and the indwelling of the Spirit, God's limitless kingdom is already at hand, in a still preliminary but nonetheless powerful and always surprising manner. To renounce the rivalries and anxieties spawned by images of scarcity is no act of blind utopianism, but founded on what is most real after all.

Nor are the practical implications to be deferred to the future. Already they are present and profound. For instance, Kenneth Boulding calls illusory the "pie" metaphor so popular among economists. He refers to the picture of "a static pie of goodies which is divided among the members of the society, presumably by a rather skillful wielding of knives. In this case the only way to help the poor would be to take away from the rich. Reality is much more complex. There is no single pie, but there is a vast pattern of little tarts, each growing or declining at its own rate."[20] Such a change in images would have an immediate effect on domestic policies, of course, even though problems of distributive justice would remain.

There are dilemmas not only in economics but also in international security which may be surmounted by a broadened vision which requires no losers. An example would be the limited nuclear test ban treaty of 1963, which penalizes no one. In fact it should benefit all signatories—and even non-signatory nations—by banning nuclear explosions anywhere other than underground. So all of us are the "winners." Such examples remind us that wisdom is a spiritual gift (1 Cor. 12:8; cf. James 3:13-18). When worldly diplomacy is blessed with wisdom it becomes the art of seeking agreements which benefit all concerned. The memory of Dag Hammarskjöld, for instance, the late Secretary-General of the United Nations, demonstrates in these discouraging times that Christian statesmanship need not be a contradiction in terms after all.[21] It can in fact become a channel of the Spirit, even in our bitterly divided world.

Thus the biblical vision can touch everyday life, even before the future kingdom of God arrives in its fullness. It can shape already our life together, freeing us from the compulsive quota mentality and one-upmanship of our cramped minds. "Spare no effort," the author of Ephesians tells us, "to make fast with bonds of peace the unity which the Spirit gives" (Eph. 4:3, NEB).

Love is the preeminent gift flowing from that future kingdom, and love is recognized by its selfless abandon. It spurns calibrated responses or partisan advantage (1 Cor. 13:4-7; Phil. 2:4-5). Like the Spirit itself, love is both a gift and a giving, a grace received and a grace in process, which must expand in irrepressible profusion. And so it transcends that ancient anxiety of works righteousness which has more recently found its home in zero-sum gaming.

Those who live in love find that in the Body of Christ each member is enhanced by the wellbeing of others, and not diminished. "If one member suffers, all suffer together; if one member is honored, all rejoice together" (1 Cor. 12:26). As the subsequent words of 1 Corinthians go on to point out, love is the clearest name we mortals have for the Spirit-given foretaste of the New Creation. It is the first installment, the downpayment of that glorious future when the whole will become greater than the sum of its parts, and at last "God will be all in all" (1 Cor. 15:28, NEB).

8

The Future as Worst Case Analysis

One reason that the human being is distinctive is because, of all the creatures God has placed on earth, humans have the ability to hope. That is to say, not only are we born biologically unfinished, but we are bestowed with the freedom at least partially to transcend ourselves and catch a glimpse of the ultimate. Immersed in the flow of time and history, we are frankly a puzzle to ourselves and not clearly definable as such. Our human essence, as Jürgen Moltmann has put it, "is hidden and has not yet appeared. 'Mankind' — the realized generic concept — is becoming, is still in process, has not yet acquired a fixed 'nature.'"[1]

Therefore our human uniqueness is not an endowment from some ancient past in Eden. And certainly it is not a present reality either — standing as we are among the shambles and sad disfigurements of modern inhumanity. Rather, our true humanity lies at the goal and end of history. And until that glorious consummation it can come to us only as a daily gift through the Son of Man, Jesus. He is the New Humanity personified in the midst of inhumanity, crucified but then risen, as the guarantor of God's promise of our humanity. The enormous contribution of a broad movement within contemporary thought, known usually as "theology of hope," has been to clarify this to the contemporary church.[2] That is, Christians should be a people who know that it is through hope that we are human.

By contrast, however, one of the pillars of the nuclear

heresy is a self-serving jaundice in envisioning the future. Indeed it is a grotesque parody of the very hope that is so basic to our humanity. This modern hopelessness bears a strong resemblance to what military planners call "worst case analysis." This phrase means that a prudent battlefield commander may choose systematically to overestimate an enemy's effective forces, while underestimating his own. On a tactical level one could argue that this conservatism is wise. But in the four decades of the Cold War it has been boosted up to the strategic and diplomatic levels, until it affects the highest centers of government policy.[3] What began as professional caution on the battlefield has become a cynicism run amuck in the capital city.

An early example of this tendency was the late John Foster Dulles, who was unalterably convinced of the inherent bad faith of communist leaders. As reported by Jerome D. Frank from an earlier case study of the Secretary of State's speeches made between 1953 and 1959, Dulles's attitude towards those leaders remained consistent:

> he interpreted all their actions as confirming this premise, seeing any apparent decrease in their hostility as a sign either of their increasing frustration or decreasing capacity, while attributing any increase in their hostility to their success and strength. Thus, he saw the Austrian treaty as evidence that the Soviet Union's policy with respect to Western Europe had failed and that the system was on the point of collapse, and ascribed their 1956 cut of 1,200,000 in armed forces to economic weakness and bad faith, in that the released men would be put to work on more lethal weapons. It followed that in either case the United States should increase the pressure—to hasten the collapse of the foe or to defend itself against their growing strength.[4]

Commenting on this study Frank, who is himself an M.D. and psychiatrist, described it as exemplifying "possibilistic thinking": the "characteristic of the paranoid person who views others' behavior in the light of the worst behavior possibility instead of the probabilities."[5] More recent examples of that same tendency are all too plentiful. For instance there is the rationale given by the U.S. director of defense research and engineering, trying to explain why the Americans were the first to put multiple warheads (MIRVs) on a single missile — which has turned out to be one of the most destabilizing escalations of the Cold War. "Our current effort to get a MIRV capability on our missiles," he said, "is not reacting to a Soviet capability so much as it is moving ahead again to make sure that, whatever they do of the possible things that we imagine they might do, we will be prepared."[6]

Three Hazards of Hopelessness

Such relentless and monumental efforts "to make sure . . . ," no matter what "they" might do, betray obsessive behavior and the sort of hopelessness that undermines our fragile gift of humanity. Moreover, it further endangers the international balance of terror — and it does so in three respects.

First, this irritating fear of the future guarantees a never-ending escalation of the arms race. Since in an era of deterrence by weapons of indescribable mass destruction there can hardly be a precedent for estimating how many weapons are "enough," each side is sure to seek an illusory safety margin. And so weapons systems multiply and the spiral towards oblivion continues. In the face of such unchecked vagaries and phantasms, there hardly seems any meaning left in the word "overkill"! By now we should have learned from history how dangerous arms races are. In a study of ninety-nine "serious disputes" among nations from 1815 to 1965, cited by Yale political scientist Bruce Russett, of those which were not preceded by an arms race, only 4 percent ended in war. But of those which were preceded by such an arms race, 82 percent resulted in war.[7] The deadly irony of hopelessness in a world of nuclear arsenals is summed up by Patrick Morgan: "Programs first developed as a hedge against the uncertainties of the future soon came to dictate it."[8]

Secondly, hopelessness guarantees a double standard in making critical judgments. The political right and anticommunist groups, in fact, do this openly and without embarrassment. Testifying before Congress in February, 1982, one of the founding members of the Committee on the Present Danger, Eugene V. Rostow, put it bluntly: "Our purpose in having nuclear weapons is defensive and deterrent, to prevent aggression against our vital national interests. The Soviet purpose . . . is to serve as the ultimate engine of a process of nuclear blackmail — a process of expansion involving the use of or the credible threat to use propaganda, terrorism, proxy war, subversion, or Soviet troops under the sanction and protection of Soviet nuclear superiority."[9]

The invidious double standard overflows into our common language as well, where it has won general acceptance. How many people would even notice, much less find objectionable, the following caricature? "The United States has a government, security organizations and allies. The Soviet Union, however, has a regime, secret police and satellites. American leaders are consummate politicians; theirs are wily, cunning or worse. We give the world information and seek influence; they disseminate propaganda and disinformation while seeking expansion and domination."[10]

The double standard makes it easy to forgive ourselves for actions that would be considered unforgivable if the other side did them. This takes on enormous significance, now that both superpowers are producing or deploying new generations of missiles with an accuracy that goes far beyond the needs of retaliation ("second strike") against an aggressor. Soon there will be the capacity of a "disarming first strike" against fortified silos and the underground command centers of the opponent. William Colby, former head of the C.I.A., has said that "the increased accuracy of the MX, and the destructive power of its 10 warheads, moves the United States to a 'first strike' capability. While we know that we would not launch such a strike, the Soviets would no doubt react to our development of that capability by accelerating their own development of an equivalent power."[11]

Of course it is our own citizens who say they "know" or are convinced "that we would not launch" a devastating sneak attack. But it is understandable why the other side might not be so generous in evaluating our intentions! In fact, as a 1978 Congressional Budget Office report admitted, "the Soviet

Union, looking at capabilities rather than intentions, might see a US second strike capability in this [former] light."[12]

Actually, *neither* side can be really sure of the other's intentions. This makes worst case analysis all the more tempting. The double standard can find ample cause for fright in inferring sinister intentions not ony from overkill capabilities, but also from loose rhetoric. Unfortunately, both superpowers have some theorists who talk recklessly about using nuclear weapons to win a "victory." Concerning this, former national security advisor McGeorge Bundy has some good advice. At the international public hearings on nuclear arms and disarmament sponsored by the World Council of Churches in Amsterdam, November, 1981, he warned against "reading and overreading what military men write for each other. It is quite easy, on both sides, to find statements about the best ways to use nuclear weapons in war. Quoting such comments from military men on the other side has been a flourishing cottage industry in each country, and you should not pay any serious attention to anyone on either side who quotes only the bellicose noises of foreigners."[13]

Then there is a third danger from the hopelessness which is cultivated by worst case analysis: it can so easily cross the line between misperception and rash action. The obsessive power of misapprehension was noted long ago by the classic writer Lucan: "So every person by his dread gives strength to rumor, and with no foundation for the existence of evils, they fear the things which they have imagined."[14] The danger is that superpower rhetoric may escalate until it generates the fatal belief that only one side can survive. On the one hand the Soviets have said, "Nuclear war is being planned by the apostles of the arms race . . . with the cold-blooded composure of gravediggers,"[15] and on the other hand President Reagan spoke in 1983 of "a plan and a hope for the long term — the march of freedom and democracy which will leave Marxism-Leninism on the ashheap of history."[16]

But what if either side carried that belief to a logical outcome in action? Likewise, if the leaders of either side were to be convinced that they possess missiles with a first-strike accuracy, then — as a congressional defense analyst testified — "they behave as though they have them. It doesn't make any difference whether they're right. It's what they believe that counts."[17] The converse is also true; rash action could result if either side believes the other possesses such deadly accuracy. The aforementioned Congressional Budget Office report concedes that discomforting possibility: "Faced with a threat to their ICBM force, Soviet leaders facing an international crisis might have an incentive to use their missiles in a preemptive strike before they could be destroyed by the United States."[18]

Beliefs based on misperceptions can have grave consequences. Impulsive steps prompted by hopelessness constitute one of the greatest perils of the post-Hiroshima age. In the words of former Undersecretary of State George Ball, "It seems safe to predict that the next war, should one break out, will almost certainly be caused by ill-considered diplomatic moves — such as brought on World War I — rather than by a deliberate aggression — such as that which produced World War II."[19] This again exemplifies the hazards of hopelessness.

A World of Boobytraps

The paradigm of the future as worst case analysis rests upon an ontology similar to but extending beyond the notions of being that we have earlier surveyed. Reality, already portrayed as an atomistic mechanism and a shrinking storehouse, now takes on an outright malicious character. Indeed, the cosmos is envisioned as an endless boobytrap. It is seen as wild and capricious in every respect — except for its unrelenting hostility to human life and values. Danger lurks around each corner and at every opportunity. Even good fortune or familiar circumstances may well be a decoy that masks some added pitfall. Thus results an insidious erosion of that primal confidence in reality, the trust in the essential goodness of the creation, which underlies Judaeo-Christian faith.

Instead arises a mindset which resembles a definition of the "neoconservative" offered by Irving Kristol: "a liberal who has been mugged by reality."[20] This epigram is a revealing insight into the notion of being which undergirds one major group of our so-called nuclear "theologians," those newly disenchanted intellectuals who in this decade have done so much to revive the Cold War. Reality, we are warned, is fond of mugging those who hope; the lesson implied is apparently that hopelessness protects the bruised psyche from further abuse.

Such cynicism, however, is incompatible with the Christian view of reality, and especially the doctrines of creation and eschatology. For self-serving hopelessness effectively blinds us to the question of the past: how could the human species have ever originated in such an inhospitable environment, in the first place? And it blinds us also to the question of the future: how may humanity come to cooperate with God's hospitable blessings?

For believers in the world as an endless series of boobytraps, such questions can hardly be asked, let alone answered. Instead, they would intimidate us by sheer cynicism into presuming that we live in spite of the cosmos, not because of it and with it. If nothing else, the ecological consequences of such an ontology would be disastrous: a crass invitation to plunder the planet before someone else does. In any case, hopelessness reduces the world at large to a stage set for some never-ending monster movie. Who knows what next will jump out at us and yell "gotcha!"? If anyone is still able to retain some interest in moral action, it must be squandered on a vigilance which borders on paranoia.

A Life of Dehumanization

Because hopelessness is intimately linked with personal psychodynamics, it is best in this chapter to vary the sequence of topics. Let us consider first, therefore, the personal and interpersonal expressions of the paradigm. In individual life, the future is sold out and betrayed by worst case thinking.

Children are the ones who feel this most keenly. Two members of the American Psychiatric Association and its Task Force on Psychosocial Aspects of Nuclear Developments make this clear in their report, "The Impact on Children and Adolescents of Nuclear Developments."[21] After reviewing research literature on the subject, as well as the Task Force's own questionnaire distributed to school students in four major cities, William Beardslee and John Mack draw the conclusion that fears of nuclear war "are having an impact on the very structure of personality itself in adolescence, particularly in the areas of impulse management and ego ideal organization."[22] That is, as the growing self learns to adjust to its surroundings and to inevitable disappointment, it needs the leverage of a reliable future which promises satisfactions. Otherwise the young person may become cynical about ordinary ideals or planning ahead. Or there may be rage at the folly of adults. If one is forced to grow up in a hopeless world, it is all too tempting to experiment with drugs or authoritarian cults, mistrust any enduring relationship, or develop a lifestyle of "get it all now."

Not just for children but for all age groups, indeed, "dehumanization" is a major sign of interpersonal hopelessness. That term encompasses two distinct but related phenomena, according to the 1964 report by the Group for the Advancement of Psychiatry.[23] In fact they actively reinforce one another. Object-directed dehumanization is the type which portrays other individuals or groups as if they were not quite part of humanity. This is done variously, by viewing them as subhuman (for instance, huns or gooks), as superhuman (for example, the superstud, the yellow peril), or perhaps as evil humans who deserve no pity. Or some may be perceived as nonhumans altogether, as no more than "consumable supplies"; to destroy them would involve us in no guilt because, as Arthur Koestler has said, "Statistics don't bleed."[24]

The other type of dehumanization is self-directed. It impoverishes one's own self-image and ability to feel empathy, which provides a convenient means of evading responsibility. "I'm only a cog in a larger machine" or "only following orders," we hear said, or "Surely 'they' [i.e., my boss, or the government] must know what they are doing."

Either way or in tandem, therefore, the self seeks protection from the future by some sort of overcompensation in the present. Both forms of dehumanization encourage the sense of helplessness, the numbing of emotional response, and the compliance with group pressures or authority figures which are characteristic of nuclearism as a whole. Dehumanization reduces relations among persons to a primitive level of fear and manipulation by threat. As such it becomes actually a parallel in microcosm to nuclearism's chief dogma, the policy of deterrence.

This view is expressed then in foreign policy development as "the rat view of human nature." Richard Barnet explains: "The official theory of human motivation is a hopelessly oversimplified derivative of the rat psychology many of the national security managers learned in college. If you want to motivate a rat give him a pellet or shock him with a bolt of electricity. In international politics it is dangerous to be overgenerous with positive inducements. That is 'appeasement.'"[25] Instead, it is negative reinforcements which are preferred (of which our arsenals have a more than generous supply), since the only language "they" understand is force.

How have these personal expressions of hopelessness come to get such influence over our lives? The psychodynamics are set in historical perspective by Carl Jung: "What we call civilized consciousness has steadily separated itself from the basic instincts. But these instincts have not disappeared. They have merely lost their contact with our consciousness and are thus forced to assert themselves in an indirect fashion."[26] As we have noted, the conscious mind or ego feels threatened by such indirect assertions. It responds with fantasies of invasion, the end of the world, or other frightful disasters — all of which are recognizably reflected in the images of our pop culture.

Preeminent among these unwanted instinctual forces is what Jung called "the shadow," that is, the part of the self which has been left aside and repressed during one's childhood quest for the ego ideal, a specific adult personality. These discarded potentialities contain some genuine value, however, and they seek from us at least recognition, a degree of reintegration. So they appear to us indirectly, in the guise of dreams, slips of the tongue, humor, fantasy, and in other circuitous ways.

Yet as adults we find it difficult to reappropriate these primal but neglected energies and learn from them. So the common way to cope with the shadow side of the psyche is by denial. That denial, however, is costly. We deprive ourselves of some positive augmentation to the self, and we shield our idiosyncrasies by "projecting" our shadow onto others.

Projection is an unconscious mechanism that occurs when some vital part of our personality is activated which is unrelated to the conscious self.[27] When we deflect our dark side by projecting it onto others, it greatly intensifies both the fear and hatred felt towards them. Those feelings reveal more about the sender, so to speak, than the receiver. In fact, "whatever form it takes, the function of the shadow is to represent the opposite side of the ego and to embody just those qualities that one dislikes most in other people."[28] It is a curious but profound truth that whatever characteristic disgusts us most about "the Other"—whether it be in a person, a racial group, an ideological party, or the opposite sex—may be the quality that offers hints about what is most needed by our own ego for its greater integrity.

But we are often unready to receive greater wholeness and learn from the uninvited message of our shadow side. Instead the ego reacts to its own alarm system, the disturbing images of invasion and cataclysm, by struggling to reassert control. After all, control is a major function of the ego. No wonder then that our preferred response to latent fears of abandonment is to create stories like *The Swiss Family Robinson* and its space-age successors. Ira Chernus showed us how fears of nuclear holocaust result in the myth of the "heroic survivors," the "big bang" followed by a fresh beginning for civilization and bold-spirited pioneers.[29] Control is the watchword! No wonder as well that the frustrating decades of defense by threat of holocaust, MAD, are being cheerfully discarded by some strategists in favor of a confidence in control: somehow nuclear war can be limited, regulated by technological reason after all, or even "won." It might even appear, under adroit media management and the reassuring tones of a likeable president, that this new emphasis on ego control has restored confidence to and in America. Such self-assurance is then commonly mislabeled by the image-makers as "hope."

The bravado of the early 1980s, however, has been purchased at the cost of a further alienation of the shadow self, both collectively and individually. For now, let us confine our attention to the latter, the interpersonal level. It is not hope, after all, but the kind of hopelessness that wears a "smiley face" which marks our lives.

To deny the existence of the inner world . . . is not

to escape its devilish aspects, but rather to fall victim to them unknowingly, and this is when evil can enter in. Evil gains power when its existence is denied. . . . To deny the reality of the unconscious is not to know oneself, and not to know oneself is to risk becoming possessed by that which we have ignored. The more split-off from consciousness, and therefore from wholeness, something is, the more malignant it will act.[30]

When disregarded, the shadow revenges itself in negative ways and gains a still more hidden power over us. Worst case thinking tempts the psyche to grasp a temporary but fragile inner unity by projecting its own struggles into the outer world. Object-directed dehumanization thus becomes the corollary of self-directed dehumanization and inner impoverishment. A vicious cycle sets in, as my ill will finds confirmation in the other person's reactions. Family quarrels, neighborhood feuds, racial or ethnic prejudice, or aggravated generation gaps may be numbered among the consequences.

Not only does hopelessness betray the future, but it betrays the very self that fears the future. As one of Jung's closest successors points out, this is

an additional disadvantage in projecting our shadow. If we identify our own shadow with, say, the Communists or the capitalists, a part of our own personality remains on the opposing side. The result is that we shall constantly (though involuntarily) do things behind our own backs that support this other side, and thus we shall unwittingly help our enemy. If, on the contrary, we realize the projection and can discuss matters without fear of hostility, dealing with the other person sensibly, then there is a chance of mutual understanding — or at least of a truce.[31]

This then is why we often find ourselves to contain an "enemy within" that collaborates with an external foe! It would seem that the unconscious wisdom within a person cannot long tolerate images of a world of boobytraps and dehumanization, but in its own blind way pushes us toward a shared future. We cannot outrun our humanity, and to be human is to hope.

A Society of Enemies

As the preceding quotation suggests, the same dynamics of worst case thinking and inner retaliation are to be found also on the social and global levels. Out of mistrust of the future and each other, factions or nations will often define it as in their group interest to accumulate a disproportionate share of the power available. Within our society, for instance, we have long observed this anxious overcompensation at work in racial or sexual discrimination, in labor/management disputes, or among successive waves of immigrant groups. But at present the international level is of special concern; there worst case analysis is running rampant. Through this model the superpowers find justification for ever greater stockpiles of weaponry, bloated budgets, and cynical erosions of international moral standards. The U.S. Department of Defense, for instance, finds it should plan ahead, not just for an adequate defense, but in readiness for what it calls the "greater-than-expected-threat" from the Soviets. No doubt strategic planners in the Kremlin return the favor.

Here too the collective shadow self is at work. Near the end of his life, Jung himself noted the comparison:

> Our world is, so to speak, dissociated like a neurotic, with the Iron Curtain marking the symbolic line of division. . . . What the West has tolerated, but secretly and with a slight sense of shame (the diplomatic lie, systematic deception, veiled threats), comes back into the open and in full measure from the East and ties us up in neurotic knots. It is the face of his own evil shadow that grins at Western man from the other side of the Iron Curtain.[32]

This concealed bond between the two global giants is made possible because, despite the well-publicized contrasts, there are also some similarities between the U.S. and the U.S.S.R.

These similarities seem more obvious to those who are outside our respective borders. "Much of the world is troubled by our affinities as nuclear superpowers, isolationists yet interventionists, materialists, technocrats, centralized and bureaucratized states, and messianic rivals utterly convinced of our own historic destiny and invincibility."[33] In fact, British historian Herbert Butterfield goes even further in the comparison:

> The greatest menace to our civilization today is the conflict between giant organized systems of self-righteousness — each system only too delighted to find that the other is wicked — each only too glad that the sins give it the pretext for still deeper hatred and animosity. The effect of the whole situation is barbarizing, since both sides take the wickedness of the other as the pretext for insults, atrocities, and loathing; and each side feels that its own severities are not vicious at all, but simply punitive acts and laudable measures of judgment.[34]

This makes the prospect of conflict between the two nations all the more dangerous. The posture of moral superiority disguises our shadow side. It also blinds us to the fact that war has always been a socially approved way of venting against outsiders those destructive impulses which are not permitted closer to home. American Indians, for instance, used to require returning warriors to undergo purification rites before reentering village life. This ought to remind us today that "what would be regarded as psychopathology at home may be called heroism abroad."[35]

The paradigm of worst case analysis is important, therefore, because it knits together these several elements of fear of the future, alienation of our shadow side, and projection of it onto enemies. We have noted that hopelessness, as part of the heresy of nuclearism, has become a particularly dangerous luxury in our time. Now that some of the psychodynamics have been described, we can appreciate why the threat to the future has become so acute. There are, at least, two additional reasons why this is so.

First, hopelessness stereotypes the opponent as "the Enemy." By doing so we foreclose the future — a future which can only exist if it is shared with that opponent. "The enemy is perceived not merely as evil, but also as operating in monolithic, consistent, rational, sinister, and purposeful ways. Each side minimizes or ignores the existence of conflicting parties and purposes within the opposing group. Also each party attributes to the other a sense of omniscience and rationality that he knows does not exist on his own side."[36] Here is object-directed dehumanization of the superhuman type, which is often embellished with apocalyptic overtones as well and a conspiracy theory of evil. The fearful stereotype becomes even more durable and resistent to correction because of these quasi-religious overtones. "Once a nation bases its security on an absolute weapon, such as the atom bomb, it becomes psychologically necessary to believe in an absolute enemy."[37]

It is difficult, even for those who are experts, to push past the stereotypes. John Steinbruner, director of foreign policy studies at the Brookings Institution, says that U.S. scholarship on the U.S.S.R. "has been highly politicized. You don't just study the Soviet Union, you take *positions* on the Soviet Union, and those positions have the quality of reigning theology. As a consequence, the field has not been all that reliable as a source of policy analysis and advice."[38] Let us pardon the disparaging reference to theology! But it is true that when foreign policy is possessed by stereotyping, it loses touch with reality and instead degenerates into deducing axioms or to ritualized incantations against evil. And when we acknowledge our shadow only as it rebounds from the silhouette of an enemy, we are cutting off the wider self from the future.

Secondly, hopelessness endangers the future because worst case thinking multiplies and feeds upon itself until it becomes a self-fulfilling prophecy. Reinhold Niebuhr's theology is well known for developing the irony of such themes. For much of his life Niebuhr was critical of pacifism, but he was equally critical about the excesses of the military mentality. "It is the business of military strategists to prepare for all eventualities," he said, "and it is the fatal error of such strategists to create the eventualities for which they must prepare."[39]

All of us, of course, tend to find what we expect. The 1964 report of the Group for the Advancement of Psychiatry, in summarizing its conclusions on conflict management, points out that there is always a risk in trying to build a relationship of trust between adversaries. "Unrealistic trust" of a stubborn antagonist is soon corrected by the other's rude behavior, so that risk is only a limited one. Unfortunately, however, "*unrealistic mistrust tends to be self-validating.*"[40] Indeed, hopelessness feeds upon itself, nurturing each grievance and magnifying each offense, with a cunning that resists any countervailing evidence.

And so a vicious circle is perpetuated by worst case thinking. Kenneth Boulding, who has long studied global issues, points out that in this cycle,

> each party in a relationship tends to create the self-image of the other in a very complex, mutual learning process. To a distressing extent each party in a conflictual relationship is a creation of its enemies. In some degree Napoleon created Bismarck, Bismarck created Clemenceau, Clemenceau created Hitler, Hitler created the Pentagon, Stalin created the CIA. Perhaps one reason for the biblical injunction to love our enemies is that they make us.[41]

Certainly stereotyping is more than idle misperception, for it serves a subterranean purpose in defining and maintaining our national identity. Again, an observation from John Steinbruner: "We view the Soviet Union as a device for defining our own values. . . . . It is a contrast, the embodiment of a lot of things we oppose."[42] As a "contrast concept," remember, the meanacing figure of "the Other" always serves to remind us of who we are *not*. It is a device to relearn the traits and roles which mark afresh the boundaries of our self-image, whether as an individual or as a group. In doing so, however, it often conceals the broader self, reinforcing the denial and projection of our darker side.

In the case of the United States, our identity historically

has been largely oriented around hope. It was first a hope for the new Israel in the New World, the "city set upon a hill"[43] to inspire the rest of humanity. Soon the national mission was scaled down to a more mundane hope: a land of opportunity, the prospects of freedom of conscience and a better life for one's family. But even in the early days the contrast concept was present, helping to consolidate a new nation's identity against perceived threats from "them" — American Indians first, then blacks, slaves and former slaves, and the succession of arriving immigrant groups. As the years have gone by, it seems that "the citizen's sense of belonging was somehow related to the vicarious exercise of national power. More and more an American came to mean someone who identified with the struggle against America's enemies."[44] Indeed we may suspect a correlation is at work: to the degree that hope has declined as the basis of our national identity, its place has been taken by fear of the Enemy. By now many citizens have come perilously close to defining "American" in mainly negative terms, as wariness against whatever is thought "un-American."

But as Boulding has told us, the projection of our shadow side is a process that is not only ongoing, but also reciprocal: "each party in a conflictual relationship is a creation of its enemies." The Soviets likewise consolidate their national identity through fear of "Western imperialism," "Wall Street capitalism," and "anti-Soviet militarism." Having endured for centuries various forms of exclusion from the international community, and now four invasions in this century, the citizens of the U.S.S.R. may be pardoned for a certain defensiveness in their intense patriotism.[45] Nevertheless, the regime has found fear of the Enemy to be a useful tool. Again, as in our own case, this worst case thinking has proved to be an effective substitute for the decline of earlier hopes for a utopian society on earth. Indeed, the following words of Richard Barnet could apply equally well to the ruling elite of either superpower: "The failure to replenish the supply of enemies is the supreme threat facing any national security bureaucracy." That is, he explains, "when old enemies disappear, mellow, or turn into allies, as frequently happens in international relations, new enemies must be found and new threats must be discovered."[46]

Both nations, therefore, act as a mirror for the other's image of the Enemy. But for each, that image is in part a projection of the shadow self, alienated and unrecognized. The conscious self is thereby impoverished and whatever collective unity gained is quite brittle. Moreover, by anticipating only the worst from the adversary we give inadvertent and piecemeal expression after all to the dark side. We do so by permitting ourselves to respond in kind—allegedly as an exception, "just this once," and only because they forced us to it.

Thus the circle of self-fulfilling prophecy is completed and readied for the next round, as each side comes to acquire in fact those vices first projected in fantasy. "In combating what they perceive to be the other's cruelty and treachery, each side becomes more cruel and treacherous itself. The enemy-image nations form of each other thus more or less corresponds to reality."[47] The cycle of hopelessness actually becomes a spiral, infecting both parties and corrupting the present as well as the future. For the future that we taught ourselves to fear, and which we wish to deny to the Enemy, becomes also a future spoiled for ourselves. Hope, by contrast, is indivisible, because the future is indivisible as well.

An Intrinsic Critique

Let us turn now to examine an internal inconsistency of this paradigm of worst case analysis. To put it bluntly: we must dispute its claim to be called "realism." The unspoken premise that the world is filled with boobytraps lies behind the model and lends it credibility. But that is after all a mere premise, a model which is a human construct. "It is no more 'realistic' always to believe the worst about every situation," says Edward Long, "than it is to believe that there is a possibility of something good emerging from it. The hard-nosed skeptic, who always sees the thorns rather than the blooms on the rosebush, is not necessarily more accurate in grasping what is real than the person who entertains hope and posits the possibility of surprise."[48]

The same metaphor is carried further by Moltmann, when he comments on Luther's coat of arms in which a heart with a cross in it is surrounded by roses. The inscription reads, "The Christian's heart walks upon roses when it stands beneath the cross." In affirming the cross, the followers of Jesus demonstrate there is a deeper reality than boobytraps and gallows. Of course, says Moltmann, the church "does not soothe and calm the tensions of brokenness and the devastations of our society, but rather it brings these to a head and confronts them with the divine transformation." Always we must look beyond the thorns, in hope. "Christianity, in the 'Yes' of faith to the cross of true love, bears the fate of the present and yet lives in the life-giving spirit of the resurrection."[49]

Why then does the monster-movie model of the world seem so credible? That image takes on the guise of reality, in large part, to the degree we create it as such. Likewise, often the reason life becomes dehumanized and populated by enemies is because of the expectations we bring to the situation. Today's grim reality, generated by yesterday's hopelessness, may not have needed to turn out that way. For example, Strobe Talbott, diplomatic correspondent of *Time*, concludes that the Reagan administration's harsh anticommunist rhetoric has simply failed to attain its declared purpose. Supposedly the tough talk was to jolt a new generation of leaders in Moscow to their senses, and make them more accommodating. However, says Talbott, "the impact of the American hard line on those internal Soviet debates and on evolution of the leadership may have been just the opposite from the one intended. The effect may have been to strengthen those men in the Politburo, the Central Committee, and the security apparatus who had been pressing a mirror-image of Reagan's own thesis: perhaps the relationships [i.e., between our two nations] may indeed be inherently, permanently, and predeterminedly bad."[50] Our worst case thinking became again a self-fulfilling prophecy.

Can it be realistic to rely on fear as our clue to tomorrow? Certainly there are dangers ahead and on all sides. But as we noted in an earlier chapter, fear tends to confuse thought rather than clarify, and threats inhibit rationality. This is just as true, indeed, when anti-nuclear groups appeal to fear or describe the grisly effects of holocaust. To do so may reinforce the very motives which drive new worshippers to nuclearism. Fear, after all, mystifies and befuddles the mind. We become preoccupied with the Enemy, which encourages us to define ourselves as victims and so avoid taking responsibility for our own actions. By nursing grievances and believing we have no power, we thereby forfeit the opportunity to confront an adversary creatively and work toward mutual solutions.

So what is "realistic," after all? If humans are future-oriented beings, as well as socially constituted, is not hope in a shared future more true to reality? Through hope we are granted the power to face both the adversary and the future, knowing that in wider reality there is room for both. Hope energizes the imagination and the will, so that problems can be defined and solutions explored. According to Fred L. Polak, sociologist at the University of Utrecht's Institute for Futurology, positive images of the future are the most potent cause of cultural change.[51] Admittedly there are also portrayals of a negative future, such as Robert L. Heilbroner's forecast of a harsh existence in the twenty-first century. He predicts that populations will be forced by shortages and pollution to fall back into several rival police states.[52] Of course it is well to take warning from ominous clues in the present. But too easily we find ourselves paralyzed with fright. It is not extrapolations from such forebodings that can mobilize a society to creativity and a new cultural synthesis, but rather the anticipations of an unprecedented and hopeful future.

Also we have seen through analytical psychology how our shadow self has become estranged from consciousness and thus projected onto the blank face of "the Other." But is it "realistic" to continue this personal impoverishment, as well as this Cold War polarization, by postulating a booby-trap world and a monster-filled future? Even on the nontheological grounds of pure self-interest, the wisdom of this paradigm is now being widely challenged. We recall Kenneth Boulding's pragmatic interpretation of the biblical imperative to love enemies because "they make us." Each side, that is, tends to grow into the image projected from the other side, in a self-fulfilling prophecy. Psychology suggests that we will not find inward health and maturity until somehow we reintegrate those alienated parts of ourself which we now glimpse only as a reflection from the latest adversary. "Augustine once observed that it is wise to love our enemies because so often we are our own worst enemy. That enemy within has to be reconciled to us in love, not vanquished with repression. The same is true about enemies without."[53] The same comment, however, could be made by any follower of Jung's depth psychology on the grounds of what the self "realistically" needs.

Finally, it can only be called the supreme realism to acknowledge that the world will either share an undivided future—or none at all! The earth has become a global village, highly interdependent in its energy and mineral resources, its shrinking margins of stored food supplies, its telecommunications networks—and in the dangerous ramifications of what once were considered only local conflicts. Survival must be a mutual effort, on a planetary scale. And this is indeed possible, once we turn to an appropriately planetary consciousness.

We noted in the previous chapter how cooperation and trust of others is generated by the assurance that we will stay in close proximity for the indefinite future. Diamond dealers and marriage partners, for instance, often trust a mere spoken promise on the most momentous matters, simply because they know they will be seeing each other again tomorrow—and for many more tomorrows. Within the context of a shared future mutual confidence among partners is nurtured, and hope can become more inventive in seeking resolutions to each old impasse. In such a context the self-validating nature of "unrealistic mistrust," which we noted above, can be transformed into an increasingly self-validating "realistic trust." And eventually, the sense of sharing a common future may alter the collective self-image of nations enough to permit a more peaceful world. In his study on how to attain a "Stable Peace," Boulding concludes that one factor is more important even than sharing a common language and culture. (After all, there have been many wars among Latin American nations, for example.) "The only guarantees of peace are compatible self-images," he says,[54] such as for instance the United States and Canada share.

Thus the paradigm of hopelessness is intrinsically flawed in its claim to tough-minded realism. As several schools of thought within psychology and political science point out, worst case thinking cannot sustain itself much longer, under the present conditions of an interdependent world. Even on a secular level, it can be argued that realism in a nuclear age requires instead a paradigm of hope.

The Biblical Hope

However, hope moves us beyond the level of an intrinsic critique of "worst case analysis," by pointing to its own transcendent ground. If we seek instead a "best case assurance" that the future does not belong to boobytraps and monster masks, we must look to God, the source and goal of all hope. Because the peaceful and unitary future we dare to hope for exceeds even our best efforts to attain, doubt always accompanies hope. Often it appears as if the forces of destruction and chaos will have the last word. So hope is akin to faith, in that it must embrace the uncertainties and terrors of history, and yet open itself expectantly to what is absolutely new and surpassing any definition of what seems possible. As the U.S. Catholic bishops have said in their peace pastoral, "To believe we are condemned in the future only to what has been the past of U.S.-Soviet relations is to underestimate both our human potential for creative diplomacy and God's action in our midst which can open the way to changes we could barely imagine."[55]

Scripture presents us with this vision of hope. It is there that the church turns for the source of its confession that the world was created in Christ, and so power is relational and nonviolent. It was there that we learned the world is graced with the bounty of the Holy Spirit, so that our life together is sustained by loving reciprocity. Now we find that Scripture bestows on us the lively hope that this world will be transformed into the kingdom of God.

From the earliest years of the Covenant of Moses, Israel expected from God some new act to establish God's sovereignty and clarify the purpose of a chosen people. First the prophets and then the apocalyptic writers expanded this hope beyond its provincial origins and into the splendor of a vision of world-encompassing righteousness. Thus Jesus had no need to explain the term when he came preaching, "The time is fulfilled, and the kingdom of God is at hand; repent, and believe in the gospel" (Mark 1:15).

But to those who followed the Galilean preacher, it soon became evident that the kingdom would not come instantaneously in a world cataclysm (Luke 17:20-21), but surprisingly piecemeal and through the mystery of a cross. In retrospect, through Jesus' resurrection, the Christian community began to sort this out. On the one hand the kingdom is anticipated in the present life of faith, received as a gift (Luke 12:52) and yet requiring wholehearted decision (Luke 9:57-62). It is prefigured in new health and wholeness (Matt. 12:28) and yet asks of us patience (Mark 4:1-32) and endurance (Acts 14:22). On the other hand the New Age is still awaited as a future event (Mark 9:1; Luke 17:24), a final vindication of God's righteousness and of human compassion (Rom. 8:21; Matt. 25:31-46).

Moreover, the hope of the kingdom of God is indeed a vision of a shared future. It represents the ultimate state of mutuality, a fellowship embracing humankind and the triune God. As such it surmounts and refutes our "worst case" fantasies. It dissolves all enemy images. This reciprocity is underlined in a key metaphor for the kingdom developed by Jesus: the messianic banquet (Matt. 22:1-14; Luke 22:30). At this "marriage supper of the Lamb" (Rev. 19:9), the table fellowship is explicitly pluralistic. In disregard for human barriers and bigotry, Jesus assures us that many "will come from east and west, and from north and south, and sit at table in the kingdom of God" (Luke 13:29). Already at the Lord's Table the church is celebrating and anticipating this ultimate communion. Indeed, the future prepared by God will bring a reconciliation which expands even to a cosmic scale, a new heaven and a new earth (Rev. 21:1-4).

Until that glorious time, biblical hope has a permeating and vivifying effect upon the here and now. Having glimpsed the promised future, we can return to the present and envision it as "in a state of pregnancy"[56] — except of course that the newness of grace exceeds any mere potentiality of nature.

Walter Wink tells of a dream he had after having led a Bible study on Ezekiel's vision of the valley of dry bones (Ezek. 37). He says he woke with this sentence ringing in his ears: "Faith is practicing the future."[57] The same should be said of hope. Here and now hope would begin the task of dismantling dangerous stockpiles as well as dehumanizing prejudices. It can do so because the anticipation of the wholeness of God's future frees us from the compulsion to manipulate others or to force our preconceptions onto the present moment. Fear of a possible worst case is replaced by love (1 Jn. 4:18). Since the future is indivisible, a blessing to be shared with all, including those who have been enemies, we are empowered to begin actualizing that solidarity in the present.

The proclamation of pardon is where this actualization begins. To become whole we have to forgive our enemies, which also means forgiving ourselves and accepting the presence of our shadow side. Here the Christian community is the practice field, the experimental space for a skill in which most of us are not yet proficient. It is in the life of mutual forgiveness that the risen Christ stands among us, and the shared future is most clearly prefigured—even inaugurated. At this intersecting point both present and future merge and become incarnate. In the midst of a world still fallen and divided, it is through forgiveness that hope is embodied and lived out. Thus, in pardon we find ourselves to be "practicing the future."

9

Faith as Official Optimism[1]

A generation ago Will Herberg described the usual common denominator of North American religion as *"faith in faith."* To illustrate he quoted a prominent member of the clergy: "I begin saying in the morning two words, 'I believe.' These two words *with nothing added* . . . give me a running start for my day."[2]

We have all heard similar statements, which often are uttered with great sincerity. They are spoken by secular as well as religious leaders, by entrepreneurs and Miss Americas, presidents and pastors, all of whom would happily lend their voices to a popular song of not so long ago: "I believe." However, is it likely that the verb is intransitive and lacks altogether an object? Usually, I suspect, there is implied at some level a reflexive pronoun: "I believe in myself." This gives the focus, if not the object, for whatever forces of cosmic benevolence that are presumed to exist. To the average person, today as well as when Herberg wrote, "to have faith" seems equivalent to something like "to have self-confidence," or "ya gotta have heart!"

Certainly this is the case in a second example, this one from outside the church. A recent interview with Mary Kay Ash, founder and chairperson of the board of Mary Kay Cosmetics, underscores the conviction that "We all have the capacity for greatness." Whenever meeting a new person, the interview reports, she imagines also an accompanying invisible sign, "MAKE ME FEEL IMPORTANT!," and she proceeds to do just that. No doubt that is a key factor in the phenomenal success of her business across the nation, in which a positive self-image is just as important as a healthy skin. But what is of greatest interest is her concept of faith — a concept which seems to be shared by her interviewer and likely by innumerable readers. "Mary Kay's philosophy rests on faith — faith in religion, in patriotism, in success and in the power of friendliness." Quite a combination! And, lest the reader overlook the indomitable self-command which seems to lie at the heart of this creedal medley, the reporter adds: "They are beliefs held in place with the same determination that controls the blond hairdo rising from her forehead like a metallic superstructure."[3]

Appearances, Credibility, and Dread

Faith in faith and a resolute but nebulous confidence have long been a part of our national character. North Americans are constitutionally committed to optimism, from the time the Declaration of Independence altered the language of John Locke to insert "the pursuit of happiness" as an inalienable right given by the Creator. The implication is that happiness should be also attainable. Or at the very least, the appearance of happiness must be maintained — and done so religiously!

There are historical reasons why this or any high technology society would seize upon the word "faith" and squeeze it into the format of simple self-confidence. It has to do with the dislocations and turmoil of Western culture in recent centuries. The early stages of industrial capitalism dismantled the remnants of medieval society, stripping away much of the tradition and old bonds of meaning that had knit life together. More and more the individual was left naked to the gales of chaos. Then the later stages of the industrial revolution added an acceleration of cultural change so great that it outstripped all normal capacities to adapt. The resulting dissonance throughout society has insured a perpetual gap between appearances on the one hand, and social realities on the other. The inevitable lag in human perceptions, together with the complexity of modern life, place therefore an unprecedented premium on images and first impressions.

The perceptual gap continues to widen. Since reality threatens to become virtually unknowable, we come to rely more and more on individualized meanings, transitory though they be. Appearances have more effect than does substance, taking on a life of their own. By now we live in an age of affluent choice among uncertainties. In our ordinary experience, packaging sells more than do contents, candidate image more than qualifications, and the customer may buy a "feeling" more than a product. A new car is not just transportation but a total experience, so we are told, and asking for the proper beverage by brand name may yield a sudden roomful of drinking buddies. This gap is compounded then by much of what passes for news nowadays. We are treated to "media events," a near incestuous reporting of opinion about impressions about other opinion — all several times removed from daily experience.

Likewise international relations have become the artful projection of image and counterimage. National leaders scramble to show resolve toward opponents, domestic as well as foreign, and to "send the right signals." Uncertain situations are to be orchestrated, if possible, to yield a desired impact. And the last thing any leader wishes to happen is to lose "credibility." Because so few events in our complex world seem able to have self-evident meaning, without an overlay of interpretation, there are never-ending contests over whose interpretation will triumph as credible. But in our shrinking and weapon-laden planet, where the time for correction of error grows ever shorter, such an intergovernmental charade is grotesque. As the Catholic bishops said in their pastoral letter on war and peace, "In a sense each is at the mercy of the other's perception of what strategy is 'rational,' what kind of damage is 'unacceptable,' how 'convincing' one side's threat is to the other."[4]

It seems a combination of technology and historical forces have dealt the Western world a double-whammy. Secularization has eroded the objective status of values, and unleashed an unmanageable pace of change. But human beings insist on wresting from life a sense of wholeness and ultimacy. So ironically that momentum of change has also necessitated new and fragmented forms of questing for the sacred. Especially this has come to mean an intensified reliance on subjective faith-judgments as one's final guide. In that specialized sense, our secularized world seems to contain very few "nonbelievers"!

The arms race follows inevitably. "Once the purpose of military spending is to create 'perception,' and weapons are procured primarily as symbols," Richard Barnet points out, "there is never enough." The superpower rivalry is less a matter of actual hardware and human bodies than it is a nuanced duel of imagery craftsmanship. Barnet continues wryly, "The entire purpose of the nuclear arsenal is to influence the behavior of six or seven Soviet leaders. As an education system, it has the highest per-pupil cost of any in the world."[5]

Objectively, of course, this is all quite absurd; either superpower could easily annihilate the other. In fact there is no longer any way to menace an opponent without endangering oneself, and the planet as well. But the absurdity is precisely the reason why appearances and bolstering is required to keep intact a nuclear "credibility." Full scale wars have become unwinnable. So the nuclear arms race becomes less a contest of armed force than a race for prestige, an expensive and risky form of psychological warfare. Instead of military strength, which has been rendered dubious by the technologies of indiscriminate destruction, the prize of the race is credibility. But credibility is ever elusive, like a will-o'-the-wisp: we have it when *we* think *they* think we mean business. Likewise it must somehow be shored up whenever we think they think we may have lost it.

Therefore, both within our country and in international affairs, manipulation of the correct images has become desperately important. We are in fact an "officially optimistic society."[6] However, there is more to it than that. Close under the sparkling surface there swims a shadowy terror: the dread of vulnerability.

The fear of helplessness stalks us, driving us even more than does the fear of death. It was Freud who observed that the unconscious mind seems incapable of imagining its own extinction, and even the conscious mind becomes aware of death only in its later stages of development. By contrast, the experience of helplessness is universal from earliest infancy.

In fact it may form the actual basis for death anxieties. Psychiatrist Sanford Gifford believes this dread of abandonment and impotence is decisive in the psychology of the Cold War.[7] Certainly it demands from us regular effort in coping and sublimation.

Moreover, it is society (whether tribe or nation state) which has a crucial role in this process. Society is the psychological extension of the self, the source and plausibility structure for our canopy of shared meaning. We rely utterly upon our group to sustain the symbols by which we live. Therefore a final vulnerability of society, an annihilation of the group, is even more terrifying to contemplate than is personal extinction. Crises such as the battlefield, accordingly, often call forth surprising heroism from quite ordinary individuals, who prefer self-sacrifice to the threat of group death.

No wonder that collective self-confidence and official optimism have become terribly important now, in the nuclear age — and perhaps in inverse correlation to any grounding they have in reality!

A World of Meaninglessness

What are the ontological assumptions behind this model of faith as official optimism, a model which masks a deeper despair? On the one hand, ultimate reality has often been depicted as a goal-directed unfolding towards greater and greater attainments. Western civilization is well known for its doctrine of progress. It started centuries ago when the purposeful traits of the Creator began to be displaced onto the created world instead, and eventually to an omnicompetent, now perfectible human nature.[8] The secular concept of progress came to replace the theological faith in Providence, effectively turning over our hopes to the technocrats of the Enlightenment and their promise of a scientific paradise on earth. The resulting vitality and accomplishments of the West, of course, have been remarkable.

But on the other hand these expectations were never fully convincing. At the same time a certain morbid gloom and self-destructive lust have plagued the Western soul, even in the hour of its greatest conquests. Self-doubt accompanied heroism, over the centuries, and genocidal massacres marked the dark underside of Western triumphs and expansion. These more sinister intuitions of reality could not be outdistanced, even at the far corners of the New World. And now in recent decades they have surfaced anew for North Americans, as history appears to conspire to rub our noses in intractable circumstances: hostage crises, economic dislocation, urban and environmental decay, and so on. We are distraught by these reminders that not all change is for the better. And so the ancient dread returns.

A world of final meaninglessness and abandonment, even nihilism, often seems to underlie and precede the famed Western image of progress. Here we begin to glimpse a terrible outcome to our earlier surveys of the implicit ontologies of a mechanistic world of scarcity as well as menace. Behind the jaunty assurances of government officials and the sprightly patter of the broadcasters, a deeper dread swells, a surging panic that possibly chaos might have the last word after all. The unspoken and unspeakable suspicion is that perhaps forward motion — like riding a wobbly bicycle — is at best a postponement of collapse.

The current apathy towards issues of peace and disarmament is especially indicative. The more acceptable the notion of winnable nuclear wars becomes to the public, the more dominant the repressed nihilism proves to be. This trend lends fresh meaning to the words of Thomas Merton: "At the root of all war is fear: not so much the fear men have of one another as the fear they have of *everything*."[9] Frenzied destruction still seems preferable to standing still long enough to face the dread, the prospect that reality might be utterly without meaning and thus human life finally at risk.

A Society of Fragile Cheerfulness

Our shared experience in society reflects the ambivalence of a "faith in faith." Visitors to this country often remark upon the pluck and high spirits to be found here, the confidence in future expansion and opportunity. In our officially optimistic society it all stands out like a hapless monotone in a choir: one note, with variations only in volume. The TV ads persuade us that reality is "the good life," a beach frolic that beckons us to just step over and join in the fun. Smiling corporate executives suggest that we "take stock" in their products, be "bullish on [their] America." Such invitations are significant. For a free-enterprise society which detaches itself from structures of tradition must rest instead upon a steady stream of images, the unrelenting efforts to shape a favorable climate for investment and marketing. Indeed the entire economy bobs and hovers over a constant flow of exuded confidence—much like the old department store demonstrations of vacuum cleaners that kept ping pong balls dancing in mid-air.

Since cheer and assurances have become so essential for the health of our economy, it follows that style and appearances are often more important than is substance. A current example is the rise of the "Yuppies" as a cultural phenomenon. The term was coined in 1983 to describe the young urban professional class, intent upon upward mobility and an affluent lifestyle. For. instance *Newsweek* quotes a twenty-eight year old Los Angeles attorney who aspires to earn $200,000 a year, has no savings, but whose investments are in a house "and her wardrobe, which she replenishes at the rate of two outfits a week. 'The way you look is very important,' [she] explains. 'Sometimes I think it is more important than what you can do.'" To stay ahead in the intensely competitive business world, she adds, "you can never rest on your laurels. I have to be bright, I have to be charming. I have to be everything."[10]

Such statements must remind us of Lifton's description of the Protean personality of a nuclear age, as well as the official optimism of an uneasy generation. The irony is that many of those now described as Yuppies were among the flower children of the 1960s, whose idealism and energies have now turned inward, lavished instead on personal careers, gourmet restaurants, and real estate deals. Jerry Rubin, for instance, who once marched at the head of the Yippies (the Youth International Party) as a war protester, has now become a figurehead for Yuppies. Having failed in their moral indignation about matters of principle, it seems that part of a generation has switched to genial affectation about matters of appearance.

There is, however, a desperate transience under the

cheery brashness that pervades American society. The shadow side is evident in the impatience with both frustration and criticism. The apparent optimism is belied by our over-reaction to the setbacks or delays which normally attend an imperfect world. Suppressed anger lashes out unexpectedly. In our cities, for instance, what is known as "urban rage" springs forth in erratic bursts of street violence, vigilante acts, or perhaps just the rude antics of many motorists in heavy traffic.

Our optimism may be shallow, but our hypersensitivity to criticism has deep roots. A century and a half ago, Alexis de Tocqueville, the distinguished French observer of the American experiment, had already noted this. He remarked on how incessant our countrymen were in calling forth compliments from foreign guests, seeking affirmation of our national virtues. Likewise nowadays such visitors are repeatedly asked, with transparently the same expectation, "Well, how do you like it here?" Our professed superiority nonetheless wishes confirmation from others. And the impatience shown to friendly criticism seems related to our impatience and consequent loss of interest when reform measures—say, in civil rights, education, or welfare reform—do not yield quick results.

Moreover our optimism bruises easily. It is curious how long and deeply grudges are held against those who ruffle our assurances. We brood over perceived betrayals, such as ingratitude in the United Nations, revolution in Central America and ("our") Cuba, and above all the indignity that has become a paradigm in our memories: Pearl Harbor, 1941. The press and the public bristle over affronts to our prized self-image, whether it come from impudent speeches by Third World leaders or impertinent challenges by domestic critics. Again and again, vehement depths of public emotion erupt in response to symbolic events such as a flag burning or the capture of American hostages in Iran or Beirut.

A comparable fury may lash out at home against those who would question the American dream. Dissenters are guaranteed civil rights, of course, but their messages may not be received graciously. We have all heard surprisingly spiteful remarks directed towards feminists and Black Power advocates, for instance, and now "freeze-niks." An example of the latter is the abuse hurled at Jonathan Schell by Michael Kinsley, editor of *Harper's*, in an embarrassing display of the very pretentiousness and "obsessive hysteria" which he attributes to the author of *The Fate of the Earth*. "Despite a lot of wacky judiciousness," charges Kinsley,

> Schell's method is basically bullying rather than argument. The pomp is intended to intimidate, and the moral solemnity is a form of blackmail. Unless you feel as anguished about nuclear war as Jonathan Schell, unless you worry about it *all the time* like him (allegedly), your complacency disqualifies you from objecting. In fact, you are suffering 'a kind of sickness' or 'a sort of mass insanity.' So shut up.[11]

A Life in Search of Reassurance

In personal life the same dynamics are at work. Even a pallid "faith in faith" is sought as a means to bolster the uncertain ego and secure it from the ravages of industrialized society. Again there are low tolerances for frustration and criticism. But beyond the platitudes of an officially optimistic society, each member is left in isolation to seek out and fashion his or her own form of psychic reassurance.

The material fruits of our cherished belief in progress are apparently not sufficient for that task. There is an alarming increase in suicides among teenagers, for example — an age group peculiarly vulnerable to the stresses stemming from a nuclear age as well as the quest for personal identity. Moreover, the rash of suicides is particularly acute in those counties in New York state, for instance, which are noted for their affluence. The same pattern is borne out by statistics on the global level. The lowest rate is found in poverty-racked Egypt (0.3 percent per 100,000 of population), and almost the highest is in Sweden (18.6 per 100,000), where the standard of living is comfortable for all.[12] To question the reason for living is an important aspect of growing up, not to mention the root of philosophy and of faith. But apparently for many youth the answers of official optimism simply do not plumb

the depths of that question. Certainly the teaching of super-
ficial cheerfulness cannot prepare those on the threshold of
adulthood for the unavoidable negative elements in life, the
tragedy, suffering, and irrationalities.

Both the liberal and the evangelical forms of popular
piety recognize the problem of finding personal meaning in
life. And both are commercially successful to the degree they
are able to shore up a person's precarious self-image in a fast-
paced world. Then there are nostrums which are less obvious-
ly "religious." For instance there are the latest arrivals in an
interminable series of human potential movements, which
promise everything from higher consciousness to stress reduction and weight control. And bookstores have shelves full of
self-help volumes that would restore confidence in our ability
to cope with everything from crumbling masonry walls to
crumbling egos. Box office hits turn out to be those films
that help us feel good about ourselves— most recently epic
adventures undergirded by a cheerful mixture of comic book
verities and violence.

There is no question that the erosion of confidence in
self and in the meaning of life is a genuine problem in a high
technology world. It is a common experience for any of us to
find the self grasping with a religious seriousness for solutions. We seek virtually any means by which self-hatred can
be displaced or inner doubts about one's role and destiny are
quieted. Of course all of us need such reintegration of the
self, since we are fallen creatures in a fallen world. But the
problem is that much of what has come to be touted as faith,
"ya gotta have heart," is instead a flimsy counterfeit. It only
displaces what it claims to display. The reassurance we desire
must have deeper roots.

An Intrinsic Critique

The paradigm of faith as official optimism is defective
because its shallow perspective, its surface sparkle, serves actually to obscure the very depths within which a life-
sustaining trust must be founded. The self-defeating inconsistency can be illustrated by the ominous new developments
in the field of nuclear strategic theory. These developments
center around the replacement of Mutual Assured Destruc-

tion (that is, deterrence) by doctrines of nuclear warfighting.

In the chapter on power as violence we have already noted Secretary of Defense Weinberger's admission in 1981 that U.S. nuclear forces should be prepared to "prevail" over the U.S.S.R., even in a "protracted" or "prolonged war." This is a departure from the earlier policy of attempting to avert war by threat of retaliation, and it has been under way for some years now. It began with the design of new missiles so accurate that they can only be considered "first strike" weapons for a surprise attack, and also with a shift towards counterforce targeting strategy. The result is that what used to be a minority view among military planners and the so-called nuclear theologians has now achieved dominance, since the later Carter years.

The clearest exponent of this confidence that nuclear warheads are militarily usable weapons has been Colin S. Gray, an important advisor of the early Reagan years. He has argued that "the United States must possess the ability to wage nuclear war rationally" and in support of the goals of our foreign policy, including the wish "to coerce the Soviet Union to give up some recent gain." Thus we should develop "a plausible American victory strategy" which would "envisage the demise of the Soviet state. The United States should plan to defeat the Soviet Union and do so at a cost that would not prohibit U.S. recovery."[13] Planning thus to win any nuclear war he initiated, a U.S. president then "should not shy away" from actually pushing the fateful button. For the same reason military leaders ought to design options so clear "that a reasonable political leader would not ever be self-deterred."[14] In other words, Gray is saying that nuclear warfighting doctrine requires commanders who are so confident that they will not "shy away" from or "be self-deterred" by the horrifying destruction they unleash!

While our leaders are quick to insist that Mutual Assured Destruction remains our *official* policy, these developments in weaponry and doctrine show that warfighting has in fact replaced MAD as our *operational* policy.[15] Psychiatrist John Mack describes the proponents of these contrasting strategic doctrines as the "thinkables" vs. the "unthinkables." "'Thinkables' believe that one should plan in terms of nuclear war actually occurring, and even for its aftermath. . . . 'Unthinkables' believe that a nuclear war, once begun, is likely to create a disaster of such magnitude that it is not meaningful to plan in terms of its actual occurrence." While the latter will look ahead no further than trying to avert war by promising Mutual Assured Destruction, the former look back to classical (prenuclear) theorists such as the much quoted von Clausewitz, with a "win" mentality that reeks with nostalgia for what was militarily possible only in earlier heydays. Furthermore, Dr. Mack holds that the main factor distinguishing these two camps is how they cope with the primal experience of nuclear dread: "The unthinkables seem more willing to experience directly, or *hold* emotionally, the reality of the nuclear danger. . . . The thinkables appear unable to experience, or . . . . have found a way to avoid its terror by reverting to older, more comfortable and familiar, warmaking thinking."[16]

The "older, more comfortable" way of thinking is of course a reappearance of our official optimism. This all too familiar paradigm helps to offset the anxiety of helplessness and the frustrations of the nuclear stalemate. Even when deterrence was still the unquestioned keystone of nuclear doctrine, it encouraged the illusion of crisis management. For, as we noted in the chapter on deterrence, decision makers together with their advisors are swayed by the pressures of "group think" into overconfidence that each crisis can be rationally managed and successfully resolved.[17] This illusion is now vastly compounded, however, by the shift from the "unthinkables" and their reliance on deterrence, in favor now of the "thinkables" and their nuclear warfighting ideas.

The shift began in the 1970s, when the United States lost its overwhelming nuclear superiority over the Soviets, entered a period of economic reverses, and bore the indignities of rebuffs and revolutions in the Third World. The ancient fear of losing control, as well as the implied humiliation, was summed up in a vivid phrase by President Nixon, in a feisty televised speech of April 30, 1970. Defending his controversial "incursion" into Cambodia, he warned that the whole world will be threatened with chaos "if, when the chips are down, the world's most powerful nation acts like a pitiful helpless giant."[18]

Therefore, as American domination of world events continued to erode, new forms of crisis management were sought. An attractive but dangerous alternative was to lower the nuclear threshold in warfare. That meant planning for "limited nuclear options" and now winnable, "protracted" nuclear wars. Apparently the risks of putting the opening round of nuclear war on a hairtrigger was considered not too high a price to pay for restoring our self-confidence, our reassertion of control in a seemingly out-of-control world.

Of course we are assured by the dispensers of official optimism that such "thinkable" initiatives are necessary for survival in the Cold War, and that it is only natural for any species to act upon the instinct of survival. But Christian theology recognizes there is more to it than that. The cunning of the human heart is laid bare, for instance, in Reinhold Niebuhr's observation: "How curiously nature and sin are involved . . . ; for human imagination transmutes nature's harmless will-to-live into a sinful will-to-power. But the will-to-power always hides behind the natural will-to-live."[19]

All this official bravado, however, serves to conceal the deep inconsistency of allegedly trying to prevent a nuclear war by preparing to win one — and doing so moreover by means of weapons which are far more effective if used first! The paradox of security in a nuclear age will not go away, even when we try to define it out of existence. There can be no "quick fix," no technical way to attain national security in a world divided ideologically and politically. Meanwhile, the guise of pragmatic, "can do" optimism is only a masquerade.

Actually, as George Kennan says, "There is no hope in it — only horror. It can be understood only as some form of subconscious despair on the part of its devotees — some sort of death wish, a readiness to commit suicide for fear of death." What presents itself as our preferred mode of so-called faith, that is, self-confidence, is actually the opposite of faith. It is in fact an "inability to face the normal hazards and vicissitudes of the human predicament," Kennan continues, indeed "a lack of faith, or better a lack of the very strength it takes to have faith."[20]

The Biblical Act of Faith

When we turn to Scripture, however, we encounter quite a different vision of reality and thus an alternate view of just what and how we trust. The enticements of official optimism were long ago rebuked in Jeremiah's words to the spiritual quacks of his day, the popular prophets of nationalism: "Thus says the Lord of hosts: 'Do not listen to the words of the prophets who prophesy to you, filling you with vain hopes; they speak visions of their own minds, not from the mouth of the Lord. They say continually to those who despise the word of the Lord, 'It shall be well with you'; and to every one who stubbornly follows his own heart, they say, 'No evil shall come upon you'" (Jer. 23:16–17; see 6:13–15; 14:13–16; 23:9–32; 28). "Behold, I am against those who prophesy lying dreams, says the Lord, and who tell them and lead my people astray by their lies and their recklessness. . . " (Jer. 23:32). Likewise in the New Testament, the peace which Jesus grants is a peace "not as the world gives" (John 14:27). This is so because, in the perspective of the Fourth Gospel, "the world" insists on being secure on its own terms and so it uses religion to ease and mask these efforts of self-affirmation (see John 1:10; 8:23; 14:17; 15:19; 17:14).

Within Scripture we find that faith has much more to do with profound mystery than heroic resolve. It is more an awe of the divine than a reassurance by the human. In contemporary language Henri Nouwen makes a similar distinction: on the one hand "the basis of all destructiveness" and of the nuclear arms race is "the illusion of control. . . . the conviction that we have to defend—at all cost—what we have, what we do, and what we think. . . . the conviction that we have to stay in control—at all cost—of our own destiny." On the other hand, "in the act of prayer, we undermine this illusion of control by divesting ourselves of all false belongings and by directing ourselves totally to the God who is the only one to whom we belong."[21]

The act of faith which Scripture portrays has little resemblance to our concern with credibility, our desperate cultivation of appearances. These are frivolous and puny gestures when measured by a hearty faith that "gives substance to our hopes, and makes us certain of realities we do not see" (Heb. 11:1, NEB). From Abraham to Paul and, yes, John of Patmos, faith has meant the reversal, the abnegation of those very mechanisms of ego protection now so highly prized by a high tech society under stress. Indeed it may call for a willingness to lose one's life and one's self (Mark 8:34–35), in an unreserved trust in the Lord of life, the Giver of selfhood.

Faith is less at home in our all-too-mortal yearnings for the securities of tribe or fatherland, and more to be found amid crisis and deep experiences of negation that clarify its nature as radical trust. It is only this biblical perspective that could sustain the sober courage which John Mack urges, if we are to escape the mentality of the so-called "thinkables" and their illusions about nuclear warfighting. We must, he says, "find a way to come to terms with the full reality of nuclear arms, to acknowledge their actual menace. . . . To move in such a direction requires a paradigmatic shift of thinking. It means living for a time with a particular kind of terror, experiencing our helplessness in the face of it, acknowledging fully the menace of the arms race and of our responsibility for the creation of this terror."[22]

Such faith is the same biblical perspective uttered by Elie Wiesel, when he appeared on the panel immediately following the famous November 20, 1983, television movie, "The Day After." Wiesel stunned the other panelists with his simple comment, "The world has become Jewish. . . ." By that he meant that "for 2,000 years, Jewish people lived in constant uncertainty, and the world now lives in constant uncertainty. For 2,000 years, Jewish lives were on the threshold of the unknown, and now the world lives on the threshold of the unknown. For 2,000 years, the Jewish people depended on the capricious impulse of a ruler, somewhere, anywhere, and now the world depends on the capricious impulse of a ruler, somewhere, anywhere."[23] Surely we Christians should struggle to renounce the current charade of appearances and stand by our Jewish brothers and sisters in learning anew the biblical meaning of faith amid crisis.

Thomas Merton guides us in recognizing how such faith is rooted in a life-embracing spirituality: "faith gives a dimension of simplicity and *depth* to all our apprehensions and to all our experiences." Rather than trying to filter all our awareness through that tiny portion of whatever we can comprehend, much less control, faith "is the incorporation of the unknown and of the unconscious into our daily life."[24] Such an act of trust must entail risk, of course. One relinquishes the compulsion to control and exposes oneself to portents of vulnerability and possible harm. But it also frees one from the incessant struggle to repress the dreadful by means of the "thinkable." A burden is lifted when one is released from the dreary treadmill of reasserting credibility and projecting confident images. Indeed, says Merton, "faith incorporates the unknown into our everyday life in a living, dynamic and actual manner. The unknown remains unknown. It is still a mystery, for it cannot cease to be one. The function of faith is not to reduce mystery to rational clarity, but to integrate the unknown and the known together in a living whole. . . ."[25]

Moreover, it is because of faith's object that the unknown can be faced so confidently. That object (which after all turns out to be The Subject!) is not a figment of the human will, reiterated and redoubled so much that it mimics divinity. Instead it is the God who revealed the divine self in covenant faithfulness. To "wait upon the Lord," in the Psalmist's phrase, is therefore an act both of patience and assurance. As theologian Heinrich Ott has said,

> Faith is a *waiting* upon God who remains free to encounter us as he wills, in ways which are always different, and in the new events and questions of human existence and history. . . . Faith, however, waits upon the God who is not only *free*, but who is also *faithful*, and whose promise, "I shall be there," always holds good. Thus faith in God is a confident waiting, not a waiting in doubt and despair, and not a tired and resigned "waiting on Godot."[26]

We wait confidently, furthermore, because the God of the covenant is the God revealed through Jesus Christ. In our previous chapters God has been identified as the Creator of all that empowers, the Giver of the Spirit that reconciles, and the Promiser of a shared future. Now we turn to the God who is faithful in "him crucified" (1 Cor. 2:2).

Because Jesus is both crucified and raised from the dead, we are invited and enabled to accept both the menacing present and the promised future. As God was in Christ giving the divine Self over to chaos and destruction, yet turning these fearsome unknowns into a triumphal procession (Phil. 2:5–11; Col. 2:15), so the followers of Christ may surrender themselves to experiences of negation, relying upon the new reality of Easter to transfigure them. For sharing in the cross of Jesus in the world is succeeded by the surpassing reality of the New Creation (Gal. 6:14–15; 2 Cor. 5:17).

Therefore, in the midst of those fears of helplessness which drive us to grasp at ever new means of controlling our destiny, we may hear the Shepherd's calming voice, "Fear not, little flock, for it is your Father's good pleasure to give you the kingdom" (Luke 12:32). And the manifold forms of official optimism, together with its supporting dread of nihilism, can be discerned as heretical, set aside, and perhaps even gently laughed at. The prospects of a cross may be accepted, as long as it is recognized as the cross of Jesus, by those who are coming to "know that in everything God works for good with those who love him" (Rom. 8:28).

PART III
Preparing for Reformation:
A New Lifestyle

10

Lifestyle as Incarnate Vision

We began our considerations of strategy with Peter Berger's observation: "It is not given to men to make God speak. It is only given to them to live and to think in such a way that, if God's thunder should come, they will not have stopped their ears."[1] Thus far we have been considering how "to think," so that our vision might be clarified. By demystifying some of the paradigms behind nuclearism, perhaps they may be replaced by more biblical models of thought.

But Berger's statement suggests more than this. How else might we prepare ourselves for a special time of confessing? If the God who is our redeemer is about to speak a mighty word of reformation to our crisis, are there further ways we may, so to speak, unstop our ears? How may we begin not only "to think" but "to live," so as to renew an orthodoxy that is worthy of the name?

Orthodoxy: Right Will or Right Thinking?

In the most recent decade of the nuclear age, the strongest voices calling for Christian renewal have come from what is usually termed the "New Christian Right." Its background is in nineteenth century revivalism and premillennialist theology, newly combined with a political activism and the language of zealous nationalism (the legacy of Phinehas). With this fresh momentum, groups such as the Moral Majority, Christian Voice, and the 700 and PTL clubs have consolidated a substantial influence in our society. For them too, the tension of living under the Bomb has prompted a new call for reformation — but of quite a different sort than that envisioned in these pages.

Warnings of crisis, however, are in plentiful supply. One example uses as a springboard the CIA's "Team B" report of 1976, which thoroughly reinterpreted previous intelligence data so as to claim a Soviet superiority in nuclear as well as conventional weaponry. Leo Cherne, chairperson of the President's Foreign Intelligence Advisory Board, thereupon drew this implication: "We are in the midst of a crisis of belief and a crisis of belief can only be resolved by belief." His next sentence, however, discloses what he actually means by belief: "'Will' depends on something most doomsayers have overlooked — crisis, mortal danger, shock, massive understandable challenge."[2] This way of interpreting the signs of the times resembles the alarm of Jerry Falwell: "The fact is that we have a 'will crisis' in this country today. We are not committed to victory. We are not committed to greatness. We have lost the will to stay strong and therefore have not won any wars we have fought since 1945."[3] In short, the problem is perceived as a loss of nerve, a shameful timidity, and so the religious response is to be an exertion of will power. The New Christian Right assumes there can be no doubt about what direction is proper for the will; all that is needed is to try harder!

For this movement, therefore, orthodoxy is construed as "right will." And it is true, of course, that the will is important. But this way of defining orthodoxy suffers from two major defects.

First, as an offspring of the American revivalist tradition, it too easily falls into the trap of voluntarism. That is, it assumes the will is the key to human nature, and that somehow the mysteries of the self can be unified and subsumed to its control.

In its secular form, voluntarism supposes the will can exert a conscious control over the various parts of the psyche. "I am the captain of my soul" is its theme song, and in its determination to dominate there is a direct parallel to the domination of technological reason over the world of nature. In its theological form, fortunately, voluntarism is less crude. It recognizes what a devious and far-ranging influence the will does have, and how crucial it is that the will be transformed by grace. But too often it errs in assuming that once the will undergoes rebirth, the other parts of the self will fall into line. Orthodoxy becomes reduced to the conversion experience itself, the changed heart, with little consideration for either matters of sound doctrine or the whole person.

Experience shows, however, that one's intellect, imagination, and unconscious are not so easily subsumed to a born-again will. In either form, in fact, the voluntarist trap echoes that Pelagian heritage mentioned in the first chapter, the presumption that somehow the human will *can* do what it *must*. Voluntarism may not require us to pull ourselves up by our own bootstraps, but it does urge a relentless redoubling of will power towards predetermined ends. Then when faced with frustration, too often the Pelagian celebration of the will prompts a hasty condemnation of oneself or of others for not believing "hard enough." By ignoring our inner complexities, including the recalcitrance of the shadow side, this simplistic notion of the psyche generates a frightful echo chamber of misplaced guilt feelings.

The second major defect of the New Right's emphasis on "right will" is that it fails even to question the direction of that will. It naively presumes the will is aimed properly; "victory" and "greatness," indeed, are Falwell's names for the divinely inspired goal. Those hearing him describe the crisis are then scolded and berated solely for not wanting this goal fervently enough. So the solution must be to agitate the will further in its proper course, to give it greater "umph" along a predetermined track, by whipping up enthusiasm through an array of revivalist techniques.

But — what if the direction itself is wrong? What if the goals, the basic aim announced for the will, be tragically misconstrued, even heretical? Someone has characterized fanaticism as redoubling one's efforts after the purpose has been forgotten. Or, in this case, it seems a purpose unexamined and indeed running counter to the gospel of the crucified and risen Lord. Intoxication with greatness and a zealot nationalist quest for victory is better suited for some Wagnerian heroism, for it seems to echo Nordic war cries from an ancient forest. Or, to vary the metaphor, it is a Dionysian flirtation with catastrophe, an ecstatic union with blind lust in the guise of a religious quest. Although in Christian garb, it is in fact a virulent form of nuclearism. The name given this movement by Lifton, appropriately enough, is nuclear fundamentalism.[4]

Both these defects, in short, indicate that regeneration requires a more profound change than the preachers of "right will" seem to have in mind. Salvation must touch more than one's will power. It must seek to permeate the whole person, including the imagination, the darker instincts, and the basic life direction. Jesus' essential message, according to the earliest gospel, summoned people to repentance because of the nearness of God's kingdom (Mark 1:15). The Greek word for repentance, *metanoia*, means far more than contrition or even change of will. It means a turning of the whole person to God, once and for all, in a total obedience that is ready to renounce any competing loyalty (Matt. 11:20−24; 10:32−39). Right will is an important part, but only a part, of that turning.

If orthodoxy should not be reduced to "right will," then what meaning does it have for our day? A second option is to interpret it as "right belief." This of course has been the more common usage of the term, long predating nineteenth-century revivalism. Maintaining with conviction the correct array of doctrines has for centuries been deemed important in Western Christianity, even essential to salvation. It may derive from the "lawyer" mentality of our Latin heritage, or the post-sixteenth century determination to reestablish once and for all the original Christianity sought by the Reformers. In any case, for centuries the churches in the West were riven by doctrinal disputes to a degree unusual among world religions. Whether through exhaustion, common sense, or spiritual maturity, this type of divisiveness has largely been reversed in recent times. In an earlier chapter we took note of the limits of official action in imposing standards, including the questionable effectiveness of theological argument. Nevertheless, some today would still define orthodoxy in terms of pure doctrine, correct theological concepts, as the goal of a new reformation.

This treatment of orthodoxy is as defective as the previous one, however. If right will is the voluntarism trap of revivalists, then right belief is the intellectualism trap of theologians. It assumes that correct concepts are the key to salvation, and that if the intellect holds the proper mental constructs, it is then that the remaining parts of the psyche will take their proper place. Once again, we are dealing with a reductionism, a telescoping of complexity into an oversimplified rubric. In this case it is a scholastic parallel to Descartes's historic presumption that clear and distinct ideas are the self-evident norm for truth.

Surely we must agree that sound doctrine is part of a mature faith. But as was the case with the previous reductionism, right belief overlooks the intricacies of the self, within even the most devout believer. It would almost seem that different facets of the psyche may each require their own conversions or transformations. At any rate, Western literature from Nathaniel Hawthorne to Sinclair Lewis is full of illustrations of how correct-believing Christians may nevertheless disgrace the name they bear. More is needed than proper concepts.

In the post-Hiroshima age, where nuclearism so easily exercises a covert sway, this problem has become particularly acute. With a terrible clarity it is evident that, in the words of Stanley Hauerwas, "we can be heretics in our lives even though our beliefs seem strikingly orthodox."[5] The present crisis should remind us that historically the church's campaigns against various heresies were not exclusively a contention about beliefs, but also a concern about the practices they entailed. I would add that when right belief is betrayed by wrong practice, it is often because of the hidden corrosive effects of paradigms in the background. Even the best of doctrines can be perverted or defaced beyond recognition if it is uprooted from the broader vision that generated it. For instance a doctrine of atonement can be twisted into a cruel and autocratic redistribution of divine punishments, if portrayed against the backdrop of a paradigm of power as violence.

Whether for this or other reasons, however, we humans do seem prone to fall grievously short of living up to sound doctrine and the redemptive reality it depicts. And admittedly, even a successful paradigm shift of the sort described in the preceding chapters, together with a renewal of imaginative vision, could provide no guarantee against hypocrisy. Right belief, as such, is an insufficient orthodoxy.

Orthopraxis as Right Living

Apparently then, neither right will nor right belief is sufficient to resist the insidious appeal of nuclearism. Important as they are, they do not encompass the total person. For it is the whole self that must be enveloped by grace, redeemed from self-centeredness, and transformed into the New Creation. It is the entire human nature that, in traditional terms, needs not only justification but also sanctification. As we sing the hymn "Rock of Ages," for instance, we confess both components of our need: "Be of sin the double cure; Cleanse me from its guilt and power." The orthodoxy required in a nuclear age should be profound as well as all-inclusive; it must embrace right will and right belief, but also right living. As Berger said, we are not only "to think" but "to live . . . in such a way" that our ears are not closed to what may come from God.

There is a name for such right living: "orthopraxis." Praxis is a word with a long history, although only recently has it come into common usage. What it describes, however, is as old as Christianity itself: (right) living, (correct) practice. It does not replace but in fact embraces and fulfills orthodoxy (correct praise and thought). For an illustration of its breadth, we may turn to the story of the young John Wesley in his early days of preaching in eighteenth century England. To his spiritual counselor, the Moravian Peter Böhler, he complained of not yet truly believing himself in the Good News he was bringing to others. Böhler's advice was, "Preach faith *till* you have it; and then, *because* you have it, you *will* preach faith."[6]

This advice might seem at first glance some cheap evasion, either through a cynical clericalism or outright hypocrisy. But its purpose was more profound. Faith is a centered act of the total person, involving speaking as well as thinking. It is risking oneself in action on a street corner as well as reflecting on one's heart in solitude. In coming to faith, the one dimension does not necessarily precede the other, although both eventually are needed. Neither concepts nor will nor even action can of themselves assure that we will be regenerated. Each of them in fact has a role in unstopping our ears so that we may be receptive to grace. But in a society known for its proficiency in subdividing and compartmentalizing, which in turn so easily invites lapses in integrity, the word orthodoxy comes to have a hollow sound. Orthopraxis, as a term, may help to grasp afresh the wholeness which God both offers and asks of us.

Traditional religions usually display this wholeness better than do those modern faiths that have adjusted to the pigeonholes posed by an industrialized society. The indigenous religions of American Indians or of Africans, for instance, know little of the modern divisions between worship and living, or between morals and ritual, for such faiths are unified around an integral vision of life. Taoism, China's oldest religion, reflects on the nature of *tao*, the "way" or "path," in this case the great way of the universe, and from this it distills a mystic wisdom of life experiences. The genius of Post-Exilic Judaism, which enabled it to survive millennia of dispersion through every conceivable culture and circumstance, was its elaboration of a total way of life that centered around obedience to Torah. Combining flexibility with faithfulness, and universality with local customs, it has endured in a way that a mere belief system could hardly have done.

Earliest Christianity likewise began in this fashion. The original designation of believers was as followers of "the Way" (Acts 9:2; 19:9, 23; 22:4; 24:14; cf. 2 Pet. 2:2, 21). This reflected Jesus' own identity: "I am the way, the truth, and the life" (John 14:6). The summons Jesus preached in Galilee was not to an orthodoxy of thinking, but an orthodoxy of following himself and his way. Indeed the word *mathetes*, disciple, means attachment to a person as a follower. So too Paul describes the faithful response to God as a "walk" in newness of life (Rom. 6:4; cf. 2 Cor. 5:7) or a walk by the Spirit (Gal. 5:16, 25; cf. Eph. 2:10; 5:2, 8, 15). And the author of the Letter to James goes so far as to say that "faith by itself, if it has no works, is dead. . . . Show me your faith apart from your works, and I by my works will show you my faith" (Jas. 2:17 − 18).

This wholistic expression of the faith has for the most part been lost in modern times. Therefore the living witness of the historic peace churches, such as the Brethren and Mennonites, is an invaluable gift to the remainder of Christendom. The Anabaptist wing of the Protestant Reformation recharted the course of faith as a way of life. Many believers' church movements have since then forfeited this distinctiveness, relegating ways of life to what the Lutheran Reformation labeled *adiaphora,* optional matters. But Christendom as a whole is indebted to the historic peace churches for retaining this encompassing vision. The simple lifestyle, the modesty which extends often to speech and plain garb, the suspicion of social rank and distinctions, all comprise a visible witness to gospel values. Conversely, they also imply a humble rebuke to the three-century rampage of the nation-state system and its ideologies of acquisitiveness and organized violence.

There is both great risk and great richness in sectarianism. But in an aimless and discordant society it is important to regain a sense of faith as right living. Outside the historic peace churches, others have recently come to grasp this wholistic vision under the rubric "experiment." Gandhi entitled his daily search for the universal laws of nonviolence "experiments in truth," a spiritual parallel to Einstein's discoveries in physical reality. "*Ahimsa* (non-violence) . . . is the only true force in life," the supreme law of the cosmos, he said, although "this cannot be proved by argument. It shall be proved by persons living it in their lives with utter disregard of consequences to themselves."[7]

The theme of experiments in truth has been picked up by James Douglass. Douglass is a Catholic peace activist whose life in disregard to consequences has led him to oppose the Trident submarine base in the state of Washington, and the "white train" that transports nuclear warheads around the nation. Since both Jesus and Gandhi discovered the deepest truth through daily experience, Douglass asks "that we discover the spiritual equation corresponding to Einstein's physical equation, and that we then begin to experiment seriously in its world-transforming reality while there is time. . . . Unless we begin to experiment with reality, in the faith that a new Reality does lie within, the opening to the new . . . does not occur."[8]

In a similar vein, Jürgen Moltmann describes hope as *"an experiment* with God, with oneself, and with history." It combines temptation and danger with intensely personal experience in plumbing the depths of human life through specific ventures of hope.[9] Living in the midst of the compulsions and drives of industrial society, the church is called by God to be a "testing grounds of the realm of freedom right in the realm of necessity."[10] Alone a Christian is vulnerable, but a life with fellow believers should form a framework that encourages the compassion and mutuality which is usually stifled by society. A final example of the metaphor of right living as "experiment" here and now comes from Jim Wallis, of the Sojourners community in Washington D.C. The urgent but risky mission of peacemaking, to which Jesus calls us, "means experimenting with the victory of Christ in our lives."[11]

Thus we have noted various examples of religion as right living, as orthopraxis. They have spanned the centuries from ancient times up until these recent calls for experimenting in real life with transcendent hope. Let us rescue the word "lifestyle," then, from its trivialization by Madison Avenue and commercial trend watchers. The term should not be wasted on the ephemeral roles and habits of what Lifton calls the modern "Protean" person, who is forever shifting to the next fashion. A faith to be lived, in the full sense of the word, is a wholistic way of life. Right living is a reflection of the righteousness of God, in whom and from whom life issues forth. Now that the nuclear age has raised before us the specter of a final ideology of totalism, Christian faith dare be no less wholistic.

Truth as Biblically Perceived

Orthodoxy as identified by right living and doing is an interpretation that matches the biblical understanding of what is truth. In Scripture truth means reality that is firm, binding, certain, and not concealed or falsified. God's Word is more than a timeless principle or a verbal communication, but a creative act that makes history (such as the Exodus) and demonstrates God's reliability (Rom. 3:3—4; 15:8). Truth is something that is acted upon, promised and then carried out by God, and so likewise the people of God must act upon any truth received. Israel knew little of the Greek dichotomy between theory and practice, between principle and application, which would open the door for a passive notion of truth. To the contrary, Israel's faith was an ordering of life at every level, a way of acting and of relating to the divine Partner of the Covenant.

No wonder the term "the Way" came so naturally to Jesus and to the earliest Christian communities. John, the author of the Fourth Gospel, emphasizes it as the doing of truth. The eternal Word (*logos*) has not simply been taught, but actually incarnate among us (John 1:1—18) as "the way, and the truth" (14:6), who sanctifies his followers in truth (17:17—19). In 1 John the author goes on to insist that for us to live in truth means not only a correct belief in Jesus as incarnate Son and Christ (1 Jn. 2:23; 4:1—3; 5:1), but also a right living in love with fellow believers (2:4—11; 3:10—18; 4:20—21). The two are indivisible, just as truth has become embodied in human form: "this is his commandment, that we should believe in the name of his Son Jesus Christ and love one another" (3:23).

So our knowledge of God, our right belief, is inextricably bound up with the immediacy and risk of living a certain way, through direct interaction with our neighbors. This is the meaning behind Peter Böhler's advice to the doubting young Wesley. In the words of a prominent Argentinian theologian, José Miguez Bonino, who has served as a vice president of the World Council of Churches, "correct knowledge is contingent on right doing. On rather, the knowledge is disclosed in the doing," rather than in advance. "We will know as we do."[12]

A generation earlier Dietrich Bonhoeffer made a similar discovery, while teaching a course on the Sermon on the Mount. In asking how a follower of Jesus can ever receive the miracle of faith, Bonhoeffer found the following two statements to be equally and simultaneously true: "*only he who believes is obedient, and only he who is obedient believes.*"[13] Not just ears are needed, but a listening that is so active that the whole self participates and acts out even what the mind has not yet fully grasped. That is why Jesus summons people whose hearts are not hardened to do more than just listen with their ears, but actively to *hear* (Mark 4:9, 23; 8:18; Luke 14:35), and thus to *follow* (Mark 1:17; 8:34; 10:21; John 12:26). "The Gospel story is not primarily a talk-text, but a praxis-text. God-talk comes in God-walk."[14]

Praxis, Liberation Theology, and Counterculture

This biblical understanding of orthodoxy as orthopraxis, of truth perceived and verified through right living, has been newly recovered in many parts of the world. Much of this has happened through several movements known collectively as liberation theology. In this gospel movement among ethnic minority and Third World Christians, the Good News is seen concretely amid situations of systematic oppression, such as in South Africa and Latin America. It emphasizes human solidarity (instead of individualism), God's activity in the world today (not God as absentee landlord), the creative possibilities for changing the future (instead of fatalism), and the special concern God has for the poor and the powerless (not a facade of impartiality which in effect gives a blank check to the powerful to exploit as they wish).[15]

Although criticized from various quarters, upon examination one will find that liberation theology is not just another form of naive do-goodism, nor is it after all wedded to violent revolution or any Marxist ideology. Many of the criticisms are misunderstandings which in fact are linked to its biblical way of apprehending truth. Centuries of scientific categories and technological reason have made us ill-prepared to appreciate that truth is a verb, so to speak, as much as it is a noun. When God's Word acts and renews itself in diverse cultures or social strata, the Word will mercifully accommodate itself to each particular situation.

Another way of saying this is that a living truth is "contextualized" to the living moment, corresponding to its special needs and opportunities. And yet it remains faithful to the character of the God of the ongoing Covenant. This is not relativism, but a divine compassion and wisdom that surpasses our time-bound minds. Perhaps by now, for instance, we have come to appreciate why Asian portraits of Jesus should have oriental features, or African Christians should praise God by means of traditional melodies. But then we should also grant that the liberating gospel may well come to peoples suffering under a subjugation we can barely understand, and bring redemption in ways perhaps unfamiliar to us.

Those of us in the so-called First World who enjoy relative affluence have much to learn from liberation theology. Especially, we can learn anew what it means to live in truth by doing the truth! This becomes even more significant for us, as we find ourselves needing liberation, indeed, from the shadow of the ultimate oppression, the Bomb and its accompanying ideology. Without paternalism or trivializing the sufferings of the poor, we can nevertheless begin to join them in yearning for "the truth [that] will make you free" (John 8:32), and seeking the lifestyle of that divine freedom. From our study of the paradigms of nuclearism that dominate our culture, then, we can appreciate the words of noted black theologian, James H. Cone, about the function of biblical stories for those suffering under slavery: "In view of their social situation of oppression, black people needed liberating visions so that they would not let historical limitations determine their perception of black being."[16]

Moreover, we can recognize just why liberation theology maintains that true knowledge cannot come from detached observation, much less armchair quarterbacking. Instead it arises in the very midst of life as it is immersed in an Exodus struggle from ever new forms of Egyptian bondage. For us, that bondage includes the technological reason that seems always ready to produce whatever new weaponry that has been imagined and then designed. It includes also an officially optimistic society that covers up new horrors with old cliches. As we seek our own Exodus, therefore, we could take some lessons from people of color around the globe. They could certainly teach the rest of us, for example, to ask persistently the *cui bono* question: just who benefits? In short, whose good is served by whatever measure is under consideration?

There is a further gift which a confessing church in a

nuclear age may receive from liberation theology and Third World Christians. We can let ourselves be reminded that living and lived truth cannot be easily verified by prior concepts or by correspondence to "reality" as conventionally conceived. The God of Scripture, after all, is veiled in majesty and thus invisible to the human eye. No one could see God, Israel learned, nor were any images or artistic replicas even to be attempted. The answer to Moses' request for divine identification, a sort of handhold on God, was simply the mysterious name (which is also a rejection of names!), "I AM WHO I AM" (Exod. 3:14). This can also be translated in the future sense, "I WILL BE WHAT I WILL BE." God's identity will be disclosed as well as vindicated in the impending acts of deliverance, which for now can only be awaited in faith and hope.

In nonbiblical language, this means that a religious statement stands or falls according to whether it permits "the entry into future truth." This phrase is explained by Dorothee Soelle, a contemporary German theologian: "The truth of Christ exists only as concrete realization, which means: the verification principle of every theological statement is the praxis that it enables for the future. Theological statements contain as much truth as they deliver practically in transforming reality."[17] Conversely, the assertions of nuclearism must be judged—and at last discredited—because of the praxis of unspeakable horror from which they originate and towards which they would condemn us.

This rediscovery of orthopraxis as lived and living truth is not to be confused with pragmatism or with various anti-doctrinal skepticisms that today compromise the integrity of Christian faith. Rather than some new fad, this emphasis is as old as "the Way" attested in Scripture. This is aptly summarized, in fact, in the famous closing words of Albert Schweitzer's study of the historical Jesus:

He comes to us as One unknown, without a name, as of old, by the lake-side, He came to those men who knew Him not. He speaks to us the same word: "Follow thou me!" and sets us to the tasks which He has to fulfil in our time. He commands. And to

those who obey Him, whether they be wise or simple, He will reveal Himself in the toils, the conflicts,
the sufferings which they shall pass through in His
fellowship, and, as an ineffable mystery, they shall
learn in their own experience Who He is.[18]

Before we move on in our reflection on right living as a
way of countering nuclearism, let us take a moment to compare another movement which was also based on lifestyle and
a new vision: the counterculture of the late 1960s. The claim
was made likewise in those days that a cultural revolution was
underway. There were hopes that the social structures of the
"establishment" were dissolving, and that a gentler, more in-
trospective and life-affirming generation was rising to replace
it. One example was Charles A. Reich's *The Greening of
America*, a book which now seems curiously dated. The
author asserted that a "Consciousness III" would soon undermine two earlier stages: both the older work ethic and the
modern corporate state. Mere reform of present institutions
was dismissed disdainfully, for "it is useless to seek changes in
society without changes of consciousness. Consciousness is
prior to structure."[19]

In retrospect we may judge the 1960s counterculture as
too self-indulgent in its individualism and too sensate in its
values. But it did draw public attention to nonviolence, ecological and human fulfillment, consciousness-raising, and a
changed lifestyle. These emphases do resemble many traits,
both of liberation theology and of the basic alternative this
book seeks to pose to nuclearism. But the counterculture failed
in its hopes. What went wrong, then? Instead of the low key
Aquarian age of the hippie, our culture has plunged into the
high tech consumer age of the Yuppie. Might that mean that a
movement against nuclearism, a confessing church which likewise relies upon a change in mental paradigms and lifestyles,
would be doomed as well to disappointment?

No flat answer can be given, of course. History remains
enigmatic, and cultural change is notoriously elusive of our
predictions. But it is fair to ask what lessons can be learned
from the miscarriage of America's "Greening." It seems to me
that there are two such lessons.

1. Any movement for a changed lifestyle rests upon deeper intuitions, whether expressed or not, of what ultimate reality is. In theological terms, every praxis implies an ontology (what is finally real?) and an eschatology (how will it all turn out?) And a lifestyle movement cannot long survive a wrong guess on these ultimate matters. It appears that what Reich named as Consciousness III was simply in error in some of these foundations. Admittedly, such a risk also attends liberation theologies and, of course, the present call for a confessional resistance against nuclear heresy — even though both of these are certainly better grounded in Scripture and the Spirit. But only time will tell — or, better said, only the providence of God will determine. If we are wrong after all, then no power on earth can help us. Meanwhile, however, we must be steadfast in following our best insights. For "faith" is the assurance of things hoped for, the conviction of things not seen" (Heb. 11:1). And since that faith is Christ-formed and Christrooted, we are summoned to unstop our ears and be receptive for that new reformation which alone can deliver us.

2. Any movement for a changed lifestyle rests also upon the joint convictions of an ongoing group, what sociologists call the plausibility structures supplied by those around us. A solitary person, quite isolated from the like-minded, would find it difficult to maintain an identity as, say, a North American in Pakistan, a Republican in a Democratic town, or a Catholic in a Baptist neighborhood. History has taught Hutterians and the Amish, and other dissenting or monastic traditions, that the support of a close-knit community is needed, if one is to believe and live differently from the surrounding culture. Faith cannot remain a merely private affair, nor can it long survive without some kind of institutional embodiment. The 1960s counterculture, however, not only lacked any institutional or collective base, but often denounced such structures as an infringement on personal self-expression. Its members spurned the very container which can carry an emerging but still fluid vision to wider circles, or to future generations.

By contrast, liberation theology is very clear on that

point. It finds its life is renewed in myriads of small action/
reflection groups or (in Latin America) Christian base communities. Likewise, a confessing church movement by definition could have no existence apart from the church. It is
through prayer and fellowship groups that it must find a base
for the wider task of seeking to reform the church as a whole.

In sum, the biblical understanding of truth as obedient
living, a "God-walk," is necessary if we are to prepare for a
special time of confessing the church's faith. I would conclude that the example of liberation theology shows the vitality of such a renewal of orthodoxy, while the miscarriage of
the counterculture and its somewhat comparable emphasis on
lifestyle can be accounted for on other grounds. Let us
therefore encourage a lifestyle in truth, a mode of right living
which will offer an unspoken and yet unmistakable alternative to the heretical claims of nuclearism.

Two Lifestyles Compared

At this point we can no longer postpone the selection of
a suitable adjective for this mode of life that contrasts to
nuclearism. To call it "non-nuclearist" is too negative by far,
since Christian living is motivated by resurrection joy, and
since nuclearism itself is a deformation, a perversion of life.
The gospel should light our path, without being first a contrast to any prior standard. Yet to speak of "Christian" vs.
"Non-Christian (nuclearist)" praxis is unsatisfactory. It
would not be well understood, at least until nuclear idolatry
has been unmasked within the churches and a clear confession offered. For now, therefore, let us adopt the adjective
"confessing," and speak of a confessing Christian lifestyle, in
distinction to its nuclearist counterparts. This terminology
would also strengthen our awareness of the theological
parallels between our own crisis and that in Germany in the
1930s and in South Africa more recently.

However, what does it really mean to live as a confessing
Christian rather than as a devotee of the Bomb? Earlier we
have contrasted some models of the two faiths. Now let us
sketch a comparable contrast between the two lifestyles. In
our present circumstances, what might each of the alternatives look like? Instead of reviewing various outgrowths of

the two opposing sets of paradigms, as already discussed in Part II, I think it better to illustrate with a single vivid example of each lifestyle.

A representative instance of nuclearist lifestyle may not be easily singled out. Nuclearism's mode of living, no less than its preconceptual models, has blended with and influenced our whole civilization. This all began, of course, long before the explosion at Almagordo in 1945. And yet a residual Christian heritage continues to impose at least some inhibitions on our public behavior. Despite this unevenness in openly expressing a nuclearist lifestyle, however, I believe examples can be found.

One instance is our society's current enthusiasm for so-called survivalism, associated with paramilitary training and weaponry. There is a new respectability for a growing subculture of machismo and commando-style combat guns. The cover story of *Newsweek*, October 14, 1985, details this trend under the title "Machine Gun U.S.A." About 500,000 military-style assault guns, including UZIs and AR-15s, are now owned by private citizens, and sales are booming. Although fully automatic weapons are supposedly regulated by federal law, conversion kits are easily available to make semiautomatics into sophisticated automatic weapons which, until recently, only elite military units would ever possess. Firing up to 1100 rounds per minute, these could by no stretch of the imagination be called sporting or hunting guns; they are designed solely to kill human beings in large numbers very quickly.

Then there is the popularity of related magazines, such as *Soldier of Fortune* (now with a circulation of 175,000), *New Breed*, or *Gung-Ho*. They also carry advertisements for schools across the country (twenty-five, by one estimate) that offer instruction in hand-to-hand combat, wilderness living, sniper techniques, and rigging booby traps. "The schools range in quality and price, from a $2,500 two-week course in Pittsview, Ala., to a 'mercenary course' that costs $300 for five days in the North Carolina woods."[20]

Let us be even more specific. This exotic way of life can be discovered at your local newsstand. Vivid detail is added by paging through, for example, the October 1985 issue of

Special Weapons and Tactics (S.W.A.T.), a bimonthly magazine. This issue contains illustrated articles on a new submachine gun available to civilians, Marine Corps recruit drilling, off-duty weapons, training in countersniping, and "Hi-Tech SWAT Gear for the Eighties." There is a sarcastic editorial attacking a new gun control bill in Congress, and also vilifying Senator Kennedy for a speech mentioning the recent surge in mail-order martial arts lethal instruments. Even more alarming are the advertisements: a great variety of semi-automatic weapons, hand guns, knives, holsters, paramilitary clothing, a practice device that gives the "actual feeling of breaking a person's leg," no trespass signs featuring brutal pictures and vigilante themes, and books such as *How to Get Anything on Anybody* and *Get Even: The Complete Book of Dirty Tricks*.

The paradigms supporting nuclearism are all here, even though nuclear weapons as such are unmentioned. The nature of power is unmistakably violent; a virtual arsenal of modern guns is displayed in loving detail, a Vietnam veteran trains college students in the wilderness in "the *brutality* or the *brute mentality* that it took to stay alive," and advertisements offer a wide variety of gadgets and books to aid survival in combat — or what is ominously referred to as "any eventuality." Also a confining world threatens to push every encounter into zero-sum gaming. The editorial rails against the frequent "ritual" in which the U.S. must "suffer through a no win situation" (implying that every situation has a winner). The lust for such victory is encouraged by military style clothing (including an Indiana Jones hat), sold "for the adventurous," and a semi-automatic carbine goes under the slogan, "In a world of compromise, some men don't."

Worst case analysis is a staple ingredient in these pages, beginning with the cover's subtitle: "For the Prepared American." A reader's letter compliments the magazine: "I get a rush of adrenalin every time I find the latest issue. Sick *yes*, but *true*" (presumably true as a portrayal of a "sick," boobytrap world). The combat training described labels hypothetical opponents quite unabashedly as the "bad guys." Several times "Commies" or "Communists" are mentioned, but there is plenty of venom left over for domestic enemies:

"our own gutless politicians," "our wimp politicians, "some civil rights attorney," "dim bulbs," your "liberal friends," and "our socialist slime." Finally, amidst the paranoia a trace of official optimism may occasionally be found. The ZX-7 submachine gun is said to be "entirely controllable," despite its heavy caliber, and those vets giving combat training to college students are actually men who "hate and fear war," but who "want their sons and daughters to be better prepared than they were in their day."

To be sure, one ought to have some sympathy for the tragic dilemmas often faced by law enforcement officers or military personnel who are conscientious. But there is no sense of tragedy in these pages of *S.W.A.T.*. Most of the contents of such a magazine instead are glorifying a lifestyle. Indeed it is a lifestyle which carries out overtly the very mindset that also is inherent in the Bomb and what it represents. When confronted with such a misshapen praxis, one can better appreciate an utterly contrasting lifestyle, namely the sectarian witness against militarism of the historic peace churches through the years. Admittedly there are risks in a principled nonconformity to the world. But in the face of the seemingly hopeless idolatry just described, such an embodied testimony is often the most faithful alternative for confessing Christians in any age.

To balance this comparison of lifestyles, now, we need some representative of a contrasting pattern, that of confessing Christians. While worthy examples could be cited also from the Anabaptist heritage, I choose a contemporary group with which I have had some contact: Koinonia Partners.

The Koinonia farm experiment, near Americus, Georgia, has for more than four decades struggled to incarnate the Christian vision. It was founded by Clarence Jordan, a native of Georgia with a big heart and homespun humor, who developed his talents in both agriculture and in New Testament Greek. From the outset the community gathered on those acres of red clay farmland has had two purposes: to live together in obedience to the Sermon on the Mount (with emphasis on peace and racial reconciliation, at a time and place which did not take kindly to such notions), and also to serve their neighbors in the deep poverty of rural Sumter

County.

The latter aim has been met through successive phases in the group's internal life. At first Koinonia assisted local farmers and sharecroppers by introducing scientific methods and new crops. But when racial hostility flared in the mid-1950s and a boycott ended most of their farming, Jordan helped the community to survive, reorganize, and find new modes of service. Now through a nation-wide mail order business in pecans and related products, they provide jobs and some further training to the unemployed. Also they are building clusters of modest but attractive homes which are then sold at cost. To date this has benefited about 140 families, who formerly lived in rural shacks in various stages of ruin. Clarence Jordan died in 1969. But to a remarkable degree a sense of his presence endures, as the community of Koinonia continues to evolve.

The several biblical paradigms which counter to nuclearism are all to be found in the ongoing life of this community. Nonviolence has been essential to Koinonia from the beginning—in fact even earlier. For young Clarence, while taking ROTC training in college, began memorizing the Sermon on the Mount. Finally, in the midst of field exercises just before being commissioned as an officer in the U.S. Cavalry, he dismounted abruptly and resigned his commission on the spot. Later at Koinonia, during the years of vigilante violence, threatening phone calls at midnight, and random gunfire from the highway bisecting the farm, the community never gave in to the temptation to violence. They responded with neither weapons nor hatred. In arguing with an old farmer who was disgusted with anyone who "wouldn't fight," Clarence explained that no farmer would respond to a mule that bit him by biting it back! "You wouldn't let that mule set the level of your encounter with him. You would get a weapon a mule couldn't use. . . . That's what Christians are supposed to do—they are supposed to use weapons of love and peace and goodwill, weapons that the enemy can't handle."[21]

Furthermore, there could be little zero-sum rivalry in a community venture which deliberately set out to embody gospel values. In the segregationist traditions of the deep South, it was long believed that progress or rights for black people could increase only at the expense of whites. Enormous fears and resentments were in the air, and for years Koinonia farm was bitterly attacked as a communist enclave of race-mixers. From the beginning, however, Clarence Jordan was dedicated to racial justice — first working as a graduate student in the inner city slums of Louisville, Kentucky, and then at Koinonia trying to build reconciliation between blacks and whites.

Furthermore, in its own group life the community was determined to give flesh to the spirit of Jesus. This evolved through several stages, first as an intentional community of families living from a common treasury and sharing work assignments, and then through several intermediate arrangements as personnel changed and the experiment was almost extinguished. Finally there was a reconstitution under the concept of "partnership." The result today is a decentralized cluster of fifty or so residents who as a group provide various ways of linking the resources of the affluent with the needs of the poor. Koinonia is not a commune, nor does it foster the intense collective behavioral energies which highly structured communal groups do, such as the Hutterian Society of Brothers (Bruderhof).[22] But its vision of human community is a wholesome combination of shared compassion, voluntary personal growth, and outreach to the wider world of humanity.

The fear inspired by worst case assumptions, next, is notably absent at Koinonia. It was founded, indeed, as a venture of trust in the future and in God's ability to work in unexpected ways. Even at the height of persecution and violent threats during the mid-1950s, members took every opportunity to seek personal reconciliation with hostile townspeople or sullen bystanders. They discovered the creativity possible in obeying Jesus' command to love those who set themselves against us as enemies.

Two illustrations will suffice.[23] When a delegation of the local KKK arrived with the warning, "we're here to tell you we don't allow the sun to set on anybody who eats with niggers," Clarence had a sudden inspiration. Using an allusion to Joshua 10:12 — 13 which seems to have been understood, he grabbed his opponent's hand and shook it vigorously: "I'm a Baptist preacher and I just graduated from the Southern Bap-

tist Seminary. I've heard about people who had power over
the sun, but I never hoped to meet one." Anger melted into
laughter, and the sun did set after all on everybody. Later,
the local Baptist church held a meeting to expel Koinonia
members for their association with Blacks. But it was
Florence Jordan (the wife of Clarence) who rose suddenly to
move the adoption of the motion for expulsion. Not knowing
then how to vote, the opposition was disconcerted by her
nondefensive goodwill.

By refusing to treat people as enemies, even when receiv-
ing obvious hatred, the members of Koinonia have demonstrated a compassion and courage born of a more inclusive vision of the future. This hope is closely linked to Clarence's
definition of faith as "a life in scorn of the consequences."
The antithesis of faith, however, shuts out the future: "Fear is
the polio of the soul, which prevents our walking by faith."[24]
This openness to the new ways of God, even when human calculations might be forbidding, has characterized Koinonia at
each successive stage of its existence. Even today, for example, the community carries no insurance (even though a building full of farm machinery was lost in a fire in July, 1985).
Typically the visitor will find its members spend little time
retelling stories of the past and its illustrious founder; they
are more concerned about new directions in spiritual renewal
and service to others.

The final paradigm of nuclearism described was faith as
official optimism. But the confessing Christian knows that
resurrection arrives only after crucifixion, and that a living
faith comes only when one has gazed into fearful depths.
Clearly the Koinonia project was not founded on conventional piety or a concern for appearances. Its members knew
themselves to be quite ordinary folk, when confronted by
danger and the threat of death; "it scared hell out of us,"
Clarence freely admitted. But the only thing more frightening
would have been to be disobedient to the way of Jesus.[25] At
the height of the persecution, when the community met all
day long for ten days to decide what to do, Florence Jordan
recalls, "There was never any feeling that we should leave.
We knew we wouldn't be the first Christians to die, and we
wouldn't be the last."[26] Clarence himself later suffered

despondency when the farm in more tranquil times was on the verge of demoralization, although he lived to see its rebirth as Koinonia Partners.

A final anecdote both shows his gentle humor and hints at the personal pain he knew. When a pastor boasted of a modern $10,000 cross atop his new church, Clarence replied that the preacher had been cheated on the price: "Time was," he said, "when Christians could get those crosses for free."[27] But out of the suffering in Sumter County arose a grounded faith that looks beyond the shadows to the light of Easter morning.

Stories and Support Groups

The contrast between the lifestyles of nuclearism and a new confessing Christianity should now be clear and stark, after surveying these two sample cases. Most of us, however, live somewhere between these extremes—neither possessed fully by the mania of the one nor rising quite to the courage of the other. For the rest of us, then, what practical ways are there to resist the pressures and culture-wide momentum of a nuclearist lifestyle? How may you and I begin to cultivate a confessional mode of living in a nuclear age? I have two suggestions: hearing stories and having a support group.

First, there is story. That is, we must again and again tell the stories of those whose lives already reflect the kingdom of God. Rather than seeking to alter lifestyles by argument or analysis, it is better simply to rehearse the lives of the (modern day) saints, lifting up their example as faithful witnesses. For they are attesting to what is after all reality.

Narratives communicate a texture and depth which the more direct language of reasoning or flat imperatives cannot. They have a self-evidencing power that is prior to any conceptual screening or evaluation. Whether through biographies, memoirs, or briefer and representative anecdotes, stories do have the immeasurable advantage of opening up and putting forward in microcosm a new thought-world. This alternate reality is in a sense irrefutable. That is, it cannot easily be dismissed as fanciful, since it has been embodied at least partially in historic persons. A story does not argue or cajole. It presents simply and incontestably a new reality. And it does so with an implicit invitation to the hearer to try it on for size, so to speak. In such a manner, the new reality grows.

Furthermore, since it is in the unrefined and thus all the more credible form of narrative, the hearers are invited to appropriate its truth at whatever level they are capable of, at the moment. Later, of course, a retelling of that story may touch the same person at a deeper level, bring new resources, and expand its significance in unforeseen ways. It is no coincidence that the narrative sections of Scripture (the gospels, much of the Pentateuch, the Acts of the Apostles) remain the most popular. Likewise the church has long recognized the value of testimonies, biographies, and martyr legends. In gentle but unrelenting manner, the story of a faithful life opens the door to a realm of fresh possibilities, a foretaste of the coming New Creation.

This robust vision offers to a person more than a general loosening of the cramped frameworks of older worldviews. It also grants a quite particular deliverance from a false self-identity. We have observed that one of the effects of nuclearism is self-dehumanization, a sense of powerlessness and futility which in turn encourages compliance with the national security establishment. We think ourselves to be nobodies, cogs in a world machine, pawns in a no-win game.

To that extent, those of us who are white can come to appreciate in some measure the cruel history of black slavery which imposed still greater destruction on the victim's self-image. Thereby one should also find new appreciation for the black gift of storytelling. This talent was a blessing to those subjugated and battered for years by a dehumanized status. In fact, says James Cone, one could argue that "the form of black religion in story was chosen for . . . sociological reasons. The easiest way for the oppressed to defy conceptual definitions that justify their existence in servitude is to tell stories about another reality where they are accepted as human beings."[28] A great deal of black theology, both historically and nowadays, is devoted to a more wholesome self-image of empowerment. For that purpose the story form is well suited. No wonder that authoritarian societies and tyrannies usually make special efforts to regulate or even censor the fiction available to a repressed populace. The appropriate story told at the right moment is a most powerful threat to coerced conformity. It may be even more so, if the story is not fictional after all, but biographical. It becomes then a subversive memory of one who undeniably existed, and who in this common life walked resolutely to the beat of a different drummer.

There is an additional way in which black religion may instruct the rest of us. For the story is most commonly told orally. Whereas much of Western society has adopted print or electronic media for its preferred modes of communication, the black tradition has always held in high esteem the art of storytelling. For a congregation the preacher has been the narrator par excellence. Indeed for all of us, whether we be in a Sunday meetinghouse, sitting around a kitchen table, or at a child's bedside, the story is best told by word of mouth. Heard from a human voice, it becomes an interpersonal event in itself, a prototypical relationship that is shaped not only by the plot but also by the distinctive personhood of the narrator and each listener. Every talented storyteller shapes the material subtly according to the situation, weaving new harmonies with the needs and receptivities of that audience. Thus the human drama being narrated is not only made more plausible by the personal presence of the narrator, but is richly compounded by a living relationship of the moment between speaker and listener. The story thus is far more than a medium through which truth is communicated; rather, in its telling it becomes a constituent part of truth itself.[29]

So confessing Christians should tell again and in ever new ways the life stories of the faithful, whose God-walk has interpreted and validated their God-talk. Let us recount the life of Gandhi, for instance, who combined steadfast nonviolence with astute political planning, and who freely accepted vicarious suffering as the path to truth that is all-reconciling. Let us go on telling the story of Martin Luther King, Jr., who through a deeply biblical vision struggled to find new ways of joining the quest for justice with a love of enemies. We rejoice that his solidarity with his people and with all who are oppressed did not preclude a witness that was universal, embracing bystanders as well as oppressors.

Let us rehearse, too, the story of Dorothy Day, who regained the biblical meaning of repentance and turned to a praxis (both new and very old!) of voluntary poverty and renunciation. The communal life she molded still serves the urban poor with hospitality, as well as bearing witness to an inhospitable society. Let us return to the story of Clarence Jordan, farmer and biblical translator, storyteller and humorist, whose feet were planted as firmly in the Sermon on the Mount as in the hard, red soil of Georgia. Through sweat, laughter, and tears he joined in building a community that lightens the darkness for us all. Let us also retell the story of André Trocmé, who led the French village of Le Chambon during the Nazi occupation into becoming quite openly a refuge for fleeing Jews. He and his townspeople refused even to lie or practice subterfuge about their work of mercy. Defying the danger, his family continued to answer the furtive midnight knock on their door with "Naturally, come in, and come in."[30]

So let us keep on telling the story in our nuclear age. There are stories from the rise of Christian conscience in South Africa—the lives of C. F. Beyers Naudé, Allan Boesak, Steve Biko, and Desmond Tutu. There are stories from the confessing church in fascist Germany—the lives of Martin Niemoeller, Dietrich Bonhoeffer, Paul Schneider—and also from the much wider circle of holocaust victims and the suffering people of God in that time of horror. The life stories go on and on, so that—in the words of the Letter to the Hebrews—"what more shall I say? For time would fail me to tell of" so many others (11:32). Biblically speaking, however, the conclusion is clear: "Therefore, since we are surrounded by so great a cloud of witnesses, let us also lay aside every weight, and sin which clings so closely, and let us run with perseverance the race that is set before us. . . "(Heb. 12:1).

Moreover, black spirituality continues to aid us in the telling of stories from the multitude of the faithful. In a stirring sermon that unites this same text from Hebrews with a roll call of modern lives of faith, Vincent Harding says that to acknowledge this great cloud of witnesses "is to know that regardless of how alone we feel sometimes, we are never alone." "I would call us to see and appreciate these folks who

are like a great cheering squad for us. In the midst of everything that seems so difficult, that seems so powerful, that
seems so overwhelming, they are saying to us: 'We are with
you,' and 'There is a way through; there is a way to stand;
there is a way to move; there is a way to hope; there is a way
to believe. Don't give up!' "[31]

This brings us to the second suggestion on how you and I
may nurture a confessional mode of living. Besides story,
there is community. That is, to cultivate a new lifestyle we
must again and again place ourselves in community with
other confessing Christians.

This second suggestion follows quite directly from the
first. For the more we retell the stories of the faithful, the
more we begin to take our frames of reference from God's
New Creation. That indeed is part of what it means to be
reborn. But we are embodied selves, and so furthermore we
do need the physical presence of the like-minded, if we are to
maintain in good repair those frames of reference. Recall that
mortal assumptions about reality are greatly influenced by
"common sense," that is, the common consensus held by the
group(s) we live with, concerning the basics of existence.
Those close to us, the "significant others," form our basic
reference group, the plausibility structure that upholds our
symbol system as believable, day after day. As humans we of
course cannot choose our parents, the country of our birth,
and our early associations. But as confessing Christians
undergoing rebirth, we can and must choose with care our
present peer groups.

The role of reference groups becomes especially crucial
for cognitive minorities — in other words, dissenting groups
whose members quite literally need one another to "know"
what the wider world disregards. The close-knit community
provides not only plausibility for the dissonant worldview,
but also mutual support in coping with ridicule or even persecution from outsiders. When the early church coined the
watchword *extra ecclesiam nulla salus* (outside the church
there is no salvation), it was not acting with imperious self-
righteousness, but indeed recognizing a sociological fact:
"only within the religious community . . . [can] the conversion be effectively maintained as plausible."[32]

History offers many examples. For 2500 years the Jewish diaspora has demonstrated how essential small communities are for the faithful. Immigrant groups of every variety, for that matter, have always sought to settle in a given neighborhood whenever there was a wish to perpetuate the old ways. Ethnic enclaves long characterized the rising cities of North America. And out on the frontier, regular visitation among far flung settlements, and also gatherings at annual meetings or annual conferences, were needed by believers (to cite but two examples), to preserve the Brethren order or Methodist mission. In short, we do need one another.

Not only to maintain right thinking (orthodoxy), but right living (orthopraxis), therefore, it is important to be a part of a community. Of course the two are intertwined. John Wesley, for instance, brought a religious awakening to England not just by his inspired preaching, but by skillfully organizing those who responded. Without the latter, he said, the former was futile. "The devil himself desires nothing more than this, that the people of any place should be half-awakened and then left to themselves to fall asleep again. Therefore I determined, by the grace of God, not to strike one stroke in any place where I cannot follow the blow."[33]

Accordingly, Wesley followed up by organizing ongoing prayer and fellowship groups — "societies" was the term common in that day. The purpose was to nurture the new faith and to express it in praxis methodically — in good "Methodist" fashion, as the label eventually developed. As the societies grew, they were subdivided into classes or bands, to preserve the intimacy of small group fellowship, worship, confession, and pastoral care. His network of United Societies expanded all over the country. The effects in England were so enduring and widespread, that they lend hope in our day for a similar shift of paradigms and lifestyle.

The lifeblood of the church in every age, indeed, has been in small, face-to-face support groups. In the early and medieval church, it was the joint intensity of devotion and discipline of the religious orders that sustained the faith amid a decaying Europe. Later, Anabaptism and believers' churches gave new energy to sixteenth century Christianity. In the following centuries it was the *collegia pietatis* (associations of piety) of Lutheran pietism, as well as the conventicles and religious societies alongside a state church in England and elsewhere. More recently Christians nurture one another by grouping themselves in prayer fellowships, koinonia cells, house churches, and mission groups. The Cursillo movement spawns small fellowships that can revitalize an adult faith in the closeness of shared pain and joy. In Latin America a massive renewal is on the rise, through thousands of *comunidades de base* (base Christian communities). There lay people provide their own collective leadership in searching the Scriptures, and through prayer and mutual support in the face of growing governmental repression.

Outside the church, of course, it is likewise well known that small groups are the best setting for any attempt to modify behavior, emotions, or attitudes. Alcoholics Anonymous, together with Al-Anon for family members of alcoholics, has proved effective as no other way has, in restoring wholeness of life to those afflicted by this problem. From this as a prototype, many comparable organizations have emerged to deal with other problems, ranging from Narcotics Anonymous to Weight Watchers. In every case the key is the personal identification one feels with a new reference group, and the readiness to receive and give mutual strength in adhering to the vision of a new reality held by that group. In similar vein, a variety of network groupings now gather and give emotional support to those burdened by some common tragedy. An example is Compassionate Partners, in which parents share the pain of having had a child killed in an automobile accident.

There are other types of examples, as well. For public demonstrations or civil disobedience the crowd often will be divided up into so-called affinity groups. The reason is that shared ideals alone may be insufficient for coping with contingencies or maintaining cohesion. The support of a face-to-face fellowship is vital, when one is under pressure. The same is true in various kinds of group therapies and consciousness-raising groups. Interpersonal contact creates its own fresh reality, and this in turn generates a powerful gravitational pull on the attitudes of each participant.

Certainly with no less seriousness, even urgency, confessing Christians should seek out each other. The impending nuclear crisis drives us to a new appreciation of that sole condition for membership which John Wesley described for his eighteenth-century equivalent of base Christian communities: "a desire to flee from the wrath to come, to be saved from their sins."[34] We do need one another, if we are to extract ourselves from the heresy of nuclearism and if we are to unstop our ears for a reformation.

A new lifestyle virtually requires support groups, an enclave of God's kingdom in a darkening world which gives corporate embodiment to the light. Outright communal living would offer the most assured framework, and every generation of the church has found such groups to be beacons in the wilderness. Koinonia Partners is but a recent instance. However, this discussion of support groups is restricted to examples which fall short of the rigor of Christian communalism, examples which are more accessible for most of us. For the moment few may be ready to risk living communally. But all of us can place ourselves somehow in Christian community, its vision and its discipline of accountability. It may be a prayer cell within a congregation, a koinonia group, or a local ecumenical fellowship such as a chapter of World Peacemakers.[35] But there is no substitute for regular and intimate fellowship with a reference group which is struggling to free itself from nuclearism and to be faithful to the gospel. To come to be in community with others who "desire to flee from the wrath to come, to be saved from their sins," and to offer themselves as building blocks of God's New Creation—this is what orthopraxis means. It is living in truth.

Hope for Reformation

The time of a new reformation is at hand. However it is not in our power to cause it to happen. If it does come and the planet is at last drawn back from the nuclear abyss, it will have been the grace of God that accomplishes it. Meanwhile we are summoned to pray, hope, and do what we can to unstop our ears. For, as Richard Barnet discovered in that encounter with the Air Force general described in our opening pages, there is "no way out of the race to destruction except somehow to transcend it."

To do so means that we prepare to listen afresh to Scripture and the Spirit, as they test and attest one another. Reading Scripture with an expectant two-fold vision, we abjure the tyranny of technological reason. And awaiting the Spirit with a firm grounding in the biblical Word, we abstain from the enticements of self-indulging ecstasies. In this way we may be led, in God's own time, to a special case for confession. Thus our hope is that the church's faith may be powerfully renewed, in our own era of nuclear crisis.

As we wait, however, we should be ready as faithful midwives. That requires some strategies, and I have suggested two. By discerning the paradigms that undergird the heresy of nuclearism we may seek to replace them with thought models that are more biblically oriented. And by recognizing the role of praxis and social context in shaping the truth, insofar as human beings can appropriate it, we may seek in community with others a confessing lifestyle that incarnates the vision.

In such ways we would embody our fervent prayer for reformation. And we would prepare ourselves and — it is to be hoped — the church itself to be midwives, through whom God may choose to work a more global transformation that will "somehow transcend" that race to destruction. And so we pray that the church as a whole may be granted a special time for confessing. To the extent that a wider awareness arises that nuclearism is indeed a covert religion and moreover a grave challenge to the gospel, then it will be recognized that the identity and mission of the church are at stake. It is at such a time of crisis (which is also, in fact, opportunity!) that the church can be reborn by confessing its faith anew.

In the days ahead, a myriad of practical decisions await us, calling upon fresh ingenuity and painstaking effort. Patience and prayer will be needed in abundance. As we begin, then, may these words from Jim Wallis go with us: "We must never lose sight of the victory of Christ in the present nuclear crisis. That victory in history is assured. It has already been won for us. We must learn to be a people who can see the world in the light of the victory of Christ."[36]

Postscript

Testimonials from Some of the Faithful
in a Nuclear Age

"Today the choice is no longer between violence and
nonviolence. It is either nonviolence or nonexistence."
—Martin Luther King, Jr.[1]

"Peace is not a thing of weakness.
It calls for heroism and action.
    Day by day you must wrest it from the mouths of
    liars.
    You must stand alone against the multitude; for the
    clamor is always on the side of the many, and the
    liar has ever the first word.
The meek must be strong."
—Stefan Zeig, Viennese poet[2]

"Sin has made us sinners—or victimizers. But it has also
made us sinned against or victims. God has acted through
Jesus Christ to save us from both sins and our enemies. It
follows that we can no more save ourselves from our enemies
than we can save ourselves from our sins. We are dependent
on God for both. Our effort to save ourselves from our
enemies is what we call the arms race."
—John K. Stoner[3]

"[Nuclear war] would be the climactic coup for him who
was 'a murderer from the start,' but would, precisely in that,
largely negate his primeval and all-encompassing deception,

'You will not die.' That lie is like the benevolent rhetoric of a wicked despot which infuses and mediates the depotism. . . . But for any who . . . see through the lie, there is something that can be set against the dominion which the collapsing lie otherwise confirms: to hear the voice of the sovereign Lord, 'Fear not, I am the first and the last, and the living one; I died, and behold I am alive for evermore, and I have the keys of Death and Hades' (Rev. 1:17 – 18); 'Because I live, you will live also' (Jn. 14:19). Not Satan's offer that we can live and not die; but God's, that, even though we die, He gives us life."
— Dale Aukerman[4]

"For the past 18 years of my life has been children — one birth child, 7 adopted children and 3 foster children. 10 of my kids are mentally retarded. . . . Tragic death cannot always be prevented. Accident or disease may kill our children while we stand helpless to do anything. But death in nuclear war is preventable. It can happen only if we allow it, and if we allow it, we will come for judgment not before the Supreme Court of the District of Columbia but before God and the murdered innocents.

It is morally incumbent upon us to defend the children. I have done so at home for 18 years. I did so on September 2nd at the White House, pouring my blood to speak against the death of nuclear weapons and for the life we could have instead — a life of reconciliation and peace. The acts through which I serve life at home are considered exemplary and noble; my nonviolent witness at the White House is considered to be criminal. After more than two years of prayer and the thought which preceded my civil disobedience and after the 76 days I have spent in the DC Jail, I cannot, in all good conscience, see the difference between the two."
— Helen Woodson, "Statement of November 15, 1982" at her trial.[5]

"Most of us build prisons for ourselves, and after we occupy them for a period of time we become accustomed to their walls and accept the false premise that we are incarcerated for life. As soon as that belief takes hold of us we abandon hope of ever doing more with our lives and of ever giving our dreams a chance to be fulfilled. We begin to suffer living deaths; one of a herd heading for destruction in a grey mass of mediocrity.

In our act of disarmament, in all its preparations and what has come since, I have found a lifeline to hope, the resurrection of hope from a living death. I resist not only the nuclear arms race, but the spiritual darkness of futility and self-pity as well. Hope is alive in the courtroom today."

— Barb Katt, sentencing statement before federal judge Miles Lord, 8 November 1984.[6]

"Even if we talk of the nuclear peril, it must be also with a smile of joy at Christ's victory."

— Jean Lasserre, French pacifist.[7]

A BIBLIOGRAPHIC ESSAY

A great deal has been written lately about nuclear weapons and the dilemmas they pose. Here we must be content with only a few suggestions. Some minimal familiarity with these matters is essential, however, and the following are important introductory sources of information. Jonathan Schell's *The Fate of the Earth* (1982) is both significant and readable; his subsequent *The Abolition* (1984) modifies his earlier political proposals. For years Richard Barnet has been a reliable guide in tracing the development of the Cold War, its dynamics and effects: *The Economy of Death* (1969), *The Roots of War* (1972), *The Giants: Russia and America* (1977), and *Real Security: Restoring American Power in a Dangerous Decade* (1981).

Concerning the sad history of arms control efforts, Alan Geyer's *The Idea of Disarmament! Rethinking the Unthinkable* is excellent and is now in a new edition (1985). Several useful anthologies have recently been issued: *Toward Nuclear Disarmament and Global Security: A Search for Alternatives,* ed. Burns H. Weston (1984); *The Nuclear Crisis Reader,* ed. Gwyn Prins (1985); and (especially useful for the classroom) *The Nuclear Predicament: A Sourcebook,* ed. Donna Gregory (1986). Readers may keep current by following such periodicals as *Nuclear Times* and *Bulletin of the Atomic Scientists.* On a more advanced level, the presuppositions behind our nuclear mentality are examined by philosophers and political scientists in *Nuclear Weapons and the Future of Humanity: The Fundamental Questions,* ed. Avner Cohen and Steven Lee (1986).

The psychological and spiritual dimensions of living

under the Bomb particularly concern us. An important early volume by concerned psychiatrists, *Psychiatric Aspects of the Prevention of Nuclear War* (1964), has been followed by *Psychosocial Aspects of Nuclear Development* (1982). For years, several medical authorities have written on the effects on daily life: Jerome D. Frank, *Sanity and Survival in a Nuclear Age: Psychological Aspects of War and Peace* (1967, reissued 1982), and various articles by John E. Mack in *Bulletin of the Atomic Scientists* and elsewhere. Schell's first book offers some useful summaries of these effects. There is a notable and moving anthology of literary and journalistic excerpts on living in the nuclear age, organized around dominant themes, *In a Dark Time,* eds. Robert Jay Lifton and Nicholas Humphrey (1984).

The most important researcher and writer on these human effects is Robert Jay Lifton. After interviewing many who lived through nuclear horror, reported in *Death in Life: Survivors of Hiroshima* (1967), he has continued to study the impact of various catastrophes on the psyche. Most important for our topic is *The Broken Connection: On Death and the Continuity of Life* (1979), a comprehensive study of the human need to maintain symbolic forms of life-connectedness; in the final chapters he turns to the climactic disruption imposed by nuclear weapons. Here is found his famed definition of "nuclearism"—although a more informal discussion of it follows in his *Indefensible Weapons: the Political and Psychological Case Against Nuclearism* (1982), co-authored with political scientist Richard Falk.

The interest of the mainstream churches on issues posed by the Bomb has ebbed and flowed over the decades. For the earlier period I have found most helpful the bibliographic essay by Ralph B. Potter, at the end of his *War and Moral Discourse* (1969). Excerpts from the recent surge of denominational pronouncements against the arms race are conveniently collected in *To Proclaim Peace: Religious Communities Speak Out on the Arms Race,* ed. John Donaghy, 2nd rev. ed. (1983). See the summaries in Judith A. Dwyer, "Catholic Thought on Nuclear Weapons: A Review of the Literature," and David A. Hoekema, "Protestant Statements on Nuclear Disarmament," *Religious Studies Review* 10:2 (April 1984):

97–107. The most notable and widely discussed single statement is that of the U.S. Catholic bishops, *The Challenge of Peace: God's Promise and Our Response* (1983); see also *Catholics and Nuclear War: A Commentary on "The Challenge of Peace,"* ed. Philip J. Murnion (1983). The latest such statement is also one of the most critical of deterrence and the mere possession of nuclear weapons: The United Methodist Council of Bishops, *In Defense of Creation: The Nuclear Crisis and a Just Peace* (1986).

For some time there have been important books on more general topics of peace, mass destruction, and the morality of warfare. Examples include the writings of John Howard Yoder and Paul Ramsey, who consistently are among the best representatives of the pacifist and just war positions, respectively. Jean Lasserre, *War and the Gospel* (1962), and Richard McSorley, *New Testament Basis of Peacemaking* (1979, 1985), remain classics on the biblical foundations. Edward LeRoy Long, *Peace Thinking in a Warring World* (1983), contrasts several popular and divisive concepts with more cooperative ways of thinking, conducive to a livable future. Arthur C. Cochrane's *The Mystery of Peace* (1986) blends biblical and Reformed theology with competent interpretations of the German church's witness against Hitler. Dale W. Brown, in *Biblical Pacifism: A Peace Church Perspective* (1986), guides us through the tradition of the Brethren and other historic peace churches.

But beyond these general works on war and peace, it has only been recently that much theological attention has turned to specifically nuclear issues. We are indebted to Dale Aukerman, whose *Darkening Valley: A Biblical Perspective on Nuclear War* (1981) plowed new ground; he is presently completing a second book. Another religious treatment of the Bomb is Denise Priestley, *Bringing Forth in Hope: Being Creative in a Nuclear Age* (1983). Within academic circles, Gordon D. Kaufman highlighted theology's peculiar position in the nuclear age, first in "Nuclear Eschatology and the Study of Religion," *Journal of the American Academy of Religion* 51:1 (March 1983): 3–14, and then in *Theology for a Nuclear Age* (1985). Lifton's studies and specifically nuclearism, however, are first discussed in their religious functions by Ira Chernus in a number of articles. Perhaps the best is his earliest, "Mythologies of Nuclear War," *Journal of the American Academy of Religion* 50:2 (June 1982); 255-73. See also *Religious Studies in the Nuclear Age: A Collection of Essays,* ed. Ira Chernus and Edward T. Linenthal, soon to be published by Cambridge University Press, and Chernus's recent book, *Dr. Strangegod: On the Symbolic Meaning of Nuclear Weapons* (1986).

In discussing a confessional approach to nuclearism, our first example is the German Church Struggle of the 1930s, culminating in the Barmen Declaration. Still highly recommended reading is Arthur C. Cochrane, *The Church's Confession Under Hitler* (1962, and reissued by Pickwick Press, 1976). See the collection of documents in *The Third Reich and the Christian Churches,* ed. Peter Matheson (1981). More advanced is Rolf Ahlers, *The Barmen Theological Declaration: The Archaeology of a Confessional Text* (1986). Our second example is a confessional response to South Africa's apartheid policies. Especially important here are the writings of John W. de Gruchy: *The Church Struggle in South Africa* (1979), *Bonhoeffer and South Africa* (1984), and edited with Charles Villa-Vincencio, *Apartheid Is a Heresy* (1983). The church there is recovering its identity through new creedal statements; see *Moment of Truth: The Confession of the Dutch Reformed Mission Church, 1982,* ed. G. D. Cloete and D. J. Smith (1984), and *The Kairos Document: Challenge to the Church* (1986). Continuing developments in that troubled land can be followed by reading the biweekly, *Christianity and Crisis*, or newsletters from the Washington Office on Africa (110 Maryland Avenue, N.E., Washington D.C. 20002).

These tragic events have led to a widening discussion of the phrase *status confessionis,* and its possible usage in the modern era. See Louis A. Smith, "The Struggle to Confess the Real Christ in the Real World," *Budapest Briefings* VI, Lutheran World Ministries (7 June 1984), and George Hunsinger, "Barth, Barmen and the Confessing Church Today," *Katallagete* 9:2 (Summer 1985): 14-27 (a series of replies will appear in a forthcoming issue). A committee was appointed by the Lutheran World Federation to study the uproar about the Dar es Salaam pronouncement of 1977, and its extensive report is in *The Debate on Status Confessionis: Studies in Political Theology,* ed. Eckehart Lorenz (1983). European attempts to apply the phrase to nuclear weapons are described there, as well as in Jürgen Moltmann, *On Human Dignity: Political Theology and Ethics* (1984).

Concerning the strategic doctrine of deterrence, the best book is probably Patrick M. Morgan's *Deterrence: A Conceptual Analysis* (1977), a profound blend of social science data and philosophical analysis. The doctrine has had its competent defenders — both in its restrained or minimalist form by Bernard Brodie, in *The Absolute Weapon* (1946) and *Strategy in the Missile Age* (1965), and in its extended or maximalist form (setting the stage for modern "nuclear warfighting" strategies) by Herman Kahn, *On Thermonuclear War* (1960), *Thinking about the Unthinkable* (1962), and *On Escalation: Metaphors and Scenarios* (1965). Geyer's *The Idea of Disarmament!* gives a fine summary and critique of both forms.

There are hardly any satisfactory answers to coping with heresies. In fact, just to raise the term invites a multitude of problems; see Walter Bauer, *Orthodoxy and Heresy in Earliest Christianity* (1971). By contrast, H. E. W. Turner thinks the term still is definable and useful; see his *The Pattern of Christian Truth: A Study of the Relation between Orthodoxy and Heresy in the Early Church* (1954), as well as J. W. C. Wand, *The Four Great Heresies* (1955). The problem of a utilitarian, "single vision" world view is a favorite twentieth-century topic of phenomenologists, existentialists, and others. But its social ramifications are presented in accessible form by Robert Bellah, *The Broken Covenant: American Civil Religion in Time of Trial* (1975), and recently (with co-authors) *Habits of the Heart: Individualism and Commitment in American Life* (1985). The analytic psychology of Carl Jung opens a way for a high tech society to regain some appreciation of the creative power of both the unconscious mind and the symbols it feeds upon. See the several readable introductory books of John A. Sanford, such as *Healing and Wholeness* (1977); for Jung himself, see *Man and His Symbols* (1968). To learn more about the modern dilemma of biblical hermeneutics, beginners might well turn to James D. Smart, *The Interpretation of Scripture* (1961), supplemented by Walter Wink, *The Bible in Human Transformation: Toward a New Paradigm for Biblical Study* (1973).

The power of paradigms in the history of science was demonstrated effectively by Thomas S. Kuhn in *The Structure of Scientific Revolutions* (1961, 1970). I accept his basic thesis, but his work has sparked considerable debate; see Gary Gutting, ed., *Paradigms and Revolutions: Appraisals and Applications of Thomas Kuhn's Philosophy of Science* (1980). Concerning the application to a seemingly intractable arms race, Michael Nagler sums it up well in "Peace as a Paradigm Shift," *Bulletin of the Atomic Scientists* 37:12 (December 1981): 49–52. As a social ethicist, Gibson Winter has long struggled with the effects of such paradigms on our common life; see for instance his *Liberating Creation: Foundations of Religious Social Ethics* (1981).

Of the paradigms selected for discussion in this book, the bewitching notion of power as violence is especially vivid. For background, see Rollo May, *Power and Innocence: A Search for the Source of Violence* (1972), and Michael Walzer, *The Revolution of the Saints: A Study of the Origins of Radical Politics* (1976). Our nation has a long heritage of attraction to such images; this is demonstrated ably by Ernest Lee Tuveson, *Redeemer Nation: The Idea of America's Millennial Role* (1968), and Richard Slotkin, *Regeneration Through Violence: The Mythology of the American Frontier, 1600-1860* (1973). I especially recommend the analyses of Robert Jewett in *The Captain America Complex* (1973, 1981) and, together with John S. Lawrence, *The American Monomyth* (1977).

There are alternate, nonviolent paradigms of power as artistic creativity (Gibson Winter) or spiritual force. For the latter, of course, Gandhi and Martin Luther King, Jr., are the modern trail blazers, but see also James W. Douglass, *Resistance and Contemplation: The Way of Liberation* (1972) and *Lightning from East to West* (1980, 1983). The biblical grounding is well summarized in John Howard Yoder, *The Politics of Jesus* (1972) and in Jean Michel Hornus, *It Is Not Lawful for Me to Fight: Early Christian Attitudes Toward War, Violence, and the State* (1980). The assorted writings of Thomas Merton on the subject are nicely assembled, together with a fine introduction by Gordon Zahn, in *The Nonviolent Alternative* (1980). For practical matters of nonviolent action, see the writings of Yoder — such as *What Would You Do?* (1983) — and of Gene Sharp — for instance, *The Politics of Nonviolent Action* (1973). A popular introduction to "civilian based defense" is found in Ron Sider and Richard Taylor, *Nuclear Holocaust and Christian Hope* (1982), chapters 13–15.

The paradigm of scarcity or "zero sum gaming" has long haunted the Western world. An acute form nowadays of that model plays off global population figures against fears about the food supply; see George R. Lucas, Jr., and Thomas W. Ogletree, eds., *Lifeboat Ethics: The Moral Dilemmas of World Hunger* (1976). Such specters are competently put in perspective by Frances Moore Lappé and Joseph Collins — briefly in *World Hunger: Ten Myths* (1982), and extensively in *Food First: Beyond the Myth of Scarcity,* rev. ed. (1978). The corrosive effects of North American competitive individualism have been analyzed by a succession of sociologists, from Robert and Helen Lynd in *Middletown* (1929) to the above-mentioned book by Robert Bellah, *et al., Habits of the Heart.* Customarily the model has been legitimated by laissez faire economic theory, but this covert faith assumption is unmasked by M. Douglas Meeks, "Toward a Trinitarian View of Economics: The Holy Spirit and Human Needs," *Christianity and Crisis* 40:18 (10 November 1980): 307–16, and in his forthcoming book, *God as Economist* (Fortress Press).

Much of our thinking is governed by implicit notions of what the future will be like. Good introductions to this vast topic are offered by Ted Peters, *Futures — Human and Divine* (1978) and *Fear, Faith, and the Future: Affirming Christian Hope in the Face of Doomsday Prophecies* (1980). A much less hopeful (and less theological) statement is Robert Heilbroner's widely read book, *An Inquiry into the Human Prospect* (1974, 1980). Such inner fears not only prompt our own dehumanization, but are easily projected onto outside figures of "the enemy." The psychology of Jung develops this insight, and a good place to begin is with John A. Sanford, *Evil: The Shadow Side of Reality* (1981). The harmful effect of stereotyping in conflict situations is well known to political scientists; see for instance Kenneth Boulding, *Stable Peace* (1978). To redress the balance we very much need books such as that edited by Dale W. Brown, *What About the Russians? A Christian Approach to the U.S.-Soviet Conflict* (1984). Moreover we are called upon to love the very antagonists who were formerly dehumanized, and William Klassen, in *Love of Enemies: the Way to Peace* (1984), presents the rich biblical evidence for this theme. For Christians, hope is the great theme about the future, and here the writings of Jürgen Moltmann are supremely important. I suggest beginning with his famous *Theology of Hope* (1967), the first and final chapters, and then his *Man: Christian Anthropology in the Conflicts of the Present* (1974) and *The Passion for Life: A Messianic Lifestyle* (1978). A somewhat different approach to hope theology is offered by Wolfhart Pannenberg, *Theology and the Kingdom of God* (1969), *What Is Man? Contemporary Anthropology in Theological Perspective* (1970), and (in greater depth) *Anthropology in Theological Perspective* (1985).

The United States has long been fond of mistaking faith for a collective optimism. The great critic of this error has been Reinhold Niebuhr; a good example is his *Beyond Tragedy* (1937). Among his followers, see Will Herberg, *Protestant—Catholic—Jew: An Essay in American Religious Sociology* (1960). An excellent critique of our official optimism is found in Douglas John Hall, *Lighten Our Darkness: Toward an Indigenous Theology of the Cross* (1976). One frightful outcome of such misplaced confidence is the current popularity of counterforce targeting and nuclear warfighting policies. A prime exponent of such strategic policies is Colin S. Gray, who (together with Keith Payne) wrote a famous essay, "Victory Is Possible," *Foreign Policy* 39 (Summer 1980): 14–27. Such policies are described and criticized in Robert C. Aldridge, *First Strike! The Pentagon's Strategy for Nuclear War* (1983), and Robert S. Scheer, *With Enough Shovels: Reagan, Bush and Nuclear War* (1983). A deeper view of faith which does not fear to admit the human darkness is, I believe, best described by Thomas Merton — for instance in *New Seeds of Contemplation* (1961).

Finally, daily life is inseparable from orthodoxy in any proper sense of the word today. This is in some contrast to the New Christian Right and its focus on right willing; see for example Jerry Falwell's *Listen America!* (1980), and for a fair but critical introduction, see Samuel S. Hill and Dennis E. Owen, *The New Religious Political Right in America* (1982). The Christian understanding of truth as obedient living is epitomized in our day by the figure of Dietrich Bonhoeffer during the Third Reich. A fine guide to his thinking is Geffrey B. Kelly's *Liberating Faith: Bonhoeffer's Message for Today* (1984); thereafter, see the writings of Eberhard Bethge — first *Costly Grace: An Illustrated Biography of Dietrich Bonhoeffer* (1979), and then the definitive biography, *Dietrich Bonhoeffer: Theologian, Christian, Contemporary* (1970). In differing cultural conditions the same theme is carried out today by various liberation theologies. Helpful introductions to these significant movements include William K. McElvaney, *Good News is Bad News Is Good News . . .* (1980); James C. Cone, *God of the Oppressed* (1975); Theo Witvliet, *A Place in the Sun: An Introduction to Liberation Theology in the Third World* (1985); Deane William Ferm, *Third World Liberation Theologies: An Introductory Survey* and *Third World Liberation Theologies: A Reader* (1986). The single finest source of such publications is Orbis Books (Maryknoll, N.Y. 10545), and an attractive catalogue is available on request.

The confessional Christian lifestyle can be seen in the biographies of individuals — see James Wm. McClendon, Jr., *Biolgraphy as Theology: How Life Stories Can Remake Today's Theology* (1974), and Dallas Lee's biography of Clarence Jordan, *The Cotton Patch Evidence* (1971). But it can also be seen in the gathering of Christian intentional communities; see Benjamin Zablocki, *The Joyful Community: An Account of the Bruderhof, A Communal Movement Now in Its Third Generation* (1971), and Jim Wallis, *Revive Us Again: A Sojourner's Story* (1983). The significance of listening to storytellers, especially for children, is explored by psychologist Bruno Bettelheim, *The Uses of Enchantment: The*

Meaning and Importance of Fairy Tales (1977). Directly or indirectly, we all depend upon intimate human contact to support whatever the mind claims as true. The dynamics of such "plausibility structures" are explained by Peter L. Berger and Thomas Luckmann, *The Social Construction of Reality: A Treatise in the Sociology of Knowledge* (1967). Their practical effects, on the other hand, are described by such books as James O'Halloran's *Living Cells: Developing Small Christian Community* (1984), and (important for our purposes) Gordon Cosby and Bill Price, *Handbook for World Peacemakers Groups* (rev. ed., 1984). The Latin American experience is documented, and on a more advanced level, in *The Challenge of Basic Christian Communities,* eds. John Eagleson and Sergio Torres (1981).

NOTES

Preface. Testimonials from Some Worshipers of the Bomb
1. *The Boston Globe*, 15 July 1980.
2. "Capsules," *The OtherSide* 21:5 (July 1985): 65.
3. *The Globe-Times* (Bethlehem, Pa.), 6 August 1982.
4. *In a Dark Time*, eds. Robert Jay Lifton and Nicholas Humphrey (Cambridge, Mass.: Harvard University Press, 1984), 64–65.
5. White House Office of Media Relations and Planning, quoted in *Christianity and Crisis* 44:4 (19 March 1984): 77.
6. Richard Barnet, *The Roots of War* (Baltimore, Md.: Penguin Books, 1972), 256.
7. *Evolutionary Blues* 1:1 (1981), 1; used by permission of the author, who of course is personally no devotee of nuclearism.

Chapter One. Nuclearism as a Religion
1. Barnet, "Of Cables and Crises," *Sojourners* 12:2 (February 1983):18, now reprinted in *Peacemakers: Christian Voices from the New Abolitionist Movement*, ed. Jim Wallis (New York, Harper and Row, 1983), 102.
2. Ibid.
3. Geyer, *The Idea of Disarmament! Rethinking the Unthinkable,* Rev. ed. (Elgin, Ill.: Brethren Press, 1985), 193.
4. Luther, The Large Catechism, quoted in *A Compend of Luther's Theology*, ed. Hugh T. Kerr, Jr. (Philadelphia: The Westminster Press, 1943), 23.
5. Tillich, *Dynamics of Faith* (New York: Harper and Row, 1957), especially chapter 1.
6. The formative study on nuclear winter is referred to—with unintended irony!—as TTAPS (after the authors): R. P. Turco, O. B. Toon, T. P. Ackerman, J. B. Pollack, Carl Sagan,

"Nuclear Winter: Global Consequences of Multiple Nuclear Explosions," *Science* (23 December 1983):1283 – 92. See also Paul R. Ehrlich, et al., "Long-Term Biological Consequences of Nuclear War," in the same issue of *Science*, pp. 1293 – 1300; Paul R. Ehrlich, et al., *The Cold and the Dark: The World after Nuclear War* (New York: W. W. Norton and Co., 1984); Mark A. Harwell, *Nuclear Winter: The Human and Environmental Consequences of Nuclear War* (New York: Springer-Verlag, 1984); Carl Sagan, "Nuclear War and Climatic Catastrophe: Some Policy Implications," *Foreign Affairs* 62:2 (Winter 1983/84): 257 – 93. A good introduction in simpler terms is offered by Thomas Powers, "Nuclear Winter and Nuclear Strategy," *The Atlantic Monthly* (November 1984): 53 – 64.

7. Schell, *The Fate of the Earth* (New York: Alfred Knopf, 1982), 119, 115. Some of his ideas were later modified in *The Abolition* (New York: Alfred Knopf, 1984).

8. Ibid., 123 – 36.

9. Quoted by Michael Mandelbaum, *The Nuclear Question* (Cambridge: Cambridge University Press, 1979), 19.

10. See Robert Jay Lifton and Richard Falk, *Indefensible Weapons: The Political and Psychological Case Against Nuclearism* (New York: Basic Books, 1982), 13 – 14, passim. A fine discussion and compilation of quotations of religious language and rites concerning the Bomb is found in James A. Aho's essay, "'I am Death, . . . Who Shatters Worlds': The Emerging Nuclear Death Cult," in *Religious Studies in the Nuclear Age: A Collection of Essays*, ed. Ira Chernus and Edward T. Linenthal, forthcoming.

11. Glover, *War, Sadism, and Pacifism* (London: George Allen and Unwin, 1946), 274.

12. Sanford, *Healing and Wholeness* (Mahwah, N.J.: Paulist Press, 1977), 87; see pp. 94 – 95, 99.

13. Winter, "Notes for a Socio-Political Religious Biography," *Religious Studies Review* 10:4 (October 1984): 329.

14. Aukerman, *Darkening Valley: A Biblical Perspective on Nuclear War* (New York: The Seabury Press, 1981; reprinted by the Winston-Seabury Press, Minneapolis), xvi.

15. Quoted in ibid., from Barth's *Church Dogmatics*, III/4 (Edinburgh: T and T Clark, 1969), 453.

16. Quoted in *Psychiatric Aspects of the Prevention of Nuclear War*, Report No. 57 (New York: Group for the Advancement of Psychiatry, 1964), 223. As early as 1946 Einstein declared,

"Science has brought forth this danger, but the real problem is in the minds and hearts of men. We will not change the hearts of other men by mechanism, but by changing *our* hearts and speaking bravely. . . . When we are clear in heart and mind— only then shall we find courage to surmount the fear which haunts the world." See Einstein, "Only Then Shall We Find Courage," *The New York Times Magazine* (23 June 1946), VI, 7.

17. See for example, Dr. Roger Walsh, *Staying Alive: The Psychology of Human Survival* (Boulder, Colo.: Shambhala Publications, New Science Library, 1984); Jonas Salk, writing in *Parade Magazine* (4 November 1984), 9; Douglas Sloan, "For the Record: Toward Education for a Living World," *Teachers College Record* 84:1 (Fall 1982): 10—13; and George F. Kennan, *The Nuclear Delusion: Soviet-American Relations in the Atomic Age* (New York: Pantheon Books, 1982), 178 and passim.

18. "Reducing the Risk of Nuclear War: What Can Scholars Do?," *Carnegie Quarterly* 30:2 (Spring 1985), 5.

19. *The Pastoral Constitution*, par. 80.

20. Quoted by Ralph B. Potter, *War and Moral Discourse* (Richmond, Va.: John Knox Press, 1969), 110. Potter's bibliographic essay (pp. 87-123) is highly recommended for background reading.

21. *The Challenge of Peace: God's Promise and Our Response* (Washington, D.C.: U.S. Catholic Conference, 1983).

22. The best published anthology commenting on the peace pastoral is *Catholics and Nuclear War: A Commentary on "The Challenge of Peace"*, ed. Philip J. Murnion (New York: Crossroad, 1983). See also Daryl Schmidt, "The Biblical Hermeneutics on Peacemaking in the Bishops' Pastoral," presentation to the Consultation on War and Peace Studies, annual meeting of the American Academy of Religion, Chicago, 8 December 1984.

23. *The Challenge of Peace*, par. 122-273.

24. Aukerman, chapter 23. His answer (p. 169): "Because God chose to let our rebellion be limitless; because He has chosen to give this culminating disclosure that apart from Him we are doomed."

25. Schell, *Fate of the Earth*, pp. 102—103, 133—34.

26. Ibid., 178.

27. Hauerwas, "Surviving Justly: An Ethical Analysis of Nuclear Disarmament," in *Religious Conscience and Nuclear Warfare:*

1982 Paine Lectures in Religion, ed. Jill Raitt (Columbia, Mo.: University of Missouri-Columbia, 1983), 8 – 13. See also Stanley Hauerwas, "Eschatology and Nuclear Disarmament," *New Catholic World* 226:1356 (November/December 1983): 250, which names Schell as a "clear case of humanistic eschatology. He would have us secure the eternality of our existence by controlling and mastering our history—exactly the same eschatological presumption that leads to our having nuclear weapons in the first place."

28. Kaufman, "Nuclear Eschatology and the Study of Religion," *Journal of the American Academy of Religion* 51:1 (March, 1983): 3 – 14.

29. Kaufman, *Theology for a Nuclear Age* (Philadelphia: The Westminster Press, 1985), 8.

30. Ibid., 39.

31. Ibid., 60.

32. His first book, *Relativism, Knowledge and Faith* (Chicago: University of Chicago Press, 1960), stakes out concerns which have continued to occupy his thinking. For astute and helpful surveys of Kaufman's subsequent development, see the review articles by Garrett Green and Douglas F. Ottati in *Religious Studies Review* 9:3 (July 1983): 219 – 27.

33. Kaufman, *Theology for a Nuclear Age*, 19, 23.

34. Kaufman, *Systematic Theology: A Historicist Perspective* (New York: Scribners, 1968), 65.

35. Cambridge: Harvard University Press, 1972.

36. Kaufman, *An Essay on Theological Method*, American Academy of Religion Studies in Religion, 11 (Missoula, Mont.: Scholars Press, 1975).

37. Philadelphia, The Westminster Press, 1981.

38. Kaufman, *Theology for a Nuclear Age,* 33 – 34.

39. See the references and discussion in my essay, "Hope and the Ethics of Formation: Moltmann as an Interpreter of Bonhoeffer," *Sciences Religieuses/Studies in Religion* 12:4 (Fall 1983): 449 – 60, especially pp. 452 – 54, 456 – 57. Also see M. Douglas Meeks, "God's Suffering Power and Liberation," *Journal of Religious Thought* 33 (Winter 1976): 44 – 54.

40. Lifton, *Death in Life: Survivors of Hiroshima* (New York: Random House, 1967).

41. Lifton, *The Broken Connection: On Death and the Continuity of Life* (New York: Simon and Schuster, 1979; republished by Basic Books, Harper and Row, 1983), 17, 18 – 35.

42. Ibid., 293-334.

43. Ibid., 298.
44. Ibid., 369. In other writings Lifton has similar but less extensive definitions of nuclearism: *Boundaries: Psychological Man in Revolution* (New York: Vintage Books, 1969), 26–27; *Proceedings of the Symposium, The Role of the Academy in Addressing the Issues of Nuclear War, Washington D. C., March 25-26, 1982* (Geneva, N.Y.: Hobart and William Smith Colleges, 1982), 73; and with Richard Falk, in *Indefensible Weapons*, ix, 87. Other writers have now taken up the term, modifying it in the process. For instance Gibson Winter, in "Hope for the Earth: a Hermeneutic of Nuclearism," *Religion and Intellectual Life* 1:3 (Spring 1984), 5-29, likewise views nuclearism as a logical and possibly terminal outcome of Euro-American technology. But he emphasizes far more the role of Western philosophy and its long tradition of abstracting the self from history and making it an autonomous subject, alienated in time and space, which then damages all relationships and leads to mortal violence.
45. Lifton, *The Broken Connection*, 369.
46. Quoted in ibid., 371.
47. Lifton and Falk, *Indefensible Weapons*, 13-14.
48. Ibid., 62-79; Lifton, *The Broken Connection*, 338-52.
49. Lifton and Falk, *Indefensible Weapons*, 78.
50. Lifton, *The Broken Connection*, 350.
51. Lifton, *Boundaries*, 30.
52. Lifton, *The Broken Connection*, 339.
53. Lifton and Falk, *Indefensible Weapons*, 82.
54. Ibid., 95.
55. Lifton, *The Broken Connection*, 296.
56. Ibid., 296-97; Lifton, *Boundaries*, chapter 3.
57. Lifton, *Death in Life*, 504.
58. Lifton and Falk, *Indefensible Weapons*, 48-52; Lifton, *The Broken Connection*, 363-68. For a survey of such research, see William Beardslee and John E. Mack, "The Impact on Children and Adolescents of Nuclear Developments," in *Psychosocial Aspects of Nuclear Developments* (Washington D.C.: American Psychiatric Association, 1982), 64-93.
59. Lifton, *Boundaries*, 31-32; Lifton and Falk, *Indefensible Weapons*, 103-104.
60. Lifton, *Boundaries*, 33.
61. Humphrey, "Four Minutes to Midnight," *The Listener* (29 October 1981): 494.
62. Lifton and Falk, *Indefensible Weapons*, 106-107.

63. See Robert K. Musil, "On Calling a Bomb a Bomb," *Nuclear Times* 1:5 (March 1983): 26–28.
64. See Roger Walsh, 39.
65. *Oxford English Dictionary* (Oxford: The Clarendon Press, 1933), VII, 584. An example is cited: more than a century ago (1880) a book was published with the title, *Dr. J. H. McLean's Peace Makers. A description of the Guns, &c., manufactured by McLean and Coloney.*
66. Lifton and Falk, *Indefensible Weapons*, 107.
67. Ibid., 14–22. These same illusions are discussed and applied by Robert Rizzo to specific instances, such as recent planning for rational and winnable nuclear war, or the Federal Emergency Management Agency's confidence in effective evacuation of entire populations. See Rizzo, "The Psychological Illusions of Nuclear Warfare," *Cross Currents* 33:3 (Fall 1983): 289–301.
68. Lifton and Falk, *Indefensible Weapons*, 25–31, 139, 176–77; see Doyle I. Carson, "Nuclear Weapons and Secrecy," in *Psychosocial Aspects of Nuclear Developments*, 34–41.
69. Mack, "Psychosocial Effects of the Nuclear Arms Race," *Bulletin of the Atomic Scientists* 37:4 (April 1981): 18–23, and with William Beardslee in *Psychosocial Aspects of Nuclear Developments*, 64–93; Carey, "Psychological Fallout," *Bulletin of the Atomic Scientists* 38:1 (January 1982): 20–24; Frank, *Sanity and Survival in a Nuclear Age: Psychological Aspects of War and Peace* (New York: Vantage Books, 1982 [1967]); "Psychological Causes of the Nuclear Arms Race," *Chemtech* (August 1982): 466–69; "Sociopsychological Aspects of the Nuclear Arms Race," in *Psychosocial Aspects of Nuclear Developments*, 1–10.
70. Schell, *Fate of the Earth,* 147–69.
71. E. L. Doctorow, "It's a Cold War World Out There, Class of '83," *The Nation* 237:1 (2 July 1983): 6. Referring to the Bomb, Doctorow insists that "in all sorts of ways, even as it sits there quietly in its silos, it is going off."
72. Kennan, "A Proposal for International Disarmament," *The Nuclear Delusion*, 176.
73. For example, the lemming behavior referred to above can better be described in traditional biblical language, as Dale Aukerman does. Jim Wallis, in *The Call to Conversion* (New York: Harper and Row, 1981), reiterates how "the Bomb has already deeply affected us. For in accepting its presence and proliferation we have already accepted the spiritual death it brings. . . . Hardness of heart . . . is the moral price we have paid for

nuclear weapons, and it pervades everything. Biblically speaking, hardness of heart is not so much the deliberate doing of evil. Rather, it is the loss of the ability to distinguish between good and evil" (p. 82).

74. Chernus, "Mythologies of Nuclear War," *Journal of the American Academy of Religion* 50:2 (June 1982): 260, 264.
75. Ibid., 256.
76. Chernus, "Mythology and Nuclear Strategy," *Dialogue: A Journal of Mormon Thought* 17:4 (Winter 1984): 33.
77. Chernus, "The Symbolism of the Bomb," *The Christian Century* 100:29 (12 October 1983): 907. See also his "Understanding Hiroshima's Symbolism," *The Christian Century* 102:24 (31 July/7 August 1985): 702-704.
78. These are found in Chernus, "Mythologies of Nuclear War," 257-64.
79. Chernus, "Imagining the 'Unimaginable,'" *Bulletin of Peace Proposals* 16:1 (1985): 79.
80. Chernus, "Mythologies of Nuclear War," 263.
81. Ibid., 266-69. See *The Effects of Nuclear War* (Washington DC: Congress of the United States, Office of Technology Assessment, 1979).
82. Arthur Katz, *Economic and Social Consequences of Nuclear Attack on the United States* (Washington D.C.: U.S. Senate Committee on Banking, Housing, and Urban Affairs, 1979), vi. Cf. the OTA study, above, pp. 109-15, 135-38.
83. Chernus, "Mythology and Nuclear Strategy," 34.
84. Chernus, "The Symbolism of the Bomb," 908.
85. This point is well argued by Hunter Brown in "The Nuclear Mirror and the Will to Identity," *Cross Currents* 33:3 (Fall 1983): 342-56.
86. Chernus, "War as Myth: The Show Must Go On," *Journal of the American Academy of Religion* 53:3 (September 1985): 449.
87. Ibid., 458.
88. Ibid.
89. *Religious Mythology and the Art of War* (Westport, Conn.: Greenwood Press, 1981). Both Aho and Chernus in turn reply upon the sociology of religion as conceived by Peter Berger; see the latter's *The Sacred Canopy: Elements of a Sociological Theory of Religion* (Garden City, N.Y.: Doubleday, 1967).
90. Gray, *The Warriors: Reflections on Men in Battle*, Perennial Library (New York: Harper and Row, 1967).
91. Ibid., 12.

92. Caillois, *Man and the Sacred*, trans. Meyer Barash (Glencoe, Ill.: The Free Press, 1959), 164.
93. Chernus, "War as Myth," 455.
94. Ibid., 460.
95. Chernus, "Mythologies of Nuclear War," 271–73; and his "The Symbolism of the Bomb," 909–910; "Mythology and Nuclear Strategy," 36.
96. Chernus, "War as Myth," 8.
97. Richard P. Hordern, "The Gospel of Peace: Theological Reflections in the Nuclear Age," *Union Seminary Quarterly Review* 39:1 and 2 (1984): 123–25.
98. Dietrich Bonhoeffer, *Letters and Papers from Prison*, the enlarged edition, ed. Eberhard Bethge (New York: Macmillan, 1972), 300.
99. See John W. de Gruchy, "Providence and the Shapers of History," *Bonhoeffer and South Africa* (Grand Rapids, Mich.: Wm. B. Eerdmans, 1984), 47–65.

Chapter Two. Nuclearism as a Heresy

1. Hauerwas, "Eschatology and Nuclear Disarmament," 250–51.
 2. Hauerwas, *Should War be Eliminated? Philosophical and Theological Investigations*. The 1984 Père Marquette Theology Lecture (Milwaukee: Marquette University Press, 1984), 51.
 3. Hauerwas, *The Peaceable Kingdom: A Primer in Christian Ethics* (Notre Dame, Ind.: University of Notre Dame Press, 1983), 29.
 4. Hauerwas, *Should War Be Eliminated?*, 53.
 5. Judith A. Dwyer, "Catholic Thought on Nuclear Weapons: A Review of the Literature," *Religious Studies Review* 10:2 (April 1984): 103 – 107. This is a companion essay to David A. Hoekema's "Protestant Statements on Nuclear Disarmament" in the same issue, pp. 97–102. Together the two review articles form a very useful summary of the recent position statements of most U.S. churches.
 6. For the background and description of this troubled chapter in the church's life, see Arthur C. Cochrane, *The Church's Confession Under Hitler* (Philadelphia: Westminster Press, 1962), and Peter Matheson, ed. *The Third Reich and the Christian Churches* (Grand Rapids, Mich.: Wm. B. Eerdmans, 1981).
 7. Bonhoeffer, "The Question of the Boundaries of the Church and Church Union," *The Way to Freedom*, ed. Edwin H. Robertson (London: William Collins and Son, 1966), 79, as translated from Bonhoeffer's *Gesammelte Schriften* (Munich:

Chr. Kaiser Verlag, 1958-1961), II, 222. See the clarifying comments of his colleague, Helmuth Gollwitzer, *The Way to Freedom*, 97-106.

8. Cochrane, 19.

9. Ibid., 237; the entire text of the Barmen pronouncements is given on pp. 237-47, and is well worth a periodic rereading.

10. As translated by Cochrane, 239.

11. For the history of such phrases, from Reformation times until the present, much of this and later paragraphs will rely on Martin Schloemann, "The Special Case for Confessing: Reflections on the *Casus Confessionis* (Dar es Salaam 1977) in the Light of History and Systematic Theology," in *The Debate on Status Confessionis: Studies in Political Theology*, ed. Eckehart Lorenz (Geneva: Department of Studies, the Lutheran World Federation, 1983), 47-94; and also Steven Schroeder, "*Status Confessionis*, Limits of the Confessing Community, and the Church's Critical Role in Society" (Paper delivered at the International Bonhoeffer Society, English Language Section, annual meeting, The American Academy of Religion, Chicago, 9 December 1984).

12. Quoted by Schloemann, 50.

13. Quoted by Schroeder, 14.

14. Ibid., 15.

15. With Germanic thoroughness, Schloemann is particularly insistent on the ambiguity of both the phrase *status confessionis* as well as its conditions. But see the more balanced and helpful summary by D. J. Smit, "What Does *Status Confessionis* Mean?," in *A Moment of Truth: The Confession of the Dutch Reformed Mission Church, 1982*, ed. G.D. Cloete and D. J. Smit (Grand Rapids, Mich.: Wm. B. Eerdmans, 1984), 7-32, especially the summary on p. 16.

16. Schloemann, 62.

17. Quoted in *The Debate on Status Confessionis*, 11.

18. Quoted in John W. de Gruchy and Charles Villa-Vincencio, eds., *Apartheid Is a Heresy* (Grand Rapids, Mich.: Wm. B. Eerdmans, 1983), 170.

19. *The Christian Century* 101:26 (29 August/5 September 1984): 793.

20. John W. de Gruchy, "Towards a Confessing Church: The Implications of a Heresy," in *Apartheid Is a Heresy*, 76; see pp. 75-76.

21. Bethge, "Appendix: A Confessing Church in South Africa? Conclusions from a Visit," in his collection of essays, *Bon-*

hoeffer: Exile and Martyr (New York, Seabury Press, 1975), 167.

22. de Gruchy, "Towards a Confessing Church," 79. We who are outsiders to the situation in South Africa are fortunate to have de Gruchy's writings to guide us. See not only his *Bonhoeffer and South Africa* and *Apartheid Is a Heresy*, but also his *The Church Struggle in South Africa* (Grand Rapids, Mich.: Wm. B. Eerdmans, 1979), and his "Bonhoeffer in South Africa: An Exploratory Essay," in Bethge, *Bonhoeffer: Exile and Martyr*, 26–42.

23. Quoted by Smit, 15–16.

24. The text is found in *A Moment of Truth*, 1–6.

25. For instance, in the 1960s, opponents of Rudolf Bultmann's existentialist interpretation of Scripture, so-called demythologizing, used this phrase in their "Confessional Movement." Also in 1980 the Central Committee of the World Council of Churches received a request to proclaim a *status confessionis* regarding world poverty.

26. Quoted in Schloemann, 70.

27. Smit, 11.

28. Schloemann, 81.

29. Brown, "1984: Orwell and Barmen," *The Christian Century* 101:25 (15-22 August 1984): 770–74. A more thorough but cautious call for a new confessing church is issued by George Hunsinger, "Barth, Barmen and the Confessing Church Today," *Katallagete* 9:2 (Summer 1985): 14–27. See also Arthur Cochrane, *The Mystery of Peace* (Elgin, IL: Brethren Press, 1986).

30. Schloemann, 58, 83.

31. Quoted in Schloemann, 73.

32. Louis A. Smith, "The Struggle to Confess the Real Christ in the Real World," *Budapest Briefings*, VI, Lutheran World Ministries (7 June 1984), 1–3.

33. Schroeder, 20: "'God's sovereignty' without 'two kingdoms' can degenerate into equation of a particular experience of certainty with the will of God and imposition of that experience on the world by force or utopian withdrawal from the world. 'Two kingdoms' without 'God's sovereignty' can degenerate into political quietism and other-worldly acquiesence in unjust decisions by temporal rulers."

34. Smit, 27.

35. *The Debate on Status Confessionis*, 129.

36. Ibid., 126.

37. Ibid., 133.
38. Ibid., 127.
39. Kumazawa, "Confessing the Faith in Japan," *The South East Asian Journal of Theology* (July/October 1966), 161.
40. Quoted in Ron Sider, *Rich Christians in an Age of Hunger: A Biblical Study* (Downers Grove, Ill.: Intervarsity Press, 1977), 58.
41. *The Debate on Status Confessionis*, 11.
42. Schroeder, 25.
43. Smit, 16.
44. Smith, 5.
45. Schloemann, 53.
46. Smit, 19. See "Findings and Recommendations" of the 1982 consultation sponsored by the Lutheran World Federation, in *The Debate on Status Confessionis*, 132.
47. *A Moment of Truth*, 5; reprinted by permission of the publisher.
48. Quoted by Jürgen Moltmann, "Discipleship of Christ in an Age of Nuclear War," *On Human Dignity: Political Theology and Ethics* (Philadelphia: Fortress Press, 1984), 129.
49. *The Challenge of Peace*, par. 120-21.
50. Childress, "Just War Criteria," in *War Or Peace? The Search for New Answers*, ed. Thomas A. Shannon (Maryknoll, N.Y.: Orbis Books, 1980), 40.
51. Hollenbach, *Nuclear Ethics: A Christian Moral Argument* (Ramsey, N.J.: Paulist Press, 1983), chapters 1-3.
52. Schroeder, 34.
53. Rahner, "History of Heresies," in *Encyclopedia of Theology: The Concise Sacramentum Mundi*, ed. Karl Rahner (New York: Seabury Press, 1975), 609.
54. Bonhoeffer, "Our Way According to the Testimony of Scripture," *The Way to Freedom*, 189 (from *GS*, II, 340).
55. de Gruchy, *Apartheid Is a Heresy*, 82.
56. G. A. Buckley, "Sin of Heresy," in *The New Catholic Encyclopedia* (New York: McGraw-Hill, 1967), 1069. Cf. Heribert Heinemann, "Heresy: Canon Law," in *Encyclopedia of Theology*, 604.
57. See the description and analysis of Lester R. Kurtz, "The Politics of Heresy," *The American Journal of Sociology* 88:6 (May 1983): 1085-1115.
58. Barth, *Church Dogmatics*, IV/3, 818-19.
59. See the 1963 Faith and Order study of the World Council of Churches, *Tradition and Traditions*, found in *Faith and Order*

Findings, ed. Paul S. Minear (London: SCM Press, 1963), 1–63. There "tradition" is held to be the human process of traditioning, "traditions" are specific patterns and usages of church life, and "*the* Tradition" refers to Christ, the living content of this process.

60. See Smit, 28–29.
61. "Armageddon View Prompts a Debate," *The New York Times*, 24 October 1984, sec. A; "Arguing Armageddon," *Newsweek*, 5 November 1984, 91.
62. Maslow, *Toward A Psychology of Being*, second edition (New York: Van Nostrand Reinhold Co., 1968), 16.
63. Ricoeur, *The Conflict of Interpretations: Essays in Hermeneutics*, ed. D. Ihde (Evanston, Ill.: Northwestern University Press, 1974), 27. Cf. Hwa Yol Jung, "Phenomenology as a Critique of Politics," *Human Studies* 5 (1982), 165–69.
64. Kaufman, *Theology for a Nuclear Age*, chapter 3.
65. See Bauer, *Orthodoxy and Heresy in Earliest Christianity*, ed. Robert A. Kraft and Gerhard Krodel (Philadelphia: Fortress Press, 1971). The controversial issues raised by Bauer are discussed in my article, "Some Theological Reflections on Walter Bauer's *Rechtgläubigkeit und Ketzerei im ältesten Christentum*: A Review Article," *Journal of Ecumenical Studies* 7 (Summer 1970): 564–74.

Chapter Three. Deterrence as Sacred Doctrine

1. Kahn, *On Thermonuclear War* (Princeton: Princeton University Press, 1960); *Thinking about the Unthinkable* (New York: Horizon Press, 1962); *On Escalation: Metaphors and Scenarios* (New York: Praeger, 1965).
2. *Time*, 5 December 1983, 39.
3. Geyer, 192.
4. JCS Pub. 1, quoted by *The Defense Monitor* 12:3 (June 1983): 5.
5. Of these area bombings, David Lilienthal, the first chairperson of the Atomic Energy Commission, said, "The fences are gone. And it was we, the civilized, who have pushed standardless conduct to its ultimate." See K. D. Johnson, "The Morality of Nuclear Deterrence," in *The Nuclear Crisis Reader*, ed. Gwyn Prins (New York: Vintage Books, 1985), 146–47.
6. Pierre Sprey, quoted by Fred M. Kaplan, *Dubious Specter: A Skeptical Look at the Soviet Nuclear Threat* (Washington, DC: Institute for Policy Studies, 1980), 41.
7. Lawrence Freedman, quoted by Geyer, 36.
8. Quoted by Johnson, 147, and Geyer, 33.

9. Quoted by Patrick M. Morgan, *Deterrence: A Conceptual Analysis*, Sage Library of Social Research, vol. 40 (Beverly Hills, CA: Sage Publications, 1977), 58–59.

10. John Steinbruner, quoted in ibid., 209.

11. Roger Fox, essay written on 25 May 1985, Moravian College, Bethlehem, Pa.

12. See Paul Joseph, "From MAD to NUTS: The Growing Danger of Nuclear War," *The Socialist Review* 61 (January-February 1982): 13–56.

13. Ellsberg, "Blind Men's Bluffs," *Nuclear Times* 3:7 (July-August 1985): 20.

14. Johnson, 144–45.

15. Geyer, "The Peace Pastoral Reconsidered," *Christianity and Crisis* 44:22 (21 January 1985): 526.

16. Morgan, chapter 2.

17. Ibid., chapter 3.

18. Ibid., 51.

19. Ibid., chapter 7.

20. Ibid., 193.

21. Quoted by Jerome D. Frank, "Sociopsychological Aspects of the Arms Race," in *Psychosocial Aspects of Nuclear Developments,* 7.

22. Morgan, chapter 4.

23. Ibid., 92.

24. Schell, *Fate of the Earth,* 202.

25. H. R. Haldeman, *The Ends of Power* (New York: Times Books, 1978), 82–83.

26. Morgan, chapter 5.

27. Ibid., 109.

28. Ibid., 121.

29. Ibid.

30. Geyer, *The Idea of Disarmament!*, 55.

31. Karl Deutsch, quoted in ibid., 53.

32. Morgan, 213.

33. Draper, in "Forum: Is There a Way Out?," *Harper's* 270:1621 (June 1985): 37.

34. See Jürgen Moltmann, *Mensch* (Stuttgart: Kreuz Verlag, 1971), 32; *Theology of Hope* (New York: Harper and Row, 1967), 285.

35. Moltmann, *Hope and Planning* (New York: Harper and Row), 1971), 105.

36. H. Richard Niebuhr, *Radical Monotheism and Western Culture*, Torchbook edition (New York: Harper and Row,

1970), 41.

37. Quoted by Morgan, 107.

38. Edward LeRoy Long, Jr., *Peace Thinking in a Warring World* (Philadelphia: Westminster Press, 1983), 16; cf. Geyer, *The Idea of Disarmament!*, 192.

39. Buber, *I and Thou* (Edinburgh: T and T Clark, 1937); Heinrich Ott, *God* (Atlanta: John Knox Press, 1974). For an Eriksonian perspective on mutuality, see Don Browning, *Generative Man: Psychoanalytic Perspectives* (New York: Delta, 1973).

Chapter Four. Coping with Heresies

1. Chernus, "Mythology and Nuclear Strategy," 34.

2. A fine example is found in Ernesto Cardenal, *The Gospel in Solentiname*, 4 volumes (Maryknoll, N.Y.: Orbis Books, 1976–82). Here Nicaraguan farmers and fishermen, from a village subsequently destroyed by Somoza's bombs, hold intense and earthy dialogues with their priest on stories and passages from the Bible.

3. See Robert N. Bellah, *The Broken Covenant: American Civil Religion in Time of Trial* (New York: Seabury Press, 1975), 72.

4. Geyer, *The Idea of Disarmament!*, 205.

5. Jung, "Approaching the Unconscious," *Man and His Symbols*, ed. Carl G. Jung, et al. (New York: Dell Publishing Co., 1968), 92.

6. Ibid.

7. See Wink, *The Bible in Human Transformation: Toward a New Paradigm for Biblical Study* (Philadelphia: Fortress Press, 1973), and *Transforming Bible Study: A Leader's Guide* (Nashville: Abingdon Press, 1980).

8. See especially Brueggemann's *The Prophetic Imagination* (Philadelphia: Fortress Press, 1978).

9. Calvin, *Tracts Relating to the Reformation* (Edinburgh: Calvin Translation Society, 1894), 37.

10. Berger, *The Heretical Imperative: Contemporary Possibilities of Religious Affirmation* (Garden City, N.Y.: Anchor Books/ Doubleday, 1980), 172.

Chapter Five. Belief, Models, and Holy Midwifery

1. Chicago: University of Chicago Press, 1961, 1970.

2. "Chunking" is the expressive term used by Bruce J. Malina, *The New Testament World: Insights from Cultural Anthropology* (Atlanta: John Knox Press, 1981), 16–17.

3. Ian Barbour, "Paradigms in Science and Religion," *Paradigms*

and Revolutions: Appraisals and Applications of Thomas Kuhn's Philosophy of Science, ed. Gary Gutting (Notre Dame: University of Notre Dame Press, 1980), 223–45.

4. Kuhn, chapter 8.
5. Philip Greven, *The Protestant Temperament: Patterns of Child Rearing, Religious Experience, and the Self in Early America* (New York: Alfred Knopf, 1977), 28, 35, and passim.
6. See Michael N. Nagler, "Peace as a Paradigm Shift," *Bulletin of the Atomic Scientists* 37:12 (December, 1981), 49–52. Also, Long, *Peace Thinking in a Warring World*, and Schell, *Fate of the Earth*.
7. Quoted as the epigraph in *Psychiatric Aspects of the Prevention of Nuclear War*, 223. Two decades ago the Second Vatican Council echoed this last sentence, with results that within Roman Catholicism are still unfolding. It affirmed that in an age of total war it is necessary "to undertake an evaluation of war with an entirely new attitude" (*Pastoral Constitution*, par. 80).
8. Barnet, *Real Security: Restoring American Power in a Dangerous Decade* (New York: Simon and Schuster, 1981), 101.
9. See Richard Barnet, "History of the Arms Race, 1945–78," in *Peace in Search of Makers*, ed. Jane Rockman (Valley Forge, PA: Judson Press, 1979), 12–24.
10. Goldstene, quoted by Norman Solomon and Ada Sanchez, "Disarmament: Beyond Illusions of Freedom," *Nonviolent Struggle for Disarmament*, National Network for Direct Action Bulletin 21 (December, 1984), 2.
11. David MacMichael, "Calling the Bluff," *Sojourners* 13:7 (August 1984), 22. Cf. Geyer, *The Idea of Disarmament!*, 90.
12. Winter, "Hope for the Earth," 6.
13. Auden, *For the Time Being: A Christmas Oratorio* (London: Faber and Faber, 1945), 66.
14. MccGwire, "The Dilemmas and Delusions of Deterrence," in *The Nuclear Crisis Reader*, 97.

Chapter Six. The Paradigm of Power as Violence

1. Klaus Hemmerle, "Power," in *Encyclopedia of Theology*, 1264.
2. Meeks, 44.
3. Lifton, *The Broken Connection*, 385.
4. This is the title of Merton's review of Robert Ardrey's *African Genesis*, now in Thomas Merton, *The Nonviolent Alternative*,

ed. Gordon C. Zahn (New York: Farrar, Straus, Giroux, 1980), 168–71.

5. *Psychiatric Aspects of the Prevention of Nuclear War*, 232. See also Hannah Arendt, *On Violence* (New York: Harcourt, Brace and World, 1970), 44–47.
6. Hobbes, *Leviathan*, I:13.
7. See Robert Jewett, *The Captain America Complex*, second edition (Santa Fe, N.M.: Bear and Co., 1984), chapter 5.
8. Quoted by Michael Walzer, *The Revolution of the Saints: A Study of the Origins of Radical Politics* (New York: Atheneum, 1976), 104; see chapter 8, passim.
9. See Ernest Lee Tuveson, *Redeemer Nation: The Idea of America's Millennial Role* (Chicago: University of Chicago Press, 1968).
10. *The Christian Century* 97:43 (31 December 1980): 1289.
11. "Living Through an Apocalypse," in *Let the Earth Hear His Voice*, ed. J. D. Douglas (Minneapolis: World Wide Publishers, 1975), 453.
12. See Richard Slotkin, *Regeneration Through Violence: The Mythology of the American Frontier, 1600*–1860 (Middletown, Conn.: Wesleyan University, 1973). This tradition and its biblical antecedents have been impressively clarified by Robert Jewett, first in *The Captain America Complex* (originally published in 1973), and then together with John S. Lawrence in *The American Monomyth* (New York: Anchor Press/Doubleday, 1977).
13. Quoted by Jewett, *The Captain America Complex*, 142.
14. Jewett and Lawrence, 188–89.
15. Ibid., chapter 1.
16. George Gerbner and Larry Gross, *Trends in Network Drama and Viewer Concept of Social Reality, 1967–73*, Violence Profile, No. 6, Annenberg School of Communications (Philadelphia: University of Pennsylvania, December, 1974). See "Life According to TV," *Newsweek*, 6 December 1982, 136–40B.
17. "True Confessions of a Pac-Man Junkie," by Steve, as told to Marion Long, *Family Weekly*, 2 January 1983, 6–7.
18. Long, 112; *The United Methodist Reporter*, 8 August 1985; *The Globe-Times* (Bethlehem, Pa.), 30 July 1985, sec. B.
19. Quotation and paraphrase by Aukerman, 36.
20. Quoted by Lifton, *The Broken Connection*, 382.
21. Gwyn Prins, "Introduction: The Paradox of Security," in *The Nuclear Crisis Reader*, xv.
22. Quoted by Lifton, *The Broken Connection*, 382. In 1961 Kiss-

inger added, "It simply does not make much sense to defend one's way of life with a strategy which guarantees its destruction"; this is quoted by K. D. Johnson, 147.

23. Barnet, *Real Security*, 71.

24. Quoted by Herbert Scoville, Jr., *MX: Prescription for Disaster* (Cambridge, Mass.: M.I.T. Press, 1981), 1.

25. Ball, "The Cosmic Bluff," *The New York Review of Books* 30:12 (21 July 1983): 37. See Kennan, 176–77, and the impressive array of similar statements by high military officers that is collected by Lous René Beres in *Mimicking Sisyphus: America's Countervailing Nuclear Strategy* (Lexington, Mass.: Heath, 1983), chapter 1.

26. *The New York Times*, 15 September 1983, sec. A.

27. Quoted by Eugene J. Carroll, "Nuclear Weapons and Deterrence," in *The Nuclear Crisis Reader*, 8.

28. See for example Langdon Gilkey, *Maker of Heaven and Earth: A Study of the Christian Doctrine of Creation* (New York: Doubleday, 1959), especially chapter 3.

29. See David Bohm, *Wholeness and the Implicate Order* (London: Routhledge and Kegan Paul, 1980).

30. Quoted in Nagler, 52.

31. Winter, "Hope for the Earth," 18. Winter supports this conclusion by describing the emerging view of the biosphere as "dynamic patterns or energy in a cosmic dance" (p. 17), and he quotes (pp. 17–18) Lewis Thomas as follows: "If this is, in fact, the drift of things, the way of the world, we may come to view immune reactions, genes of the marking of self, and perhaps all reflexive responses of aggression and defense as secondary developments in evolution, necessary for the regulation and modulation of symbiosis, not designed to break into the process, only to keep it from getting out of hand."

32. May, *Power and Innocence: A Search for the Source of Violence* (New York: Norton, 1972), 105–19.

33. Walter Grundmann, "*dynamai/dynamis*," in *Theological Dictionary of the New Testament*, ed. Gerhard Kittel (Grand Rapids, Mich.: Wm. B. Eerdmans, 1964), II:293.

34. Ibid., II:299.

35. See for instance John Howard Yoder, *The Politics of Jesus* (Grand Rapids, Mich.: Wm. B. Eerdmans, 1972), for a leading exposition of Jesus' ethic. The early church, although eventually pushed to what seemed an irreversible series of compromises, certainly accepted this as the definitive teaching of Jesus and thereafter of the Holy Spirit; see Jean Michel Hor-

nus, *It Is Not Lawful for Me to Fight: Early Christian Attitudes Toward War, Violence, and the State*, rev. ed. (Scott-
dale, Pa.: Herald Press, 1980).

36. See Gibson Winter, *Liberating Creation: Foundations of
Religious Social Ethics* (New York: Crossroad, 1981), especially pp. 102–103, 117–18.

37. Thomas Merton, "Gandhi and the One-Eyed Giant," *Gandhi
on Non-Violence: Selected Texts from Mohandas K. Gandhi's
Non-Violence in Peace and War*, ed. Thomas Merton (New
York: New Directions, 1965), 13.

38. Quoted by Gordon C. Zahn in his introduction to *The Nonviolent Alternative*, xxix.

39. Merton, "Blessed Are the Meek: The Christian Roots of Nonviolence," in *The Nonviolent Alternative*, 213.

40. For a Christian interpretation of this Gandhian category, see
James W. Douglass, *Lightning from East to West* (Portland,
Ore.: Sunburst Press, 1980). This has been reissued in 1983 by
Crossroad Publishing Co.

41. See the recent writings of Gene Sharp—for instance *The
Politics of Nonviolent Action* (Boston: Porter Sargent, 1973),
and *Making the Abolition of War a Realistic Goal* (New York:
Institute for World Order, 1981). Also Ron Sider and Richard
Taylor, *Nuclear Holocaust and Christian Hope* (Downers
Grove, Ill.: InterVarsity Press, 1982), chapters 13–15.

42. Merton, "Blessed Are the Meek," 213.

Chapter Seven. Life Together: a Zero Sum Game

1. Harry F. Waters, "What TV Does to Kids," *Newsweek* (21
February 1977), 62–70.

2. See Garret Hardin, "Lifeboat Ethics: The Case Against Helping the Poor," *Psychology Today* (September 1974): 38–34,
123–26; George R. Lucas, Jr., and Thomas W. Ogletree, eds.,
Lifeboat Ethics: The Moral Dilemmas of World Hunger (New
York: Harper and Row, 1976).

3. Fuller, *Utopia or Oblivion: The Prospects for Humanity* (New
York: Overlook Press, 1969), 286.

4. See Frances Moore Lappé and Joseph Collins, *World Hunger:
Ten Myths*, 4th ed. (San Francisco: Institute for Food and
Development Policy, 1982), 8, 53.

5. Barnet, *The Roots of War*, 96–97.

6. Quoted in ibid., 99.

7. Quoted in Roger Burbach, "Revolution and Reaction: U.S.
Politics in Central America," *Monthly Review* 36:2 (June

1984): 6-7.

8. Interview by Karen Elliot, *The Wall Street Journal* (3 June 1980), 95-98.

9. See Geyer, *The Idea of Disarmament!*, 95-98.

10. Quoted by Frank, "Sociopsychological Aspects of the Arms Race," 7.

11. Quoted by Lifton, *The Broken Connection*, 159n.

12. Salk, in *Parade Magazine*, 4 November 1984, 9.

13. Dorion Sagan, "The Evolution Revolution," *Bostonia* 59:1 (February/March 1985): 46.

14. William F. Allman, "Nice Guys Finish First," *Science 84* 5:8 (October 1984): 24-32.

15. MccGwire, 85.

16. See Ronald J. Sider, ed., *Cry Justice! The Bible on Hunger and Poverty* (New York: Paulist Press, 1980).

17. Gager, *Kingdom and Community: The Social World of Early Christianity* (Englewood Cliffs, N.J.: Prentice-Hall, 1975), 140.

18. See M. Douglas Meeks, "Toward a Trinitarian View of Economics: The Holy Spirit and Human Needs," *Christianity and Crisis* 40 (10 November 1980): 307-16; Jürgen Moltmann, "Pentecost: There Is Enough for Everyone," *The Power of the Powerless* (New York: Harper and Row, 1983), 127-35.

19. Sider, *Rich Christians in an Age of Hunger*, 101.

20. Boulding, *Stable Peace* (Austin, Texas: University of Texas Press, 1978), 76.

21. See James Wm. McClendon, Jr., "Dag Hammarskjöld — Twice-Born Servant," *Biography as Theology: How Life Stories Can Remake Today's Theology* (Nashville: Abingdon Press, 1974), 39-64.

Chapter Eight. Future as Worst Case Analysis

1. Moltmann, *Hope and Planning*, 80.

2. Most important, I believe are the writings of Jürgen Moltmann, whose first major work gave the label for this cluster of movements: *Theology of Hope.* In addition to the essays in *Hope and Planning*, Moltmann's vision of human nature is found in his following works: *Der verborgene Mensch* (Wuppertal-Barmen: Jugenddienst, 1961); "Man and the Son of Man," in *No Man Is Alien*, ed. J. R. Nelson (Leiden: E. J. Brill, 1971); *Theology of Play* (New York: Harper and Row, 1972); *Man: Christian Anthropology in the Conflicts of the Present* (Philadelphia: Fortress Press, 1974); *The Passion for*

Life: A Messianic Lifestyle (Philadelphia: Fortress Press, 1978). Another contemporary German theologian, Wolfhart Pannenberg, analyzes the nature of humanity from a somewhat different hope perspective in *What Is Man? Contemporary Anthropology in Theological Perspective* (Philadelphia: Fortress Press, 1970), and *Anthropology in Theological Perspective* (Philadelphia: Westminster Press, 1985). From the Roman Catholic side, the writings of Johann Baptist Metz and to some extent Karl Rahner also contribute to hope theology.

3. See Raymond L. Garthoff, "Worst-Case Assumptions: Uses, Abuses and Consequences," in *The Nuclear Crisis Reader*, 98-108.

4. Frank, *Sanity and Survival in the Nuclear Age*, 128-29.

5. Ibid., 130.

6. Quoted in Geyer, *The Idea of Disarmament!*, 92.

7. Russett, "The Contribution of Political Science," in *Proceedings of the Symposium*, 91-92.

8. Morgan, 209.

9. Quoted in *Has America Become Number 2? The US-Soviet Military Balance and American Defense Policies and Programs* (Washington DC: The Committee on the Present Danger, n.d.), 1.

10. Steven F. Cohen, "Sovieticus," *The Nation* 238:18 (12 May 1984): 568.

11. Quoted by John C. Bennett, "Nuclear Deterrence is Itself Vulnerable," *Chrisianity and Crisis* 44:13 (13 August 1984): 298.

12. Quoted by Robert C. Aldridge, *First Strike! The Pentagon's Strategy for Nuclear War* (Boston: South End Press, 1983), 38.

13. Bundy, "Deterrence Doctrine: A Need for Diversity," *Christianity and Crisis* 41:22 (18 January 1982): 387.

14. *De Bello Civili.* 1. 480.

15. Quoted by Walsh, 25.

16. Address to Members of Parliament, London, 8 June 1983; now in Strobe Talbott, *The Russians and Reagan* (New York: Vintage Books, 1984), 102.

17. John M. Collins, as quoted by James Fallows, *National Defense* (New York: Random House, 1981), 156.

18. Quoted by Aldridge, 38-39.

19. Ball, 37.

20. Quoted by George Hunsinger, "Karl Barth and Liberation Theology," *The Journal of Religion* 63:3 (July 1983): 247.

21. William Beardslee and John Mack, in *Psychosocial Aspects of*

Nuclear Developments, 64–93.

22. Ibid., 89.
23. *Psychiatric Aspects of the Prevention of Nuclear War*, 245–56.
24. Quoted in ibid., 254.
25. Barnet, *The Roots of War*, 99.
26. Jung, "Approaching the Unconscious," in *Man and His Symbols*, 72.
27. See John A. Sanford, *Evil: The Shadow Side of Reality* (New York: Crossroad Publishing Co., 1981), 59; chapter five, "The Shadow," is an excellent introduction to the subject.
28. M.-L. Franz, "The Process of Individuation," in *Man and His Symbols*, 182.
29. Chernus, "Mythologies of Nuclear War," 257–59.
30. Sanford, *Healing and Wholeness*, 101.
31. Franz, 181–82.
32. Jung, "Approaching the Unconscious," 73.
33. Geyer, *The Idea of Disarmament!*, 184.
34. Quoted in ibid.
35. Sanford, *Evil*, 61.
36. *Psychiatric Aspects of the Prevention of Nuclear War*, 261.
37. Patrick Blackett, quoted in *In a Dark Time*, 27.
38. Quoted in "Reducing the Risk of Nuclear War," 4.
39. Quoted in Geyer, *The Idea of Disarmament!*, 93.
40. *Psychiatric Aspects of the Prevention of Nuclear War*, 289.
41. Boulding, 17–18.
42. Quoted in "Reducing the Risk of Nuclear War," 4.
43. See John Winthrop's famous sermon, "A Modell of Christian Charity," preached in 1630 by the first leader of the Massachusetts Bay Colony just before they landed in the new world. *Winthrop Papers* (Boston: The Massachusetts Historical Society, 1931), 2:294–95.
44. Barnet, *The Roots of War*, 255.
45. See Dale W. Brown, ed., *What About the Russians? A Christian Approach to the U.S.-Soviet Conflict* (Elgin, Ill.: Brethren Press, 1984).
46. Barnet, *The Roots of War*, 97.
47. Frank, "Psychological Causes of the Nuclear Arms Race," 467.
48. Long, 67.
49. Moltmann, *Hope and Planning*, 150.
50. Talbott, 78.
51. Polak, *The Image of the Future*, trans. and abridged by Elise Boulding (New York: Elsevier Scientific Publishing Co., 1973). For a summary and theological critique of some contemporary

futurologists, see Ted Peters, *Futures — Human and Divine* (Atlanta: John Knox Press, 1978).

52. Heilbroner, *An Inquiry into the Human Prospect* (New York: W. W. Norton and Co., 1974).
53. Long, 93.
54. Boulding, 17.
55. *The Challenge of Peace*, par. 258.
56. Eric Fromm, *Revolution of Hope* (New York: Harper and Row, 1968), 13.
57. Wink, "Faith and Nuclear Paralysis," *The Christian Century* 99:7 (3 March 1982): 236.

Chapter Nine. Faith as Official Optimism

1. Some of the material in this chapter has appeared in an earlier form in my essay, "Faith as Official Optimism: A Nuclearist Heresy," *Christianity and Crisis* 44:12 (9 July 1984): 271-73; used by permission.
2. Herberg, *Protestant — Catholic — Jew: An Essay in American Religious Sociology* (Garden City, N.Y.: Anchor Books/ Doubleday, 1960), 89.
3. Elizabeth Kastor, "Mary Kay Says Everyone Should Feel Important," *The Sunday Globe* (Bethlehem, Pa.), 23 December 1984, sec. E.
4. *The Challenge of Peace*, par. 136.
5. Barnet, *Real Security*, 39, 27.
6. See Douglas John Hall, *Lighten Our Darkness: Toward an Indigenous Theology of the Cross* (Philadelphia: Westminster Press, 1976), chapters 1-3.
7. Gifford, "Death and Forever: Some Fears of War and Peace," *The Atlantic Monthly* 209:3 (March 1962): 88-92.
8. See Hall, chapter 1, and Langdon Gilkey, *Reaping the Whirlwind: A Christian Interpretation of History* (New York: Seabury Press, 1976), part I.
9. Merton, *New Seeds of Contemplation* (New York: New Directions Books, 1962), 112.
10. Quoted in "The Year of the Yuppie," *Newsweek*, 31 December 1984, 19.
11. Kinsley, "Nuclear Holocaust in Perspective," *Harper's* 264:1584 (May 1982): 9, and now reprinted in *The Apocalyptic Premise: Nuclear Arms Debated*, ed. Ernest W. Lefever and E. Stephen Hunt (Washington D.C.: Ethics and Public Policy Center, 1982) 247.
12. George S. Hendry, "Possible Reasons for Teen-Age Suicide,"

New York Times, 16 November 1984, sec. A.

13. Colin S. Gray and Keith Payne, "Victory Is Possible," *Foreign Policy* 39 (Summer 1980): 14, 26, 21.

14. Gray, "Nuclear Strategy: The Case for a Theory of Victory," *International Security* (Summer 1979): 57.

15. See Aldridge, passim, and also Robert S. Scheer, *With Enough Shovels: Reagan, Bush and Nuclear War* (New York: Vintage Books, 1983).

16. Mack, "Psychosocial Effects of the Nuclear Arms Race," *Bulletin of the Atomic Scientists* 37:4 (April 1981): 22, 21.

17. See Morgan, chapter 7.

18. Nixon, quoted by George C. Herring, *Ameria's Longest War: The U.S. and Vietnam, 1950*-1975 (New York: John Wiley and Sons, 1979), 231.

19. Niebuhr, *Beyond Tragedy: Essays on the Christian Interpretation of History* (New York: Charles Scribner's Sons, 1937), 103.

20. Kennan, 199.

21. Nouwen, "Letting Go of All Things: Prayer as Action," *Waging Peace: A Handbook for the Struggle to Abolish Nuclear Weapons*, ed. Jim Wallis (New York: Harper and Row, 1982), 202.

22. Mack, 23.

23. Wiesel elaborated on his initial comment in an address delivered at Moravian College, Bethlehem, Pa., 13 February 1985.

24. Merton, *New Seeds of Contemplation*, 135.

25. Ibid., 136.

26. Ott, 58.

Chapter Ten. Lifestyle as Incarnate Vision

1. Berger, 172.

2. Quoted by Jerry Saunders, *Peddlers of Crisis* (Boston: South End Press, 1983), 198.

3. Falwell, *Listen America!* (Garden City, N.Y.: Doubleday and Co., 1980), 10.

4. Lifton, in *Indefensible Weapons*, 80–99.

· 5. Hauerwas, letter to the author, 17 September 1984.

6. 28 February 1738, *The Journal of John Wesley*, ed. Nehemiah Curnock, 8 vols. (London: The Epworth Press, 1909–1916), 1:442.

7. *Gandhi on Non-Violence: Selected Texts from Mohandas K. Gandhi's Non-Violence in Peace and War*, ed. Thomas Merton

(New York: New Directions Publishing Co., 1965), 25.

8. Douglass, *Lightning East to West*, 5, 14.

9. See Moltmann, "On Hope as an Experiment: A Postlude," in *The Experiment Hope* (Philadelphia: Fortress Press, 1975), 186–90.

10. Moltmann, "The First Liberated Men in Creation," in *The Theology of Play* (New York: Harper and Row, 1972), 70.

11. Wallis, *The Call to Conversion*, 106.

12. Miguez Bonino, *Doing Theology in a Revolutionary Situation* (Philadelphia: Fortress Press, 1975), 90, 98–99.

13. Bonhoeffer, *The Cost of Discipleship*, rev. ed. (New York: Macmillan Co., 1963), 69.

14. Frederick Herzog, *Justice Church: The New Function of the Church in North American Christianity* (Maryknoll, N.Y. Orbis Books, 1980), 3.

15. Good introductions to liberation theology, its promise and its problems, can be found in the work cited above by Miguez Bonino; also, William K. McElvaney, *Good News Is Bad News Is Good News.* . . (Maryknoll, N.Y.: Orbis Books, 1980); Gerald H. Anderson and Thomas F. Stransky, eds., *Mission Trends No. 3: Third World Theologies* (New York: Paulist Press, and Grand Rapids, Mich.: Wm. B. Eerdmans Publishing Co., 1976); Gerald H. Anderson and Thomas F. Stransky, eds., *Mission Trends No. 4: Liberation Theologies* (New York: Paulist Press, and Grand Rapids, Mich.: Wm. B. Eerdmans Publishing Co., 1979).

16. Cone, *God of the Oppressed* (New York: Seabury Press, 1975), 60.

17. Soelle, *Political Theology* (Philadelphia: Fortress Press, 1974), 76; the preceding phrase is quoted from Jürgen Habermas, a philosopher of the Frankfurt school of ideology critique.

18. Schweitzer, *The Quest of the Historical Jesus: A Critical Study of Its Progress from Reimarus to Wrede* (New York: Macmillan Co., 1959), 403.

19. Reich, *The Greening of America* (New York: Bantam Books, 1971), 362.

20. "Mercenary Schools Offer Gun Training, 'Adventure,'" *The Sunday Globe* (Bethlehem, Pa.), 30 June 1985, sec. A.

21. Quoted by Dallas Lee, *The Cotton Patch Evidence* (New York: Harper and Row, 1971), 58. Most of my material about Clarence Jordan and Koinonia farm is derived from this invaluable source. The quarterly newsletters from Koinonia are another source. Copies of these, together with the mail order

brochures and information about their excellent products, are available on request from Koinonia Products, Route 2, Americus, GA 31709.

22. See Benjamin Zablocki, *The Joyful Community: An Account of the Bruderhof, A Communal Movement Now in Its Third Generation* (Baltimore, Md.: Penguin Books, 1971), and compare my essay, "Koinonia, 1976: An Experiment in Community, Revisited," *Cross Currents* 25:3 (Fall 1975): 283-87.

23. Lee, 37-38, 78-79.

24. Ibid., 143-44. See note 7 above and Gandhi's "experiments in truth."

25. Ibid., 38-39.

26. Ibid., 115.

27. Ibid., 186.

28. Cone, 60.

29. Bruno Bettelheim has a fascinating discussion of how narrating fairy tales can aid children to attain progressively higher levels of self-understanding. This has implications, of course, for religious education of all ages. See his *The Uses of Enchantment: The Meaning and Importance of Fairy Tales* (New York: Vintage Books, 1977), 28, 58-59, 150-56.

30. See Philip Hallie, *Lest Innocent Blood Be Shed: The Story of the Village of Le Chambon and How Goodness Happened There* (New York: Harper and Row, 1979); the closing words are found on pp. 120, 128, 287.

31. Harding, "In the Company of the Faithful: Journeying Toward the Promised Land," *Sojourners* 14:5 (May 1985): 16.

32. Peter L. Berger and Thomas Luckmann, *The Social Construction of Reality: A Treatise in the Sociology of Knowledge* (New York: Doubleday and Co., 1967), 158.

33. Wesley, quoted by Bill Kellermann, "To Stir Up God's Good Trouble," *Sojourners* 13:3 (March 1984): 22.

34. Quoted in ibid.

35. This national network has an excellent manual which offers to groups a pastoral guidance for both the inward journey and the outward journey of the spiritual life. It is *Handbook for World Peacemakers Groups*, by Gordon Cosby and Bill Price, and is available from World Peacemakers, the Church of the Savior, 2025 Massachusetts Ave., N.W., Washington D.C. 20036.

36. Wallis, *The Call to Conversion*, 107.

Postscript. Testimonials from Some of the Faithful in a Nuclear Age

1. King, *Stride Toward Freedom: The Montgomery Story* (New

York: Harpers, 1958), 224.

2. Quoted in Geyer, *The Idea of Disarmament!*, 197.
3. "Capsules," *The OtherSide* 21:5 (July 1985): 65.
4. Aukerman, 216–17.
5. Quoted by Hunsinger, "Barth, Barmen, and the Confessing Church Today," 27.
6. *Harvest of Justice: Newsletter of the Gaudete Peace and Justice Center* (January 1985), 2.
7. Quoted by Aukerman, xvii.

Index